CHAMBERS'S
GUIDE
TO
SCOTLAND

by
MARY JACK
AND
JOHN L. BLAIR

W. & R. CHAMBERS LTD.
EDINBURGH & LONDON

CONTENTS

*Jacket: Colour photograph by W. S. Thomson of
Edinburgh.*

Opposite: Yachting on the Clyde.

Grateful acknowledgement is made to all who have provided illustrations for this book; in particular to the Scottish Tourist Board, *Scotland's Magazine*, *The Scotsman*, The North of Scotland Hydro-electric Board, Publicity Committees in Dundee, Perth and Rothesay, as well as to Messrs. Graham Cowie, W. S. Thomson, Alasdair Alpin MacGregor, Ian Craig, F. G. Sykes, P. Jeffrey Smith, Morris Allan, V. A. Firsoff, M. A. Steen, Miss B. C. Crichton, Paul Shillabeer and the executors of the late Sir John Stirling Maxwell

FIRST PUBLISHED 1957
REVISED EDITION 1963
REVISED EDITION 1967

PRINTED BY J. AND J. GRAY
212 CAUSEWAYSIDE, EDINBURGH

INTRODUCTION

SCOTLAND is small, her maximum length being but 274 miles; but so rich is the variety of scene which she offers that visitors often discover their time is too short. Only a few outstanding districts are mentioned here, all within reach of main centres, and to see these, at least, may give some idea of the contrasts to be found in this land.

The Borders.—The Borders are the pleasant green counties of southern Scotland—Peebles, Selkirk, Berwick, Roxburgh and Dumfries—where the hills are gentle and Tweed and Teviot flow. It is a land of ancient abbeys (Dryburgh, Jedburgh, Melrose), of grim keeps and fortresses (Hermitage Castle, Neidpath Castle), relics of a stormy history of bloody forays against the English, but a land, too, of myth and legend, recorded for us by such writers as Sir Walter Scott and James Hogg, the Ettrick Shepherd. The Border towns of Hawick, Kelso, Jedburgh, Galashiels, Melrose (with nearby Abbotsford House), Selkirk and Peebles are easily accessible from Edinburgh (Hawick, 51 miles, being the farthest distant); but each one is itself an excellent centre for the district. Also regarded as Border country is part of the more southerly county of Dumfries, including the towns of Moffat, Lockerbie, Ecclefechan and Dumfries itself (77 miles from Edinburgh by road) with its ancient bridge and its associations with Robert Bruce and Robert Burns. This, too, is the town from which to explore westwards into Galloway.

Loch Lomond.—Loch Lomond can be reached within an hour by road from Glasgow by the Clyde to Alexandria and thence to Balloch. The road on the western shore is the more popular; it is narrow, and throughout the summer months a continuous line of cars and buses weaves round the countless bends at a moderate, sight-seeing speed to Luss, Tarbet and to Ardlui at the head of the loch (24 miles). The eastern shore is reached by branching off across country at Balloch to Drymen (or from Glasgow, through Bearsden to Drymen, about 18 miles), turning left there to Balmaha, a favourite haunt of boating enthusiasts, and Rowardennan, where the loch road ends.

A visit to the *Three Lochs* is a pleasant afternoon tour, the lochs being Lomond, Long and the Gare Loch. At Tarbet on Loch Lomond the road crosses over a narrow neck of land to Arrochar at the top of the salt-water Loch Long, where the impressive Cobbler towers. And so down Loch Long and across to the top of the Gare Loch, the third loch, which is in fact an arm of the Firth of Clyde, extending 7 miles from Garelochhead to Helensburgh.

The Trossachs, in Perthshire, is one of the most renowned of Scotland's beauty spots, and is described elsewhere. From Glasgow and Edinburgh there are day excursions by bus, for example, a tour via the Trossachs, Loch Katrine and Callander, returning by either of the Forth road bridges to Edinburgh. There are also various holiday tours from London centred on this area. By car the shortest route from Glasgow is through Milngavie, Strathblane, Killearn to Aberfoyle. Callander, 9½ miles, and Aberfoyle, 4 miles from the Trossachs, are excellent centres.

The Pass of Glencoe is reached by continuing from Ardlui at the head of Loch Lomond to Crianlarich, branching west to Tyndrum, then north through Bridge of Orchy and the Moor of Rannoch to Kingshouse, in all about 32 miles. The road through the glen runs for some 14 miles to Ballachulish through some of the wildest and most awesomely impressive country in Scotland. Here stand the massive craggy heights of Buchaille Etive Mor (the Great Shepherd of Etive), Bidean nam Bian and the Three Sisters. The return journey may be made along the lovely Loch Linnhe to Connel Ferry, east along Loch Etive, the Pass of Brander to Dalmally and, completing the circle, back to Crianlarich. Oban, mainly thought of as the centre for the islands of the Inner Hebrides, is also an ideal base from which to visit Glencoe and indeed to explore the whole county of Argyll.

Deeside.—Deeside with its Royal associations is one of the most popular parts of Scotland. It is approached most easily from Aberdeen, but the visitor using Perth as a starting point can contrast the wild Grampian country, which he must cross, with the rich beauty of hill, forest and river which is Deeside. First, the road from Perth is through the Valley of the Tay, passing the fruit-growing town of Blairgowrie, then up into the hills and Glenshee to the celebrated S-bend known as the Devil's Elbow and Cairnwell, the highest point on any road in Britain. The Dee, which has risen far up in the Cairngorms, is reached at Braemar and followed from there all the way to Aberdeen, past Crathie Church, through Ballater, Aboyne, Banchory and Crathes. Balmoral Castle can be viewed from the road between Braemar and Crathie Church. Seven miles west of Braemar, at the Linn of Dee, is the beginning of the Lairig Ghru, the famous pass through the Cairngorms to Aviemore.

Northwest Scotland.—The vast grandeur of northwest Scotland is best approached from Inverness. A memorable journey is that taken across country from Inverness to Gairloch—74 miles of moor, loch and mountain scenery, by the Beauly Firth to Muir of Ord, Loch Garve, Achnasheen, and through Glen Docherty to Kinlochewe (where a road runs southwest through Glen Torridon to Loch Torridon). The route now winds along the shore of Loch Maree, one of Scotland's most beautiful lochs; Slioch towers on its farther shore. From the loch it is about 10 miles by way of Kerrysdale to Gairloch.

Glen Affric, one of the most beautiful glens of Scotland, is reached from Inverness by following Loch Ness to Drumnadrochit and branching west through Glen Urquhart to Cannich, the focal point of extensive hydro-electric workings. In Glen Affric birch-covered mountains surround the glen through which the Affric flows into Loch Affric. The road ends here, and the return journey is by Strath Glass to Struy Bridge and thence to a point just outside Beauly where the main road sweeps over Beauly Bridge east to Inverness. This circular tour is in all 56 miles.

Skye.—Skye is the island, it is said, to which all visitors return. A primitive, savage land, dominated by the bare Black Cuillin, it is reached by steamer from Kyle of Lochalsh to Kyleakin, or from Mallaig to Armadale. A walker's and climber's paradise, Skye can also be enjoyed by a road which circles the island from Broadford to Sligachan, Portree, to Kilmaluag in the north, round to Uig where is the memorial to Flora MacDonald, south and west to Dunvegan, south again to Bracadale, and so to Sligachan. A shorter tour runs from Sligachan to Portree, Bracadale and back to Sligachan. The surface of these roads is not first class, but is quite adequate.

How to Come to Scotland

There are excellent direct services by rail, road and air from London to Edinburgh and London to Glasgow, either by day or by night, with usually increased frequencies during the summer months, and with convenient connections to other parts of Scotland and the outer islands.

For example, the famous day train, "The Flying Scot" completes the journey from London (King's Cross) *via* York and Berwick to Edinburgh in six hours—passing through some excellent scenery en route—whereas the air journey between these two capital cities occupies eighty minutes. Similar services operate between London

3

and Glasgow, the rail route being from Euston via Crewe, and the air trip to Abbotsinch airport.

There are also direct daily flights from Manchester and Birmingham to Glasgow, with connections to Edinburgh.

Passengers who prefer motor-coach road transport will find a choice of convenient and cheap services principally from London, Manchester or Liverpool to Glasgow or Edinburgh, with many road connections beyond.

Visitors from Ireland have the option of an overnight sea passage by comfortable steamers either between Dublin and Glasgow or Belfast and Glasgow. The shortest sea passage lies between Larne and Stranraer.

There are also daily direct flights from Dublin to Glasgow and Edinburgh (flying time approximately 70 minutes) or between Belfast and Glasgow (45 minutes).

For travellers from Europe, there are some direct flights to either Glasgow or Prestwick, and excellent air services from all European International Airports, *via* London.

Visitors from Canada or the United States will no doubt prefer to use one of the many transatlantic direct flights to Prestwick, or if sea travel is preferred, one of the Atlantic liners calling at Greenock.

Details of these services and other information (accommodation, car-hire, etc.) may be obtained from any Travel Agency.

For cars the usual routes from England into Scotland are (1) to Edinburgh by Newcastle, crossing the Border at Carter Bar, and (2) to Glasgow by Carlisle, crossing the Border at Gretna Green. There are numerous variations, however, and advice should be sought from the A.A. or R.A.C.

NOTES FOR TOURISTS IN SCOTLAND

Roads in Scotland are in the main good, but in the Highlands, and especially in the northwest, they are often very narrow. The surface of secondary roads may be rough in places but should present no great difficulty to careful drivers; there are passing places on most of them.

Petrol.—Outside the towns pumps in the Highlands are scarce, and it is not always easy to buy petrol on Sundays.

Hotels.—In the larger towns these are of good standard. North and west of Inverness the visitor to outlying districts will find comfort rather than luxury, and will do well to recognise this fact. As Scotland is becoming increasingly popular with tourists, accommodation should, if possible, be arranged beforehand. A useful handbook, *Where to Stay in Scotland* (3/6), is published by the Scottish Tourist Board.

Ferries.—In the Highlands many ferries do not operate on Sundays. Information can be had from the Automobile Association.

Licensing Hours.—Generally, alcoholic drinks are unobtainable on weekdays before 11 a.m., between 2.30 and 5 in the afternoon, and after 10 p.m.; obtainable, however, from licensed grocers during normal business hours. On Sundays the permitted hours are 12.30 to 2 p.m. and 6.30 to 10 p.m. (hotels only, public houses being closed).

History.—Ancient Scotland had five different peoples—the Picts, the Galloway Picts, the British (who were refugees from the south), the Angles, and the Gaelic-speaking Scots from Ireland. Of these the Scots, who gave Scotland her name, overcame the others, and in 843 the kingdoms were consolidated under Kenneth Macalpin. From this date the history of Scotland is largely the history of her relations with England. Many and bitter were the contests, first with Plantagenets and then with Tudors. Scotland's struggle for independence produced two outstanding national heroes—William Wallace and Robert the Bruce. Wallace led his countrymen to victory against Edward I at Stirling, but was later defeated at Falkirk, captured and executed in London in 1305. Robert Bruce was crowned at Scone in 1306, and in 1314 scored a heavy Scottish victory at Bannockburn. Under the Stewart kings Scotland's fortunes waned; from 1371 every new king was a minor, and this led to internal struggles for power among the Scottish nobles. James IV, the strongest and most gifted of the Stewarts, in whose reign the arts flourished, was killed at the disastrous battle of Flodden in 1513, and his granddaughter, Mary, Queen of Scots, was executed by the English Elizabeth. Under her son, James VI, the crowns of Scotland and England were united in 1603. Meanwhile the Reformation was spreading, and with John Knox the Protestant religion was established in Scotland. Defence of Presbyterianism led to further struggles with England. So bitter were religious controversies that, when the Civil War broke out in England, at first the Scots (Covenanters) joined forces with the English parliament against the King, Charles I. But another national hero, James Graham, Marquis of Montrose, led a Highland army in a series of brilliant victories over the King's enemies before his final defeat at Philiphaugh.

After the execution of Charles I and the defeat by Cromwell of

Charles II, Scotland suffered English invasion and occupation until 1660 when Charles was enthusiastically restored to the throne. The Catholic reign of James VII was popular in neither Scotland nor England and led to the acceptance of the Dutch William as king by all except the Highland supporters of the Stuarts led by Claverhouse, Viscount Dundee. Victorious at Killiecrankie, Dundee himself was killed and the rising was suppressed. The clan chiefs swore allegiance, all except Macdonald of Glencoe, who was six days late; his people were massacred by the Campbells and the King was held responsible.

Scotland's economic position at this time was poor, due mainly to the refusal by England to grant her free trade except on condition that she accept a total union with England. And so in 1707 came the "end o' an auld sang" with the union of the parliaments. This took place by no wish of the Scottish nation as a whole, and its unpopularity was forcibly expressed in the Jacobite risings. Bravely the Highlanders rallied to the side of the exiled Prince Charles Edward in his fight to regain the throne, a fight which ended in the disastrous battle of Culloden in 1746. The sternest measures followed: the old clan system in the Highlands came to an end for ever with the disarmament, eviction and enforced emigration of the Highland people.

From the 18th century on, Lowland Scotland prospered, central Scotland becoming an industrial area of first importance. Scotsmen made outstanding contributions to the Industrial Revolution— James Watt with his separate condenser for the steam engine; James Neilson with his invention of the hot blast in iron manufacture; David Dale by building his cotton mills in Lanarkshire where Arkwright's new water frame should function; and William Symington, Henry Bell and Robert Napier with their advances in steam navigation.

In some quarters the tendency is to regard Scotland, administered as she is from London, as a part of England. But Scotland will always regard herself as a separate nation. At the Union she retained two institutions which are fundamentally different from those of England—her law and her church. There are many who hope that one day she may have her own parliament again in Edinburgh.

ABOUT THE SCOTS

Language.—In Scotland, contrary to the belief of some tourists even today, there is no language difficulty. Gaelic, it is true, is still spoken in parts of the Highlands and Islands, but even there the people are bi-lingual. (A short list of Gaelic terms found in place-names is at the end of this volume.) The Scottish accent does not exist as such—as in all countries the accent varies from district to district. There is the musical lilt of the island speech, the sing-song tones of the east, the broad, slovenly, rather ugly speech of Glasgow, and in Inverness, the unaccented "four-square" English which is said to be the purest in Britain.

Character.—Popularly the Scot belongs to one of two types: either he is dour, phlegmatic, thrifty, reliable and humourless—the Lowlander; or he is wild, romantic, poetical, alternating between gaiety and melancholy—the Highlander. This is an exaggerated conception of the Scottish character, but it has been fostered by the Scots themselves with the help of native writers. Though basically true some qualification is needed. The sullen-seeming dourness of the Lowlander is born of an age-old struggle with the land combined with shyness, and an inherent stubborn independence; underneath there is true kindliness. Nor is he a humourless man. The Scot's type of humour is perhaps not that of the Englishman, but he has a fine sense of the ridiculous and the grotesque. Scottish "dry" humour, hard to define, is at its best a wit quietly expressed and quietly received, but with appreciation on both sides. The "pawky" or sly type, attri-buted to Scots by writers of the Kailyard School (Ian MacLaren, J. M. Barrie, etc.), is a sentimentalised humour. It is practised but not always with success. In Glasgow, humour is lively, cheeky, often noisy and may, as has been suggested, owe a little to the Irish element in the city.

As for the Highlander, brave and romantic, he too exists, and to the emotional qualities already listed may be added a fine sensitivity and inborn courtesy. But the dour determination of the Lowlander is in sharp contrast to the strong *laissez-faire* attitude to life which often characterizes the Highlander and Islander. This shows itself most notably in a complete disregard for time.

One characteristic is ascribed to the Scots as a nation—meanness. Scottish meanness is a music-hall myth; it has been the subject of countless jokes and has been laughed at by the Scots themselves. Basically the Scots are a thrifty race, and this stems from their poverty of former times, but no people can be more generous or more hospitable to the stranger within their gates.

Loch Benevean (Glen Affric)

SCOTLAND

ABBEY ST. BATHANS, a picturesque hamlet on the Whiteadder, 7 miles NW. of Duns. The east and north walls of its church are part of an ancient nunnery chapel.

ABBOTSFORD, Sir Walter Scott's stately mansion, 3 miles W. of Melrose, Roxburghshire, built (1817–21) on a farm called (Cartley or sometimes Clarty) Hole. Abbotsford is open to the public during the summer months, contains not only fascinating souvenirs of Scott (the Raeburn portrait, Chantrey bust, his study with his desk, armchair and table) but also many interesting Scottish relics which he gathered under his roof.

ABBOTSINCH, former naval air station, 7 miles W. of central Glasgow, site of Glasgow's new civil airport (1966), with new motorway to link it to city centre.

ABERCHIRDER, an agricultural village of Banffshire, 9 miles S. of Banff, colloquially but obscurely called "Foggie Loan".

ABERDEEN

SCOTLAND'S third city and her largest holiday resort, an ancient and historic royal burgh, busy seaport and centre of the fishing industry, also by virtue of its situation, commercial capital of the north-east, on the east coast some 145 miles NNE. of Edinburgh. The older part (Old Aberdeen), on the River Don, contains two of its finest buildings, King's College and St. Machar's Cathedral. The New Town, with the harbour and docks, fish market, shopping centre and residential areas, stands mainly on the Dee.

Aberdeen is built on two rivers, the Dee and the Don, both famous for their salmon and their scenery. Between the rivers lie the "Golden Sands"—two miles of bathing beach with an esplanade, putting and tennis, as well as a ballroom and restaurants. Union Street is a broad and handsome thoroughfare, and a really good shopping centre. At the foot of Union Street, in Castle Street, is the imposing granite-built Town House (19th century) incorporating the tower and spire of the 14th century Tolbooth. Here are preserved the Royal Charters from the time of William the Lion; also the most complete set of Burgh Records in Scotland, ranging back for five or six centuries—with only one volume missing.

Nearby, in the Castlegate, is the old Jacobean Mercat Cross with medallions of Scottish Kings, and a marble unicorn on top. Here too, in Broad Street, is Marischal College, a splendid modern structure housing one of the two colleges which together form the University of Aberdeen. It is reputed to be the finest granite building in the world, and is certainly one of the largest. Its size is not oppressive. Perpendicular lines and Gothic pinnacles (perhaps also the tone of the light-grey Aberdeen granite) carry its great bulk upwards with unbelievable lightness and grace. Across the courtyard from the great archway is the Mitchell Tower (233 ft.), and other interesting features are the Library, Graduation Hall and Portrait Gallery.

Opposite Marischal College is Provost Skene's House, an old Scottish turreted mansion, open as a period house and museum, with its period garden. Another old house—oldest in Aberdeen—is Provost Ross's House in the Shiprow, maintained by the National Trust. Then halfway up Union Street are the East and West churches of St. Nicholas, before the Reformation one church of St. Nicholas. Both churches have since been rebuilt. Note, however, the curious little 15th century Chapel of St. Mary (crypt of the east church, and part of the original building) with its fine stone vaulted roof, carved panels and stalls. It was formerly used as a prison-house for witches. Crossing the bridge in Union Street one may go, via Union Terrace, to Schoolhill, where are the

Aberdeen Harbour.

Art Galleries with their interesting collection of sculpture and art. Sightseeing of a different kind takes one to the harbour and its extensive docks and quays; also (around 7 o'clock in the morning!) to the fish market. Westward of Union Street are the handsome suburbs of the New Town, climbing the banks of Dee among gardens and woods. Houses are built mainly of granite. Old Aberdeen lies on the Don. Here is St. Machar's Cathedral (14th century founded 12th), and King's College with its lantern and crown. The Cathedral with its twin towers and short, rounded sandstone spires is a landmark. Worthy of note are its great seven-light west window and round-arched doorway; massive round piers supporting the pointed arches of the nave; and flat heraldic ceiling of painted oak, bearing the arms of St. Margaret, Pope Leo X, the Emperor Charles V and many more—40 shields in all.

Outstanding in King's College is the chapel, all that remains of the original college, founded by Bishop Elphinstone in 1494. The tomb of the founder is here, also a memorial tablet to Hector Boece. Note the fine, Flamboyant west window, canopied stalls, exquisite carving; and the 16th century Bishop Stewart's pulpit carved with the heads of Scottish kings. The tower, surmounted by its crown and lantern dates from 1636. Other college buildings are more modern.

Around the Cathedral is the Chanonry. The Don flows under

the 14th century Brig o' Balgownie nearby.

The city has many beautiful and well-tended parks, the largest, Hazlehead, a delightful 800-acre stretch of gardens, park and woodland, including a breezy 18-hole golf course and also one of 9 holes. Others are the Duthie Park, Johnston Gardens, Stewart Park, Victoria and Westburn Parks and Union Terrace Gardens.

Excellent hotels and boarding houses cater for the visitor, whose interest is held by a succession of notable events, of which the highlight is the Royal Braemar Gathering (see BRAEMAR).

Facilities for sport include golf at Hazlehead, the Links and Balnagask, fishing (salmon and trout) on the Rivers Dee, Don and Ythan, climbing on Bennachie, Hill of Fare, Morven, Lochnagar and among the high peaks of the Cairngorms. Tennis, bowls and putting are available in practically every park and playing field in the city.

For indoor recreation there are theatres, cinemas, ballrooms, ten pin bowling and a long programme of concerts, lectures, flower shows, country dancing displays, etc. throughout the year.

Communications are good by road, rail or air (see DYCE). There are many tours to the Aberdeenshire coast, the Scottish Highlands, Deeside and Donside, while Aberdeen is a port of call for motor vessels cruising to Orkney and Shetland.

ABERDEENSHIRE, a county bounded N. and E. by the sea. In the SW. it contains part of the Cairngorms (Ben Macdhui 4,300 ft., Cairntoul 4,241 ft., Braeriach, on the Inverness-shire boundary, 4,248 ft.). The rivers Dee, Don, Ythan and Deveron flow into the North Sea. The chief towns are Aberdeen, Peterhead, Fraserburgh, Inverurie and Huntly. The north-east district (Buchan) is famed for its cattle-rearing. Agriculture and fisheries are important.

SCOTTISH GARDENS

During the summer months hundreds of famous Scottish Gardens are open to the public. A small admission charge is made and tea is generally served. Full information can be obtained from the General Organiser, Scotland's Gardens Scheme, 26 Castle Terrace, Edinburgh, 1.

ABERDOUR, a small but popular resort on the Firth of Forth, about 15 miles NW. of Edinburgh with a pretty, wooded shore and bathing facilities; it has a camping site, golf course (18-hole), tennis, bowls, fishing and boating.

ABERFELDY, a small town and salmon and trout fishing resort near the River Tay (here crossed by a fine General Wade Bridge, 1733). The original muster of the Black Watch (1725) is commemorated by a monument. The three Falls of Moness nearby are said to have inspired Burns to write "The Birks (Birches) of Aberfeldy". Fishing is available on the Tay and on Loch na Craige to the S. There is golf, tennis, bowls, and winter sports.

ABERFOYLE, a pleasant village and resort 27 miles N. of Glasgow. A good but steep route runs over the "Duke's Road" to the Trossachs and other roads lead to the Lake of Menteith and via Loch Ard and Loch Chon to Inversnaid. Scott's novel *Rob Roy* is remembered in the Bailie Nicol Jarvie Inn. Golf, fishing and pony-trekking are available. To the south is Dunshee, the fairy knowe, where the Rev. Robert Kirk, who wrote "The Secret Commonwealth of Elves and Fairies" (1691) was taken by the fairies. Just off the "Duke's Road" above the village is the David Marshall Lodge, built by the Carnegie Trust, and used as a free resting place by many tourists each year.

ABERGELDIE CASTLE, 6 miles W. of Ballater, was a favourite residence of Edward VIII when Prince of Wales.

ABERLADY, a pleasant village and resort on Aberlady Bay (wildfowl sanctuary), 2 miles S. of Gullane in East Lothian. It has a hotel reconstructed from an old coaching inn, golf (Kilspindie, 18-hole—others within easy reach) and bowls. A mile or so NE. is Luffness golf course, and to the SW. Gosford House in its beautiful grounds.

ABERLEMNO, a village 6 miles NE. of Forfar with interesting Pictish sculptured stones.

ABERLOUR, a small village on the Spey, about 15 miles below Grantown.

ABERNETHY, a historic Perthshire village, ancient capital of the Picts, 8½ miles SE. of Perth. Most notable antiquity is its 74 ft. high Round Tower, said to date from the 8th or 9th century. Only two others are known in Scotland, one in Egilsay (Orkney) and the other in Brechin.

ABINGTON, a pretty village 14 miles S. of Lanark.

ABOYNE, 30 miles WSW. of Aberdeen, is a delightful village resort famous for its Games (highland gathering). Records set up at Aboyne are regarded as genuine because the competition field is flat! The village has a

Abernethy Tower.

golf course, village green and the partly 17th century Aboyne Castle, seat of the Marquis of Huntly.

ACHARACLE, a small fishing resort at the SW. end of Loch Shiel, southern terminus of the loch steamer.

ACHILTIBUIE, a small resort in fine scenery on Baden Bay, opposite the Summer Isles.

ANGLING IN SCOTLAND

For the full possibilities of angling in Scotland one should buy *Scotland for Fishing*, an excellent publication (3s.) of the Scottish Tourist Board. The following fishing waters are among the most noble available:

RIVERS:
Alladale (Ross and Cromarty).
Carron (,,   ).
Cassley (,,   ).
Creek (Lewis).
Grimerstra (Lewis).
Laxay (Lewis).
Oykel (Ross and Cromarty).

LOCHS:
Loch Leven.
Loch Maree.
Loch of Stenness (Orkney).

Loch Achray.

ACHNACARRY, See Arkaig.

ACHNACLOICH, a woody hamlet on Loch Etive, 3 miles E. of Connel.

ACHNASHEEN, a remote hamlet of Wester Ross, 27½ miles W. of Dingwall; on road and railway, which continue SW. to the Kyle of Lochalsh. Achnasheen has good fishing, and makes a charming holiday place as well as a touring centre.

ACHNASHELLACH, a forest of Ross and Cromarty, in Glen Carron, dominated by Sgurr Ruadh (3,142 ft,) and other peaks.

ACHRAY, LOCH, a beautiful loch in the Trossachs between Lochs Katrine and Vennachar.

AFFRIC, GLEN, a wild and lovely glen in NW. Invernessshire, traversed by the Affric, which may be ascended from Invercannich. In its lower part, called Chisholm's Pass, narrow and richly wooded, it opens out, and the new 'hydro-electric' road skirts Loch Benevean to Loch Affric, its shores clothed with magnificent Scots pines said to be 400 years old. Here at Affric Lodge the old road ends, but a track continues beneath Mam Soul (3,862 ft.) and Cairn Eige (3,877 ft.—

Nature Reserve) to Altbeath, whence it is possible to descend to Loch Duich in Wester Ross. Loch Affric is the head of an extensive hydro-electric scheme but is itself little affected.

AILORT, a sea loch of SW. Inverness-shire, with Kinloch-ailort at the head. It is fed by the short River Ailort, which flows out of Loch Eilt.

AILSA CRAIG, a large rock-islet (over 1,000 ft. high and some 2 miles round) at the mouth of the Firth of Clyde, *c.* 10 miles W. of Girvan, noted for its innumerable sea birds, (especially solan geese and puffins), its lighthouse and its granite quarries (supplying the material for Ayr-shire's curling stones); also for the remains of an old tower. The fairly arduous climb to the top is rewarded with magnificent views.

AIRDRIE, a small burgh 11 miles E. of Glasgow, practically continuous with iron-working Coatbridge 2 miles W. A long main street passes imperceptibly from one to the other. There are attractive parks, gardens and playing fields. Both towns are important industrially.

AIRLIE, the name of a castle 5 miles to the NE. of Alyth (Perthshire), former seat of the late Dowager Countess of Airlie.

AIRTH, a picturesque old village on the banks of the Forth, 8 miles SE. of Stirling, at one time a busy sea-port. Near here was the royal dockyard of King James IV. Traces of the old docks can still be seen. Created a burgh of barony in 1597, the Mercat Cross erected 100 years later is still in good order.

ALDER, BEN, a mountain (3,757 ft.) overlooking Loch Ericht from the W.

ALE, a tributary (Selkirk and Roxburghshires) of the Teviot.

ALEXANDRIA, a town in the Vale of Leven, *c.* 3½ miles N. of Dumbarton. Its industries include dyeing, bleaching and textile printing. Salmon, sea-trout and brown trout are taken in the River Leven.

ALFORD (ah'ford), a village 1 mile S. of the Don in the Howe of Alford (see below), 26 miles W. of Aberdeen, with salmon and trout fishing in the Don. There is a pleasure park with facilities for tennis, bowls, cricket, football and a children's corner, skating and curling ponds and a riverward stretch of woodland with delightful walks. Near by was fought the battle of Alford (1645) in which Montrose defeated the Covenanters under General Baillie.
A little to the NW. is Bridge of Alford (fishing).

ALFORD, HOWE OF, 10-mile stretch of the Don Valley, roughly centred on Alford, sheltered by hills, pleasantly wooded, and guarded at either end by a narrow defile. In its progress through the Howe the river drops 80 ft., with many fine salmon pools and trout-fishing reaches.

ALLOA, a manufacturing town (beer, yarn, engineering and light industries) and port on the Forth. Alloa Tower (13th century) stands in the grounds of Alloa House here.

ALLOWAY, a village, now situated within Ayr town boundary, birthplace of Robert Burns. Here one is able to see the thatched cottage—indeed the very room—in which he was born, furnished approximately in the style of the period. Relics include his family Bible, and MSS and rare editions of his works. A mile on is the roofless Alloway Kirk, scene of the witches' dance in *Tam o' Shanter* and close by the Burns Monument and Tea Gardens. The monument is a graceful copy of an Athenian temple; from the tea gardens one has a view of the lovely little Auld Brig o' Doon, for which Tam rode so wildly with the witches at his heels! Near here, too, is Mount Oliphant Farm, where Burns spent some years of his childhood.

ALNESS, a village on the River Alness, 2 miles W. of Invergordon. It has distilleries, a picturesque golf course, and a bowling green.

ALTNAHARRA, an angling spot near the west end of Loch Naver (Sutherland).

ALVA, a wool town of Clackmannanshire, with a glen of the same name and, in it, a waterfall.

ALYTH (ay'lith), a market town and resort of Perthshire, near the Angus border, with facilities for fishing and golf. The falls of Reekie Linn are here, also a Pictish fort traditionally associated with Queen Guinevere.

AMULREE, a small, pretty hamlet of Perthshire, 10 miles from Dunkeld on the Crieff road. There is fishing in Loch Freuchie and the River Bran.

ANCRUM, a village 4 miles NW. of Jedburgh (Roxburghshire) on the Ale Water, with nearby, the battlefield of Ancrum Moor (1545), also called Lilliard's Edge in honour of a heroine of the battle.

ANGUS, formerly Forfarshire, an eastern county washed by the North Sea and the Firth of Tay. Between the Sidlaw Hills and the Grampians is the rich plain of Strathmore (the Howe of Angus). Agriculture and fishing are important, and linen and jute are manufactured in the towns, of which Dundee, Arbroath, Brechin and Montrose are the largest. Forfar is the county town.

ANNAN, a royal burgh near the mouth of a like-named river on the Solway Firth. Carlyle was educated and taught at the old Grammar School here. The town has engineering and other industries, as well as Chapelcross nuclear power station nearby. Picturesque Annandale stretches NNW. to the Devil's Beef Tub (*q.v.*)

AN TEALLACH ("the forge"), a small range (3,483 ft.) to the S. of Loch Broom (Ross-shire).

ANSTRUTHER, the name given to the three royal burghs of Kilrenny, Anstruther Easter and Anstruther Wester, a group of small fishing and agricultural places in the East Neuk of Fife, on the Firth of Forth. There is golf (9-hole course), tennis, bowls and angling. "Anster Fair" is a gala occasion. Anstruther Easter was the birthplace of the great Scottish divine, Dr. Thomas Chalmers. Most interesting building is probably the 16th century manse of the Auld Kirk. An old stone coffin found here was said to be that of St. Adrian (see May, Isle of).

APPIN, a western district of Argyll, including Lismore Island, scene of the historic murder of Colin Campbell of Glenure, for which James Stewart ("James of the Glen") was hanged, a miscarriage of justice which caused a great outcry in the West. On a tiny island in Loch Linnhe is Castle Stalker, built as a hunting-lodge for James IV by a Stewart of Appin. At the mouth of little Loch Laich is the village of Port Appin, with a pier and steamer service to Lismore.

APPLECROSS, a fishing village of Wester Ross in the Inner Sound opposite the island of Raasay. A sculptured stone is the only relic of St. Moalrubha, who built a chapel here in the 7th century. The West Highland School of Adventure for Boys is established at Hartfield House. The road to Applecross, through the Bealach-nam-ba (cattle pass) over Tornapress Hill, is the steepest in Britain, rising to over 2,050 ft. in 5 miles. The views over Ross-shire, Skye and the Outer Hebrides are fine.

ARBROATH

A TOWN and popular seaside resort of Angus, 15 miles NE. of Dundee, famous for its large and architecturally interesting 12th century Abbey Church, and the fine rock scenery round its coast. It has a small harbour, an engineering industry and manufactures of jute, sailcloth, etc. Arbroath caters for visitors with a seaside golf course and a large and well-equipped swimming pool.

The Abbey, begun in 1175, twice burnt by the English, was the scene of a bold Declaration of Independence by the Three Estates (1320). After the Reformation it was allowed to fall into decay. Mainly Early English in style with Norman and later influences apparent in, *e.g.*, the round-headed, deeply-recessed west doorway, the ruins comprise the south wall of the nave, south transept (fairly complete) and the Chapter House; the Abbey Pond with its flanking tower, and the Abbot's House, used as a museum. Among the

monuments is part of an effigy (doubtfully) representing William the Lion, founder of the Abbey, who is buried here. The round window facing the sea in the south transept was formerly lighted as a guide to ships. To the south is the solitary rock stack known as the Pint Stoup.

ARBUTHNOTT, a village 12 miles SW. of Stonehaven, has a fascinating 13th century church, the chancel of which (with the priest's chamber above) is part of the original structure. The famous Arbuthnott Missal, Prayer-book and Psalter (Paisley Museum) are said to have come from here. Arbuthnott House stands near by in lovely grounds rising from the Bervie Water.

ARD, LOCH, a small and beautiful loch 3 miles W. of Aberfoyle.

ARDENTINNY, a pretty hamlet on Loch Long, Argyllshire.

ARDEONAIG (ar-jo′nayg), a loch-side place on Loch Tay.

ARDERSIER, a pretty fishing village on the south shore of the Moray Firth, 7 miles W. of Nairn, with a golf course. Two miles NE. on a promontory of the Firth stands Fort George, built as a Hanoverian barracks after the '45. Chanonry Point, with its conspicuous light-house, stands across the Firth, but the ancient ferry from Ardersier no longer operates.

ARDGOUR, a mountainous district to the NE. of Morven in Argyll, thinly populated, but with much stormy inter-clan history in the past.

ARDLUI, a resort at the N. end of Loch Lomond below Ben Vorlich. Near it is the Pulpit Rock, where open-air services were once held.

ARDNADAM, a small resort and yacht-building place on the Holy Loch (Firth of Clyde).

ARDNAMURCHAN POINT, most westerly point of the Scottish mainland, on the Ardnamurchan peninsula, with a wild and hilly hinterland. There is a lighthouse near the point.

ARDOCH, a great Roman station with, in places, fine ramparts and ditches, 8 miles NE. of Dunblane.

ARDRISHAIG, a large, pleasantly wooded village at the Loch Fyne end of the Crinan Canal. It has facilities for boating, bowls, tennis, fishing, and a cinema, steamer services to the Clyde in the season, bus communication with Glasgow, Oban and Campbeltown. Like its near neighbour, Lochgilphead, Ardrishaig was formerly engaged in the herring fisheries.

ARDROSSAN, a sunny, well-situated town and port on the Ayrshire coast, *c.* 18 miles NW. of Ayr. It has an excellent harbour and regular cargo and passenger sailings to Arran, Isle of Man and Ireland. Industries include oil refining, ship-building, ironfounding and metal manufacture. There are fine bathing sands, golf, tennis, bowls, and splendid sea-fishing; and a fascinating collection of Ayrshire literature in the Wood Memorial Library.
Ruins of Ardrossan Castle (captured by the English, re-taken

by Wallace, finally destroyed by Cromwell) are of interest, especially the ancient well and the so-called "Wallace's Larder". Horse Island is just off-shore. The coast road offers delightful walks and good views of Arran.

ARGYLLSHIRE, western seaboard county between Inverness-shire and the Clyde estuary, including Mull and other islands of the Inner Hebrides. The county is mountainous with such outstanding summits as Bidean-nam-Bian, Buchaille Etive, Cruachan, Ben Arthur and Ben More. The county town is Inveraray.

Dunoon, Tobermory, Oban and Campbeltown are famous resorts, and there are numerous historic castles and monuments.

Other notable places include Fingal's Cave, Iona and Glencoe. For the sportsman there are salmon and trout fishing, shooting and stalking, swimming, bathing, boating, golf, tennis, bowls around the larger centres and some of the smaller ones as well, mountaineering in Mull and the mainland.

Argyll's Bowling Green is the mountainous area between Loch Long and Loch Goil. Camden P.L.

ARISAIG, a fine coastal hamlet, 38 miles W. of Fort William.

ARKAIG, LOCH, a long narrow loch joined to Loch Lochy (Great Glen) by the short River Arkaig. Here, according to tradition, is hidden the treasure of the Jacobites. At the Loch Lochy end of the loch is a famous beech avenue called the "Dark Mile" or "Black Mile". Lochiel, whose seat is at Achnacarry

FAMOUS CLIMBS

BEN NEVIS,
 Gardyloo Gully.
 Rubicon Wall.
 Slav Route.
BLAVEN RIDGE, SKYE,
BIDEAN-NAM-BIAN,
 Church Door Buttress.
BUACHAILLE ETIVE MOR,
 Crowberry Gully.
 D-Gully Buttress.
 North Buttress.
 Rannoch Wall.
 Ravens Gully.
CUILLIN,
 Crack of Doom Chimney.
 Main Ridge.
LOCHNAGAR,
 Parallel Buttress.
 Tough Brown Ridge.
SGOR NAM FIANNAIDH,
 Clachaig Gully.

Overleaf: Bass Rock and Tantallon Castle.

near by, is said to have planted those trees before joining Prince Charlie.

ARKLET, a small loch and glen between Lochs Katrine and Lomond.

ARMADALE, a place near the south end of Skye with a modern castle (1815), and steamer connection with Mallaig.

ARMADALE, a village on the north coast of Sutherland, 24 miles W. of Thurso. At Kirtomy point, to the NW., formation of the rocks makes a long covered waterway open at either end, a natural curiosity.

ARRAN, a large island and holiday resort in the Firth of Clyde with magnificent scenery and rugged contours which form a grand feature of the Clyde. It has a good local service of buses and is catered for by steamers from Ardrossan and Fairlie, with cruises from Clyde ports in summer. A car ferry operates, and fast trains run from Glasgow to connect with steamers. A good coast road goes round the island. The chief places are Brodick, Lamlash, Whiting Bay, Corrie, Lochranza (*qq.v.*). The culminating point is Goat Fell (2,866 ft.) and other attractive places are Glen Rosa, Glen Sannox, Glen Monamore,

Arran: Glen Rosa.

Arran: Lochranza.

Catacol, Pirnmill, Machrie Bay, Kildonan Castle, Lagg, Sliddery and Blackwaterfoot. There are fine hill and rock climbs, the flora is of exceptional interest and there are tumuli and standing stones notably at Tormore, near Machrie.

Arrochar.

ARROCHAR, an attractive resort at the head of Loch Long, often used as a base for the ascent of Ben Arthur (The Cobbler).

ARTHUR, BEN, a mountain at the head of Loch Long, called "The Cobbler" from a fancied resemblance of its craggy top to a cobbler at work, offers every kind of climb from the fairly easy to the well-nigh impossible. The best base is Arrochar.

ASHIESTIEL, formerly a home of Sir Walter Scott (1804–12), W. of Galashiels.

ASSYNT, a beautiful loch in Sutherland with the ruined Ardvreck Castle on its shore, scene of Montrose's betrayal in 1650.

ATHELSTANEFORD, a village *c*. 2 miles N. of Haddington. Traditionally the burial-place of the Saxon King Athelstane—hence the

English-looking place-name, which however is pronounced el'shin-ford.

ATHOLL, formerly a district in the N. of Perthshire, whose inhabitants had the secret of the celebrated Atholl Brose, a compound of honey, whisky and other ingredients.

ATTOW, BEN, a mountain (3,383 ft.) at the head of Glen Affric, which may be ascended from Altbeath at the head of the glen.

AUCHINBLAE, a pretty village and inland resort of Kincardineshire, 11 miles SW. of Stonehaven, delightfully situated among hills and woods on the banks of the Luther Water. It has facilities for golf (9-hole course), tennis, bowls and fishing in the Luther. Beauty spots in the neighbourhood are Strathfinella and the Castle and Glen of Drumtochty, (W.)—the first taking its name from Fenella, wife of the Mormaor of the Mearns, lady of the so-called Green Castle, an earthwork or mote 6 m. to SW.

AUCHINCRUIVE, a mansion-house 3 miles NE. of Ayr housing the important West of Scotland Agricultural College. Hard by is the Hannah Dairy Research Institute.

AUCHINLECK, a village 2 miles NW. of Cumnock (Ayrshire) with Auchinleck House, seat of the Boswell family and birthplace of James Boswell.

AUCHTERARDER, a royal burgh and market town of Perthshire, 14 miles SW. of Perth. It dates from the 12th century, has important cattle markets and a woollen industry, and consists largely of a very long main street. It has facilities for golf and fishing.

AUCHTERMUCHTY, a royal burgh and quaint old inland town,

10 miles W. of Cupar in the Howe of Fife. Places of interest within easy reach include Falkland Palace and Lindores Abbey, and good loch and river fishing is available in the neighbourhood.

AUCHTERTOOL, a village of Fife between Dunfermline and Kirkcaldy.

AULDEARN, a village 2 miles E. of Nairn; scene of a victory of Montrose over the Covenanters. Inshoch Tower (ruins) is near by.

AULTBEA, a village on the east shore of Loch Ewe, Wester Ross, 2 miles SW. of Gruinard Bay It has a Royal Navy Boom Defence Depot and N.A.T.O. oil fuel depot.

AVICH, a river and loch of Argyllshire to the W. of Loch Awe into which the river flows. The ruined castle in the loch figures in Fingalian legend.

AVIEMORE, "gateway to the Cairngorms", a small village and wintersports resort on the River Spey in Inverness-shire near the borders of Banff, presently being developed as a tourist centre by the provision of a multistorey luxury hotel, covered ice rink, heated swimming pool, cinema, bowling alley, conference hall, restaurants and new shopping precinct.

AVOCH (auch), a fishing village on the Black Isle, on Inverness Firth.

AVON (aan), a stream, a remote loch and a mountain (Ben Avon; 3,843 ft.) of the Cairngorms. The stream, giving name (Glenavon) to a deer forest here, flows out of the loch, which is on the NE. descent from Ben Macdhui, E. through Glen Avon and N. through Strathavon to the Spey at Ballindalloch.

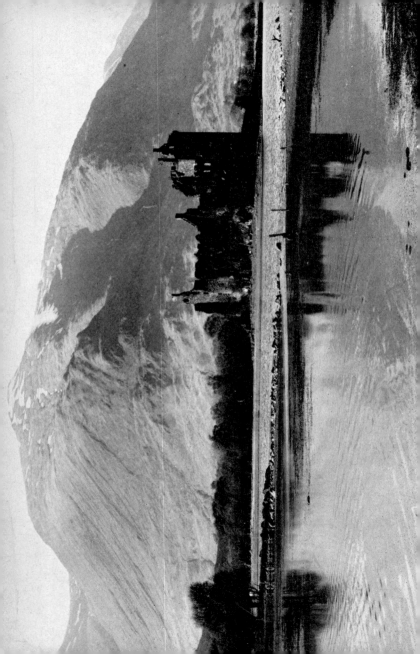

AWE, LOCH, a freshwater loch of central Argyll, running from Dalmally in the NE. to Ford, near the head of Loch Craignish, in the SW., very narrow except at its N. end, where it widens to a lovely sheet of water dotted with wooded islets. Here on a promontory is the most notable of its castles, Kilchurn, an ancient Campbell stronghold dating from 1440. Westward an arm of the loch narrows to the Pass of Brander, to flow as the River Awe into Loch Etive. Of the islets, Inishail ("isle of rest") is the site of a nunnery. Fraoch Eilean, literally "heather island", is associated in legend with the dragon-slaying hero Fraoch in the old Celtic tale of the Daughter of Maeve. On the shores of the loch are Lochawe, Port Sonachan, Ardchonal Castle, Portinisherrich, Ford, Cladich, Taychreggan and a number of smaller hamlets— including New York! Loch Awe is the centre of an important hydro-electric scheme of considerable technical interest (pump-storage; reversible pump/turbines). See also Cruachan.

AYR

A N old historic town on the Ayrshire coast, county town of Ayr, also a popular seaside and holiday resort, a fishing and agricultural centre, busy industrial town and port at the mouth of the River Ayr; it has many associations with Robert Burns.

There is a large holiday camp on the Heads of Ayr; attractive shops, cinemas, theatre, Palais de Danse, ice rink; esplanade and good bathing sands. The racecourse is a great attraction, with four race meetings in the season. Also one has golf, tennis, bowls, angling, boating, bathing, sea-fishing, children's amusements, bands, etc. in the Lower Green, and summer entertainments in the Pavilion. Road and rail communications are good, and Prestwick's famous airport is only 4 miles away. There are frequent bus tours and steamer sailings to the Clyde coast, Arran and Kintyre.

A royal burgh since 1202, Ayr has a rich history. Here Wallace started the War of Independence by burning some English soldiery in the "Barns of Ayr". Bruce held a parliament here in 1315 to determine the Scottish succession. Cromwell built his great fort above the harbour, incorporating the 12th century church of St. John, which he used for the storing of arms. Fragments of the old church remain, though the fort has practically disappeared.

Opposite : Kilchurn Castle by Loch Awe, W. S. Thomson.

Ailsa Craig from the Ayrshire Coast.

Old St. John's was replaced (1665) by the present parish church, which itself has features of interest. It is reached from the High Street at Wallace's Tower, a more modern version of an ancient tower in which, traditionally, Wallace was immured. Near by is the Tam o' Shanter Inn (museum) and up the street Burns's statue. The lower town, about the River Ayr, has many evidences of antiquity, including the "Auld Brig" sung by Burns. In the newer part are the Town and County Buildings, Wellington Square, Belleisle House and grounds and some pleasant residential suburbs among gardens and trees. There are further associations with the poet Burns near the town (see Alloway, Catrine, Mauchline, Mossgiel, Tarbolton).

AYRSHIRE, a western seaboard county with a long coastline. A farming, industrial and holiday county, famous for its Ayrshire cows and early potatoes, its golf, airport and racing yachts, and sharing with Dumfries the title of Land of Burns.

For the tourist, interest centres in the golf courses and golden sands of its famous resorts,

Largs, Saltcoats, Ayr, Prestwick, Troon and the rest. Inland, the Glen Trool National Forest Park is of great beauty. The old divisions of Ayr still bear their ancient names— Cunninghame (north), Kyle (centre, between the rivers Irvine and Doon) and Carrick (south).

AYTON, a small place on the Great North Road, 5 miles SW. of Eyemouth (Berwickshire).

BADENOCH (baed´nohh), a mountainous district of Inverness-shire, gave name to the infamous Wolf of Badenoch. (See Loch-an-Eilean).

BALALLAN, a village of Lewis, near the head of Loch Erisort, centre of the island's tweed industry. There is angling, sailing, and delightful walks. On an island in the loch are the remains of a Columban church.

BALCARRES. See Kilconquhar.

BALERNO, a village to the SW. of Edinburgh, a good starting point for Pentland walks.

BALGONIE, a village of Fife, 5 miles W. of Leven, has an old church. Near by are the formidable ruins of Balgonie Castle.

BALGOWNIE, BRIG O'. See Aberdeen.

BALLACHULISH (bhaile aig a Chaolas, "township on the narrows"), a village on Loch Leven in N. Argyll, 15 miles S. of Fort William. It was formerly noted for its slate quarries, which are now of less importance. There is a monument here to James Stewart, hanged for his supposed share in the Appin murder. The surrounding scenery is magnificent. The ferry to North Ballachulish in Inverness-shire saves 20 road miles on the Fort William route. There are facilities for mountaineering, trout and salmon fishing, hiking, boating, and coach tours to places of interest. Glencoe is 1½ miles away.

BALLANTRAE, a fishing port, former smugglers' haunt and small seaside resort of south Ayrshire, at the mouth of the River Stinchar. There is golf, tennis, angling, boating, sea-fishing, as well as touring by car or bus. Points of interest are the ruins of Ardstinchar Castle, and Sawney Bean's Cave, introduced into Crockett's *Grey Man*. Three miles to the N. is Bennane Head and Knockdolian Hill (869 ft.), a local landmark.

BALLATER, a town and resort of Aberdeenshire, gateway to "Royal" Deeside and the splendidly picturesque upper reaches of the river. It is a pleasant little place with fishing in the Dee, golf and tennis, and numerous shops with "By Royal Appointment" signs. Also a good touring centre, especially for walkers.

BALLINDALLOCH, a village at the junction of the Avon and the Spey, 13 miles NE. of Grantown on the Elgin road. Buses run from here to Tomintoul and Craigellachie. Dalnasheugh Inn is close by, on the banks of the Avon. Ballindalloch Castle—also on the Avon—is one of the finest baronial structures in this much castled area, with some of its older features still intact.

BALLINLUIG, a road junction for Aberfeldy and Killin at the meeting of the Tay and Tummel (Perthshire).

BALLOCH, an increasingly popular resort of Dunbartonshire, *c.* 5 miles N. of Dumbarton, picturesquely situated at the foot of Loch Lomond. There is angling in Loch Lomond and the River Leven, boating, hill-walking, touring and cruising. Near here is the entrance to Balloch Park. There is a tea-room in Balloch Castle; the ancient castle (site is nearby) was a seat of the Earls of Lennox. To the NE. is the little wooded village of Gartocharn with an interesting church, and a few miles beyond, just E. of the bridge over the Endrick Water, is Kilmaronock church, on or near the site of a cell of St. Maronnan (see Scott's *Lady of the Lake*).

BALLOCHMYLE. See Catrine.

BALMACAAN, a hamlet 1 mile S. of the River Urquhart near Loch Ness. It has a college of Celtic Art.

BALMACARA, a peaceful village on the shores of Lochalsh in Wester Ross. The district around (estate of Balmacara) belongs to the National Trust, the mansion-house being used as a secondary boarding school for boys, with agricultural subjects, and Duncraig Castle is similarly employed for girls, with emphasis on domestic science.

BALMACLELLAN, a village of Kirkcudbrightshire, 2 miles NE. of New Galloway.

BALMAHA, a place on the east side of Loch Lomond, like Balloch, it has a very successful Cruising Club.

BALMERINO, a Fifeshire village with famous abbey, near Newport.

BALMORAL CASTLE, the Queen's private residence and estate, delightfully situated on the River Dee. The Castle, a handsome structure of "white" granite in the Scottish baronial style, was built by Prince Albert, consort of Queen Victoria, about the middle of the last century. It is the Highland home of Queen Elizabeth and her family, frequently in residence here. Balmoral Estate is extensive, and includes Ballochbuie Deer Forest and the estate of Bachnagairn, purchased by George VI in 1947. Except when royalty is in residence, the grounds on certain days are open to visitors.

BALQUHIDDER (bal-whidder), a picturesque place 12 miles NNW. of Callander. There is shooting, good loch fishing, climbing and hiking. Rob Roy MacGregor, the celebrated Highland outlaw and freebooter whose exploits are told in Scott's novel *Rob Roy*, is buried in the churchyard here. To the N. and W. are the Braes of Balquhidder.

BALWEARIE. See Kirkcaldy.

BANAVIE, a village near Loch Eil at the south-west end of the Caledonian Canal.

Opposite: Balmoral Castle.

BANCHORY (ban'cor–i), 18 miles W. of Aberdeen, is a charming village with an interesting perfume factory. It stands among woods and meadows on the N. bank of the River Dee, and has a golf course. Near by is the picturesque Bridge of Feugh, over the Water of Feugh, a tributary of the Dee.

BANFF, an ancient royal burgh, and decayed seaport, county town of Banffshire, on the Moray Firth, at the mouth of the Deveron, with its sister town, Macduff, opposite on the east side of the estuary (Banff Bay). There is a popular, well-appointed caravan site at Banff Links, to the W. of the town, and an attractive golf course extending up the riverside, on which stands Duff House, a former residence of the dukes of Fife, a fine building by Robert Adam (senior) dating from 1730, but no longer occupied. Banff has facilities for putting, tennis, bowls, sea-fishing, angling (salmon, sea- and brown trout). It is a good touring base, with buses to Fraserburgh, Huntly, Aberdeen, Buckie, Elgin, and Inverness.

Banff is notable for its interesting old houses. There is a church yard with small remains of an ancient church, and vestiges of a castle (birthplace of Archbishop Sharp in 1618).

Some 2 miles S. is the old Bridge of Alvah at a picturesque gorge on the river.

BANFFSHIRE, a north-eastern county on the Moray Firth, mountainous in the S. where on the boundary lie the Cairngorms and Ben Macdhui. The chief rivers are the Spey and the Deveron. Agriculture, forestry, distilling, fishing, and boatbuilding, engineering and woollen manufactures are carried on. Banff is the county town.

BANNOCKBURN, a small town 3 miles SSE. of Stirling. To the W. took place the Battle of Bannockburn (1314) in which Bruce, by defeating the English, won Scotland's independence. At the Borestane, overlooking the battlefield, stands an equestrian statue of Bruce, unveiled by the Queen in 1964. A Rotunda shows the plan of battle, and there is a restaurant.

BARCALDINE. See Creran.

BARR, a resort on the River Stinchar, *c.* 7 miles SE. of Girvan (Ayr), with angling for salmon, sea-trout and brown trout.

BARRA, the southernmost of the larger islands of the Outer Hebrides, separated from Eriskay and South Uist by the Sound of Barra, famed for its white sands, for Kisimul Castle, seat of Clan MacNeil (on Castle Bay in the SW.) and for its songs. The location scenes for the film "Whisky Galore" were shot here. Beneath the castle walls is Castlebay, chief place on the island and a fishing port. There is a steamer connection with Oban, as well as air and sea links with Glasgow and the Clyde.

BARRHEAD, a manufacturing town 7 miles SW. of Glasgow.

BARRY LINKS. See Monifieth.

BARVAS, a village on the west coast of Lewis, near the head of the little Loch Barvas. There is a sandy beach, and trout and salmon fishing. Barvas has a small pottery industry.

BASS ROCK, THE, a rocky islet in the Firth of Forth, opposite Canty Bay and Tantallon Castle, 2 miles E. of North Berwick. "The Bass" is 350 ft. high and about a mile round, has a lighthouse and wears a perpetual fluttering mantle of seabirds, chiefly solan geese (gannets), but also gulls and guillemots, cormorants, kittiwakes and a host of others including the amusing little puffins. An episode in R. L. Stevenson's *Catriona* is set here. St. Baldred (7th century), missionary to the adjacent mainland, had a retreat on the Bass. In the 17th century thirty-nine Covenanters were imprisoned in its fortress (ruins can still be seen), and later in the century some Jacobites, who, however, overcame their guards and took possession of the islet. The Bass Rock is encircled by motorboat excursions from North Berwick (landings only by arrangement).

BATHGATE is an industrial town of West Lothian, c. 18 miles W. of

Gannets on the Bass.

Edinburgh. Sir James Y. Simpson (of chloroform fame) was born here in 1811. It has large automobile assembly and other works.

BEARSDEN, former residential community of Dunbartonshire, c. 4 miles NW. of Glasgow, became a separate burgh in 1958.

BEATTOCK, a village at the N. end of Annandale, 2 miles S. of Moffat.

BEAULY, a pretty wooded village of Inverness-shire, on the Beauly near its entrance to the Beauly Firth. On the river, noted for its salmon fishing, are the picturesque Falls of Kilmorack (5 miles SW.), and two hydro-electric dams in the Kilmorack and Aigas gorges. Beaufort Castle is the home of Lord Lovat, Chief of the clan Fraser.

BEITH, a small Ayrshire town, 15 miles SW. of Glasgow, noted for its beautiful furniture.

BELHAVEN, a coastal village of East Lothian with fine sands.

BELL ROCK, or Inchcape Rock, a rock off the Firth of Tay with a lighthouse on it. It is said to have taken its name from a bell anciently placed there (see Southey's Ballad, "The Inchcape Rock").

BEMERSYDE, a hamlet, mansion and estate of Berwickshire, to the NE. of Newton St. Boswells, seat of the Haig family.

BENBECULA, an island of the Outer Hebrides, between North and South Uist; connected with the former by the North Ford causeway, and with the latter by viaduct over the narrow, islanded Benbecula Sound. A road runs from north to south of the island; air services to Abbotsinch Airport (for Glasgow).

BENDERLOCH, or Ledaig, a village on a wide bay 2 miles N. of Connel Bridge in the district of Benderloch (Argyll), lying between Lochs Etive and Creran.

BENEVEAN, LOCH, a hydro-electric reservoir below Loch Affric (*q.v.*), in beautiful scenery. A tunnel (3 miles) brings to it water from Loch Mullardoch. (*q.v.*)

BENMORE ESTATE (Argyll-shire), north of the Holy Loch. The gardens (which now belong to the Forestry Commission) contain a vast collection of trees and shrubs, and are open to visitors.

BENNACHIE, a mountain (1,733 ft.) of Aberdeenshire, N. of the River Don near Inverurie, a land-mark and the subject of the nostalgic old Scots song, "*O gin I were where Gadie rins, at the back o' Bennachie*".

BERNERA, an island in Loch Roag, on the west coast of Lewis. It is noted for its stone circles and fine white sands.

BERRIEDALE, a village on the east coast of Caithness.

BERVIE. See Inverbervie.

ANCIENT COMMON RIDINGS AND FESTIVALS

HAWICK
  Common Riding: June
SELKIRK
  Riding of the Marches:
  June
LANARK
  Lanimer Day: June
PEEBLES
  Beltane Festival: June
LINLITHGOW
  Riding of the Marches: July
GALASHIELS
  Braw Lad's Gathering: July

ANNAN
  Riding of the Marches:
  July
LANGHOLM
  Common Riding: July
LAUDER
  Common Riding: August
SANQUHAR
  Riding of the Marches:
  August
INNERLEITHEN
  Cleikum Ceremony:
  August

Exact dates are published annually by the Scottish Tourist Board.

BERWICK-UPON-TWEED
(ENGLAND)

A SEAPORT and municipal borough at the mouth of the Tweed, forming with the adjoining Spittal and Tweedmouth the county of the borough and town of Berwick-upon-Tweed.

Because of its strategic position at the mouth of the Tweed, on the main line of communication between the two countries, it was fought over for centuries—sacked, burnt, besieged, captured and recaptured, until at last, in 1482, it rested with the English. After the Union it became a kind of neutral zone; official documents made mention of "England and Scotland and Berwick-upon-Tweed".

The ancient castle (burnt by the English in 1174) is gone, pulled down to make room for a railway station! There still remains the 15-arched bridge begun in 1611, the parish church, dating from 1648, fragments of the defence walls built by Edward I, and the more extensive relics of the Elizabethan walls.

Berwick to-day is a peaceful fishing town and seaport, with a broad modern bridge carrying the Great North Road over the Tweed, fine sands and swimming pools, golf (links lie between the town and the North Sea); tennis, bowls, boating, salmon and trout fishing in the Tweed and Whiteadder.

To the NW. (2 miles) is Halidon Hill, scene of a disastrous Scottish defeat at the hands of the English (1333).

BERWICKSHIRE, a border county separated from England for the most part by the lower course of the Tweed and having in the N. the broad uplands of the Lammermuir Hills, which run W. from St. Abb's Head and attain 1,749 ft. in Meikle Says Law on the N. boundary. Many sheep are reared in these uplands, while the Merse (the fertile lowland between the Tweed and the Lammermuirs) is a rich farming district. In the W. the Leader Water runs through Lauderdale to the Tweed. Duns is the county town; Eyemouth, Coldstream, and Lauder are the burghs.

BETTYHILL, a village on the Pentland Firth, named from a bygone Countess of Sutherland. It has salmon fishing in the Naver, and fine coast walks.

BHUIRD, BEN-A-, an eastern mountain (3,924 ft.) of the Cairngorm group.

BIDEAN-NAM-BIAN, a mountain (3,766 ft.) to the S. of Glencoe (Argyllshire).

BIGGAR, a pleasant country town near the E. boundary of Lanarkshire, and a bracing upland holiday resort with golf, good fishing, and touring facilities. It is a royal burgh.

With a wide main street and no particular air of antiquity, it yet has an old church dating from the Middle Ages, and the ruins of a feudal castle. In more modern times it was the home of W. E. Gladstone's ancestors, and the birthplace of Dr. John Brown (*Rab and His Friends*).

Biggar is a route centre, with roads running to Edinburgh and Newcastle, and a link between E. and W.

BIRKHALL, a royal residence near Ballater.

BIRNAM, a charming little village and resort on the River Tay opposite Dunkeld (*q.v.*) whose amenities it shares. Here grew the famous Birnam Woods which marched against Macbeth, and while little remains of these, the district is still well wooded. There is a ruined hill fort on Birnam Hill where King Duncan is said to have held his court. Near Birnam House is a "hangman's oak", where summary justice was dealt to wild clansmen descending from the hills.

BIRRENS. See Ecclefechan.

BIRSAY, a hamlet near Birsay Bay in the N. of the mainland of Orkney with a ruinous earl's palace, and traces of antiquity on Brough Head, an islet off the coast.

BLACKADDER, a tributary of the Whiteadder (Berwickshire).

BLACK ISLE, THE, a large peninsula of Easter Ross, bounded by the Cromarty, Beauly and Moray Firths, its base running roughly from Dingwall to Beauly. A hilly, well-wooded region of mainly agricultural character, with a marked ecclesiastical interest. Cromarty, Fortrose and Rosemarkie are within its bounds.

BLACKNESS, a decayed port in the Forth, 15 miles WNW. of Edinburgh, with an ancient castle.

BLACKWATERFOOT, a seaside resort of Arran, with a golf course. King's Cave near by is said to have sheltered Robert Bruce. There is good bathing, fishing and pony-trekking.

BLACK ROCK OF NOVAR. See Dingwall.

BLADNOCH, a village to the SW. of Wigtown, with ruins of Baldoon Castle near by.

BLAIR ATHOLL, a delightfully situated village on the River Garry, 7 miles NW. of Pitlochry, with salmon and trout fishing, and pony-trekking. Blair Castle, seat of the Dukes of Atholl, dates in part from the 13th century, has been held by Montrose, Claverhouse, Cromwell's faction and (during the '45) by Prince Charles Edward. The castle is open to the public.

The Firth of Forth at Blackness Castle.

BLAIRGOWRIE, a prosperous small burgh of Perthshire, on the River Ericht, 5 miles NW. of Coupar Angus. Centre of a raspberry growing area; has rayon and jute, agricultural machinery, canning and frozen-fish packing industries. There is an excellent golf course and facilities for pony-trekking, skiing, etc.

BLAIR, MOUNT, a mountain (2,441 ft.) N. of Blairgowrie.

BLAIRMORE, a small resort on the west coast of Loch Long (Argyll).

BLAIRS COLLEGE (Roman Catholic), is about 5 miles SW. of Aberdeen. It is a handsome modern building, uniquely distinguished in the possession of the Douai portrait of Mary Queen of Scots, also some notable relics of the famous Scots College at Paris.

BLANTYRE, the birthplace of David Livingstone (1813–1873), Scotland's great missionary-explorer, a mining and textile village 9 miles SE. of Glasgow on the River Clyde. Blantyre is interesting also as the site of a Priory, of which there are only scanty remains.

The house in which Livingstone was born, and from which, as a boy, he went daily to work in the mills, is incorporated in the National Memorial, which includes a museum with many fascinating relics of his life and work. Rose gardens slope to the river, and tea-rooms are a useful amenity for tourists.

BLAVEN (blay'ven), a mountain (3042 ft.) in Skye near the head of Loch Slapin, an inlet on the E. of Loch Scavaig, an impressive landmark and of interest to climbers.

BOAT OF GARTEN, a

pleasant small resort on the River Spey, 5 miles N. of Aviemore. Formerly a ferry (since replaced by a bridge) crossed the river at this point—hence the name. There is good fishing, tennis, and golf. It is also a winter sports centre, with a ski school. The farm of Tulloch in the vicinity gave its name to a well-known Highland reel.

BODDAM, a granite-built fishing village with hotel, of east Aberdeenshire, 3 miles S. of Peterhead, near Buchan Ness.

BONAR BRIDGE, a beauti-

fully situated village, 13 miles NW. of Tain on the Kyle of Sutherland. Industries are salmon fishing and tourism. There are facilities for golf and angling. Bronze Age remains may be seen in the neighbourhood.

BO'NESS or Borrowstounness, a manufacturing town (fertilisers and chemicals) and port on the Firth of Forth in a coal-mining district.

BONAWE, a village on the south shore of Loch Etive, near Taynuilt. There is a ferry across the loch to Bonawe Quarries, near which is the ancient Ardchattan Priory (now part of the mansionhouse) with its interesting burial ground. Ardchattan has associations with Robert the Bruce, and was the site of the last Gaelic parliament.

BORERAIG, on the north-west coast of Skye. Here a cairn commemorates the famous college of piping of the MacCrimmons (hereditary pipers to the MacLeods of Dunvegan in past centuries). The rent of one penny is paid by the present College of Piping to the local laird during Skye Week (end of May).

BORTHWICK, a small place 10 miles SSE. of Edinburgh with a massive ruined castle, having associations with Mary Queen of Scots, Bothwell and Cromwell.

BOTHWELL, a pleasant residential village on the Clyde, 2 miles NNW. of Hamilton on the Glasgow road, noted chiefly for its ruined castle (12th century) and (restored) 14th century church. It was the birthplace of Joanna Baillie, the poetess (1762–1851). Across the river from Bothwell is Blantyre.

The Royal Braemar Gathering Topix.

At Bothwell Brig here, the Covenanters were severely beaten by Monmouth in 1679.

BOWLING, a village at the Clyde end of the now disused Forth and Clyde canal, 2½ miles up the Clyde from Dumbarton. Surrounded by an oil depot is a memorial to Henry Bell, who put the first steamer on the Firth of Clyde.

BOWMORE, the chief village on Islay, a small market town, fishing village and port on Loch Indaal. It has a curious round white church, with a small round tower, on a hill above the harbour.

BRACADALE, LOCH, an islanded loch in the W. of Skye, with the village of Bracadale on an eastern arm. It has glorious cliff scenery.

BRACO, a village 10 miles N. of Stirling on the Crieff road, chiefly noted for its proximity to the large Roman Camp of Ardoch (*q.v.*).

BRAEMAR, 8 miles W. of Balmoral, stands 1,100 ft. above sea-level, a bracing little mountain village in magnificent surroundings, with the Clunie

Water flowing through it. Historic highlight is the raising of "The Standard on the Braes o' Mar" by the Earl of Mar in 1715. The site of this event is now occupied by a hotel. Here, too, Robert Louis Stevenson wrote part of *Treasure Island*.

An event in the Scottish social calendar is the Royal Braemar Gathering, usually attended by the Queen and a party from Balmoral. The village then presents a gay appearance, and hotel accommodation is severely taxed.

This is a famous centre for winter sports, also for climbing —a favourite base from which to tackle Lochnagar, some 12 miles SE.

BRAERIACH, a mountain (4,248 ft.) of the Western Cairngorms. SW. of Braeriach lie the Wells of Dee.

BRAID HILLS. See Edinburgh.

BRAN, (1) A river of Perthshire, tributary of the Tay followed by the road from Amulree to Dunkeld, its valley known as Strath Bran. (2) A river of Ross-shire flows through Strath Bran into Loch Luichart.

BRANDER, PASS OF, a romantic gorge through which the River Awe flows from the hydro-electric barrage at the north end of Loch Awe to Loch Etive. It is overlooked by Ben Cruachan from the N.

BRANXHOLM TOWER, a ruined tower 4 miles SW. of Hawick.

BREADALBANE, an ancient district of north-western Perthshire, gave title to a branch of the Campbells. The Breadalbane hydro-electric scheme makes use of the river Lyon headwaters (with Lochs Lyon and Daimh as reservoirs), and also the waters of Lochs Earn and Lednock.

BRECHIN, a pleasant country town and agricultural centre of Angus, prettily situated on the South Esk, 8 miles inland from Montrose, noted for its 12th century cathedral and especially for the Round Tower adjoining it. It has some manufactures of linen, jute, rayon, and agricultural machinery, light engineering and distilling. There is a good 18-hole golf course, and angling in the North and South Esk, West Water and Cruik. Brechin is a splendid touring base, particularly for the Angus glens.

Brechin Castle is remembered in history for its gallant stand against the English armies of Edward I. Brechin cathedral, which is also the parish church, is mainly Early English; it has considerable architectural beauty without and within, and possesses many ancient relics. But its chief glory is the Round

HIGHLAND and other GAMES

May — September

LOCHORE	. . .	May	STRATHPEFFER . .	August
PITLESSIE	. . .	May	TAYNUILT . . .	August
ALLOA	. . .	June	NAIRN . . .	August
PERTH	. . .	June	MOREBATTLE . .	August
MARKINCH .	. .	June	INNERLEITHEN . .	August
CUPAR .	. . .	June	STRATHDON . .	August
CERES .	. . .	June	MURRAYFIELD (Edinburgh)
CROOK OF DEVON	.	June		August
KIRKCONNEL	. .	June	KINLOCHRANNOCH .	August
STRATHMIGLO	. .	July	CRIEFF . . .	August
OXTON	. . .	July	GLENFINNAN . .	August
ALVA .	. . .	July	NETHY BRIDGE . .	August
JEDBURGH .	. .	July	MILNGAVIE . . .	August
LUSS .	. . .	July	WHITTINGHAME . .	August
DUNBEATH .	. .	July	BALLATER . . .	August
AIRTH	. . .	July	DRUMNADROCHIT .	August
FORT WILLIAM .	.	July	COWAL (Dunoon) .	August
KELSO	. . .	July	SHOTTS . .	September
DINGWALL .	. .	July	ABOYNE . .	September
LOCHEARNHEAD .	.	July	ROYAL BRAEMAR GATHERING
DORNOCH .	. .	August		September
BRIDGE OF EARN	.	August	DUNBLANE . .	September
INVERKEITHING .	.	August	PITLOCHRY . .	September
ABERLOUR .	. .	August	ARGYLLSHIRE .	September
			OBAN . .	September
			BIRNAM . .	September

Exact dates obtainable from Scottish Tourist Board Office.

41

Tower at its south-west corner—one of only three in the country; he otthers are at Abernethy and Egilsay in Orkney. It is 87 ft. high and dates from about the 10th century, a relic it is believed, from the early Celtic church which preceded the cathedral on this site.

BRESSAY, an island of Shetland separated from Lerwick by Bressay Sound, having off its east coast Noss, a famous bird sanctuary.

Brechin Cathedral and Round Tower.

BRIDGE OF ALLAN, a spa and health and holiday resort on the Allan Water, 3 miles NNE. of Stirling. There is excellent salmon and trout fishing in the Allan Water, as well as golf, tennis, bowls, and boating.

The town stands in the beautiful woods of Airthrey Castle (a little to the S.), where Scotland's newest university is being built. Eastwards lies Dumyat (1,375 ft.), a shapely, climbable hill offering lovely and rewarding views. To the NW. is the great estate of Keir (former seat of the Stirling family) with its fine mansion and beautiful park and gardens.

BRIDGE OF BALGIE, a hamlet near the head of Glen Lyon (Perthshire).

BRIDGE OF CALLY, a small town and winter sports centre to the N. of Blairgowrie (Perthshire).

BRIDGE OF EARN, a small resort 5 miles S. of Perth.

BRIG O' DOON. See Alloway.

BRIG O' TURK. See Trossachs.

BRITTLE, a sea inlet and stream at its head, the latter flowing through Glen Brittle, in the south of Skye.

BROADFORD, a village 8 miles SW. of Kyleakin, on Broadford Bay (Skye). It is a good touring centre and road junction, linking with practically every part of the island. To the W. are the Red Hills (Ben na Cailleach 2,403 ft.; Ben Dearg 2,323 ft.).

BROAD LAW, a mountain (2,754 ft.) 10 miles SW. of Peebles.

BRODICK, a seaside resort on Brodick Bay on the east side of Arran, of which it is the unofficial capital. To the N. is Brodick Castle opened by the National Trust for Scotland to visitors. Goatfell is often climbed from here. Brodick has an 18-hole golf course, tennis courts, bowling and putting greens, fine sands and water-ski-ing facilities.

BRODGAR, RING OF. See Orkney.

BROOM, LOCH ("loch of showers"), a sea-loch in Wester Ross, 15½ miles long, with Ullapool on its north-east shore. Into its wide estuary opens Little Loch Broom (from which it is separated at one point by an isthmus only 1 mile wide) and lovely Gruinard Bay. The River Broom flows into the southern end of Loch Broom.

BRORA, a town on the east coast of Sutherland, at the mouth of the Brora, which flows out of Loch Brora. It has a small coal mine, first opened in 1598, a tweed mill, distillery and brickworks. There is a golf course, angling facilities and sea-bathing.

BROUGHTON, a pleasant Peebles-shire village, c. 8 miles E. of Biggar; a favourite holiday place. It has associations with Prince Charlie.

BROUGHTY FERRY. See Dundee.

BROXBURN, a West Lothian mining village, 11 miles W. of Edinburgh, skirted by the Edinburgh–Glasgow road (A8).

BRUAR, a stream of northern Perthshire, which flows through Glen Bruar and forms in its lower course three series of romantic falls (Falls of Bruar) near Struan.

BUCHAILLE ETIVE MORE, a mountain (3,345 ft.) at the head of Glencoe, famous for climbing.

BUCHAN. See Aberdeenshire.

BUCHAN, BULLERS OF, a vast "pot" or cauldron in the Buchan cliffs (east Aberdeenshire). The Bullers (i.e., Boilers) are 50 ft. across, 200 ft. deep, with perpendicular rock walls of varying thickness. The sea enters by a natural opening at the foot, into which, in fine weather, it is possible to row a boat. Dr. Johnson did this and was duly impressed.

BUCHAN NESS, a headland with lighthouse on the North Sea near Boddam, 3 miles S. of Peterhead; the most easterly point of Scotland.

BUCKHAVEN AND METHIL, two busy Fife coal ports combined in a single burgh, near the mouth of the River Leven, on the Firth of Forth. There are oilsilk, brick-making, and coalmining industries.

BUCKIE, a considerable fishing port on the Moray Firth, 21 miles W. of Banff. It has a large busy harbour with a high sea wall, effectively approached from the Square, and a fish-curing industry.

BUDDON CAMP. See Monifieth.

BUNESSAN, a small place on the west coast of Mull with granite quarries.

Kyles of Bute.

BURGHEAD, a fair-sized fishing village and commercial port on the Moray coast, 8 miles NW. of Elgin, with good sands and golf. It has a B.B.C. transmitter, and is the site of the Outward Bound Moray Sea School. It is visited also for its antiquarian interest: remains of extensive fortifications have been brought to light, among them the "Roman Well", a large rock-chamber enclosing a spring of water and a cistern. In January there is a well-known fire festival, the "Burning of the Clavie".

BURNMOUTH, a picturesque fishing village at the cliff foot near Eyemouth (Berwickshire).

BURNTISLAND, a royal burgh and seaport of Fife, on the Firth of Forth, 9 miles E. of Dunfermline. It has important shipbuilding and aluminium industries. Rossend Castle is associated with Mary Queen of Scots. There is a fascinating 16th century church. Burntisland has a swimming pool and a golf course.

BURRAFIRTH, a wild sea-inlet of Unst (Shetland).

BURROW HEAD, a promontory of Wigtownshire.

BUTE, an island in the Firth of Clyde, hilly in the N., fertile in the centre and S. It contains the popular resort and royal burgh of Rothesay, the smaller resorts of Port Bannatyne and Kilchattan, numerous remains of antiquity (including a vitrified fort at Dunagoil), and the seat of the Marquis of Bute at Mount Stuart. The Kyles of Bute are the beautiful straits separating the N. of the island from Argyll.

BUTESHIRE, an island county in the Firth of Clyde, includes Bute, Arran, and the Cumbraes. Rothesay (Bute) is the county town.

CABRACH, a Banffshire village near the Aberdeenshire border, 8 miles SE. of Dufftown. The lady of the Scots song, "Roy's Wife o' Aldivalloch", had her home at a farmhouse near by.

CADZOW. See Hamilton.

CAERLAVEROCK, a village 6 miles SE. of Dumfries, with an ancient ruinous castle of the same name at some distance to the S. of it nearer the Solway shore. It was a stronghold of the Maxwells.

CAIRNBULG, a fishing village of NE. Aberdeenshire (see Fraserburgh).

CAIRN EIGE, a mountain (3,877 ft.) of SW. Inverness-shire between Glen Affric and Glen Cannich.

CAIRNGORMS, a mountain group named from one of its summits (see below) in the central Highlands, giving name to the beautiful brown or yellow rock crystal found here. The chief peaks are Cairn Gorm (4,084 ft.) and Ben Macdhui (4,300 ft.) ascended from Aviemore via Glenmore Lodge; Braeriach (4,248 ft.) and Cairn Toul (4,241 ft.) ascended from Aviemore via Loch Einich. Its central area is a National Nature Reserve (62 sq. m.). The group is crossed by the Lairig Ghru, a desolate pass from Rothiemurchus to Braemar. Loch Avon and Loch Etchachan lie high upon the slopes of Cairn Gorm and Ben Macdhui respectively. On the Cairn Gorm the new "Ski Road" allows access by cars to a height of 2,000 ft.

CAIRNSMORE OF DEE, CAIRNSMORE OF FLEET, two hills of central Galloway (1,600 and 2,331 ft. respectively).

CAIRN TOUL. See Cairngorms.

CAITHNESS, a county at the north-east tip of Scotland; a "lowland" county beyond the Highland Line, generally flat and treeless. In the NE., however, it rises into high headlands —Holburn, Dunnet and Duncansby Heads, with much fine rock and cliff scenery. Fishing and agriculture are basic industries, there is an important nuclear power station at Dounreay near Thurso. Wick, on the E. coast, is the county town. Angling is a favourite sport where the rivers (notably the Thurso) are well stocked with salmon, and the numerous small lochs with trout. In the S. near the Sutherland border are the mountains of Morven (2,313 ft.) and Scaraben (2,054 ft.).

CAITHNESS, ORD OF, a bold rocky ridge and headland forming the south border of Caithness. On a cliff a little to the N. is the "deserted village" of Badbea, whose evicted people were among the first settlers of New Zealand.

CALEDONIAN CANAL, traverses the Great Glen from Banavie (near Fort William) to Clachnaharry (Inverness), linking Lochs Lochy, Oich and Ness. Begun by Telford in 1803, it took some forty-five years to complete, and was formerly much used, not only by fishing and cargo vessels, but also by small steamers. Now it is little frequented, although steamers still take tourists seeking the Loch Ness Monster from Inverness. Progress through the canal is slow, particularly at the Fort William end, where the steep ascent is made by a series of locks called "Neptune's Staircase", considered one of Telford's engineering masterpieces.

CALGARY, a small place on Calgary Bay on the west coast of Mull, which gives its name to Calgary in Canada.

CALLANDER, a favourite holiday place, 16 miles NW. of Stirling, on the River Teith, chief gateway to the Trossachs, and an important touring centre. It has hotels and other tourist accommodation, climbing, fishing, golf, tennis and bowls.

Bracklinn Falls, on the Keltie, are NE. of the village. There are remains of a Roman camp near Callander. Short tours can be taken to many of the places named by Scott in "The Lady of the Lake". They include Coilantogle Ford, the mustering place of Clan Alpine, and the Brig o'Turk.

CALLANISH, STANDING STONES OF, near the head of east Loch Roag (west coast of Lewis), a fine example of a prehistoric stone circle. With its radiating "arms", Callanish is 400 ft. long from north to south; it has 47 stones in all, including a giant monolith 18 ft. high.

CAMBUSKENNETH. See Stirling.

CAMBUS O'MAY, a small place on Deeside to the E. of Ballater.

FAMOUS	RIVERS	
TAY	. .	117 miles
SPEY	. .	110 miles
CLYDE	. .	106 miles
TWEED	. .	96 miles
DEE	. .	90 miles
FORTH	. .	66 miles

W. S. Thomson.

Campbeltown.

CAMPBELTOWN, only town in the Kintyre peninsula (Argyll), the charter dates back to Robert the Bruce; later Stuart kings granted the burgh to the Argyll Campbells, in whose honour its name was changed from Kiolkerran to Campbeltown. In 1700 it was created a royal burgh. Main industries are fishing and distilling. An ancient Celtic cross stands in the main street. In the Bay is Davaar Island, which can be reached on foot at low tide. Davaar has a lighthouse, ecclesiastical associations with St. Barr, and some interesting caves.

CANOEING IN SCOTLAND

Beginners. — Annan, Dee (Galloway), Forth, Ken, Nith, Leven (Loch Lomond to Clyde).

Practised.—Awe (caution), Clyde (caution), Dee (caution), Ness, Oich, Orchy, Shiel, Spey, Tay, Tweed (caution).

CAMPSIE FELLS, a range of hills in Stirlingshire, S. of the Endrick Water. The highest point is Earl's Seat (1,895 ft.). Campsie Glen is on its east side. Fintry, Killearn and Campsie are villages among its foothills.

CANISP (2,786 ft.), one of Sutherland's "fantastic" mountains, 5 to 6 miles ESE. of Lochinver. Like Suilven and Stac Polly, it owes its impressive isolation to the sandstone-on-gneiss formation of this geologically interesting region.

CANNA, a small island to the SW. of Skye with its own pier and harbour. Compass Hill (690 ft.) is composed of magnetic rock.

CANNICH, a river of Inverness-shire, flows from Loch Mullardoch through Glen Cannich to join the Glass at Invercannich (*q.v.*). The Affric Hydro-electric scheme has greatly influenced local life.

CANONBIE, a village on the Esk near the Scottish border, 5 miles S. of Langholm.

CARDRONA, a small place 4 miles E. of Peebles on the south bank of the Tweed, noted for its fine old keep and standing stone.

CARDROSS, a leafy village about halfway between Helensburgh and Dumbarton, standing a little way back from the Clyde Estuary. In Cardross Castle (no longer existing) Robert the Bruce died.

CARFIN, a village 2 miles NE. of Motherwell, a place of pilgrimage for its Grotto to Our Lady of Lourdes.

CARFRAEMILL, a well-known hotel on the Edinburgh–Lauder road about 5 miles NW. of the latter.

CARLETON CASTLE. See Lendalfoot.

CARLOPS, a small village in the foothills of the Pentlands some 15 miles SW. of Edinburgh. Has associations with Allan Ramsay.

CARLUKE, a town 6 miles NNW. of Lanark with a mining industry, but also engaged in fruit-growing and preserving.

CARNOUSTIE, a seaside resort 10 miles ENE. of Dundee, with 2 first-class golf courses and fine sea-bathing facilities.

CARNWATH, an old and interesting town of Lanarkshire, on the Carnwath Burn 6 miles ENE. of Lanark. It has a fine old church, parts of which date back to antiquity, and slight relics of Cowthally Castle, ancient seat of the Somervilles. In the main street is the old Halle Cross.

CARRADALE, a small resort and fishing place on the east coast of Kintyre (Argyllshire).

CARRBRIDGE, a village 22 miles SE. of Inverness. It stands high (850 ft. above sea-level) among hills and pine woods and near the River Spey. Touring and ski-ing centre.

CARRICK. See Ayrshire.

CARRON, a sea inlet (Loch Carron) of Wester Ross with a small river and glen of the same name at its head.

CARRON, a Stirlingshire village adjoining Larbert and Stenhousemuir. It contains the famous Carron Iron Works.

The Campsie Fells.

CARSEBRECK, a famous curling centre, 6 miles SW. of Auchterarder (Perthshire).

CARSE OF GOWRIE, a rich arable tract along the north bank of the Tay estuary W. of Dundee.

CARSPHAIRN, a village 10 miles NNW. of New Galloway.

CARSTAIRS JUNCTION, a railway junction (separating the main Edinburgh and Glasgow lines), 5 miles NE of Lanark.

CARTER BAR, a high point on the Scottish border where the road from the S. enters Roxburghshire.

CASTLECARY, a small place 6 miles W. of Falkirk with a castle of the name and a Roman fort.

CASTLE DOUGLAS, market town at the north end of Carlingwark Loch, 10 miles NE. of Kirkcudbright. Near by on an island in the Dee is the ruinous Threave Castle (National Trust) once seat of the Douglases.

CASTLE KENNEDY, a ruinous castle 3 miles E. of Stranraer (Wigtownshire) with interesting gardens.

CATRINE, a village 12 miles ENE. of Ayr near which is Ballochmyle House (now a hospital), setting of Burns's "The Lass o' Ballochmyle".

CAWDOR. See Nairn.

CERES (seers), a Fifeshire village with an ancient bridge, 3 miles SE. of Cupar, noted for its Games.

CHAPELCROSS, 3 miles NE. of Annan, is the site of an electricity-producing nuclear power station.

CHEVIOT HILLS, a hill-range on the border between England and Scotland, extending 35 miles SW. from Roxburghshire into Northumberland. The highest point is The Cheviot (2,676 ft.) in Northumberland. The grazing is excellent and there is a Cheviot breed of sheep. A main road crosses the range at Carter Bar.

CHIRNSIDE, a village 8 miles WNW. of Berwick, with a Norman doorway in its church.

CLACKMANNAN, county town of Clackmannanshire, on the River Devon, E. of Alloa.

CLACKMANNANSHIRE, the smallest county of Scotland, extending from the Ochil Hills to the Forth. Ben Cleuch (2,363 ft.) is the highest point. There are coal-mines, woollen mills, distilleries and breweries. Alloa is the largest town; Alva, Clackmannan, Tillicoultry and Dollar are other towns.

CLATTERINGSHAWS LOCH, See Glen Trool National Forest Park (p. 281).

CLOCH, THE, a well-known white lighthouse and landmark on the Firth of Clyde opposite Dunoon.

CLOVA, GLEN, a glen in Angus ascended by the route (in parts a track only) from Kirriemuir to Braemar.

CLOVENFORDS, a village to the W. of Galashiels with renowned vineries.

CLUANIE, a hamlet, glen and loch (hydro-electric dam) in SW. Ross, between Glen Moriston and Glen Shiel.

The Clyde near Hyndford Bridge.

Shipyards of the Clyde.

CLYDE, a river and firth in the W. of Scotland. The river, from its source in the Daer Valley, flows through upland moors, then through the vale of Lanark, before it enters on its last phase as a great world waterway, with several miles of docks and quays and large shipbuilding yards. Glasgow, Port Glasgow and Greenock are on its banks. In its upper reaches it is a fine fishing stream, with a number of small towns and villages on its banks.

The three falls comprised in the Falls of Clyde near Lanark, Cora Linn, Bonnington Linn and Stonebyres Linn, though depleted in volume by a hydro-electric scheme, are still charming. Beyond Dumbarton the river widens considerably, and at Gourock becomes the Firth of Clyde famed for its seaside resorts. The Clyde fortnight in summer is an event in the yachting calendar. (See Dunoon, Largs, Rothesay, etc.).

CLYDEBANK, a busy industrial town of the Clyde, contignons to the City of Glasgow. Here are the famous John Brown's Shipyards (Queen Mary, Queen Elizabeth and a third "Queen" under construction) and the extensive Singer Sewing Machine Factory. Clydebank suffered in a two-day blitz in 1941.

CLYDESDALE, a part of the Clyde basin, often taken to be that between Lanark and Bothwell, giving name to a famous breed of horses reared here.

CLYNDER, a yacht-building village near Garelochhead (Dunbartonshire).

COATBRIDGE, an industrial town E. of Glasgow (iron, tinplate, general engineering).

COBBLER. See Arthur, Ben.

COCKBURNSPATH (kŏ′burnzpath), village of Berwickshire between the Lammermuirs (q.v.) and the sea, near the East Lothian border. Has a village cross and an interesting old church with a beacon tower; remains of another (Norman) 2 miles E.; and the ruins of a fine 15th century church in the grounds of Dunglass House. Cockburnspath is on the Great North Road.

COCKENZIE, a fishing village and holiday place on the Firth of Forth, E. of Prestonpans, site of a large new power station.

COCKPEN, a parish of eastern Midlothian. In it formerly stood Cockpen House, associated with Lady Nairn's song, *The Laird of Cockpen.*

COLDINGHAM, a village 1½ miles S. of St. Abb's Head on the Berwickshire coast, visited for the still beautiful ruins of Coldingham Priory. Built in the 12th century on the site of an ancient (7th century) nunnery dedicated to St. Ebba, the Priory has features of exceptional architectural interest, including the fine Early English arcading of the north and east galleries of the (restored) Choir —in use as a parish church. The walled-up skeleton of a woman (presumed to be a nun) was found here about the beginning of last century— suggesting to Scott an episode in *Marmion.*

COLDOCH. See Doune.

COLDSTREAM, a small Berwickshire town, on the Scottish Border, *c.* 11 miles SW. of Berwick, chiefly famous for the Coldstream Guards, raised here in 1650 by General Monk. Noted also in earlier times for its "Gretna Green" type weddings. There is fishing in the River Tweed.

COLINTON, a residential village on the south-west outskirts of Edinburgh with Colinton Dell, a pretty wooded valley on the Water of Leith.

COLINTRAIVE ("swimming narrows"), a small place on the Kyles of Bute, where in former times cattle were made to cross the Narrows by swimming; now a vehicular ferry crosses the Kyles at this point. A road leads N. through Glendaruel to Strachur.

COLL, an island 7 miles W. of Mull (*c.* 12 miles by 4 miles), mainly agricultural, with a lobster-fishing industry. The east coast is rocky, the west coast deeply indented with intriguing sandy beaches, delightful for bathing or sun-bathing. There is excellent fishing, shooting (snipe, woodcock, etc.). Coll has considerable historic and antiquarian interest, and an ancient castle dating from the time of Robert the Bruce, if not earlier.

COLONSAY, a small island N. of Islay, with Oronsay as a satellite to the S. Scalasaig, Garvard and Kiloran are hamlets on Colonsay. Kiloran has a fine bathing beach. Oronsay (linked at low tide with the larger island) has a ruined priory and a Celtic Cross; also (like Coll) some rare specimens for the botanist.

COMRIE, a charmingly situated resort on the River Earn, 6½ miles W. of Crieff. Hotels; fishing, tennis, golf. Glen Lednock lies to the NW., and a hill-track runs through it to Ardeonaig on Loch Tay. In the glen are some fine waterfalls, including the Deil's Cauldron, a natural curiosity. Only "fault" in this pleasant little place is the geological one which subjects it to recurring earthquakes!—these however, so slight that they rouse interest rather than alarm.

Colonsay: Kiloran Bay.

The Coolins, Skye.

CONNEL (FERRY). 5 miles NE. of Oban, a pleasant village at the mouth of Loch Etive, over-looking the famous Falls of Lora. 1½ miles away is Dunstaffnage Castle (see Oban). Connel Bridge—"the Forth Bridge in miniature"—carries road and railway over the Narrows to Benderloch and the north.

CONON, a river of Ross-shire, flowing from Loch Luichart (*q.v.*) to the Cromarty Firth near Dingwall. Conon Bridge, an angling village, stands near the mouth; within the river basin is a whole series of important hydro-electric under-takings based on a catchment area of 345 sq. m. These have involved the creation of several new lochs (Glascarnoch, Vaich, Meig, Orrin, Achonockie), and the development

of others (Luichart, Fannich), and the building of power stations at Grudie Bridge, Luichart, Torr Achilty, and elsewhere.

COOLINS, CUILLIN, CUCHULLIN, a magnificent mountain range of Skye, famous for climbing, its best known peak Sgurr nan Gillean (3,167 ft.) ascended often from Sligachan.

CORA LINN. See Clyde.

CORPACH, a village on Loch Eil to the NW. of Fort William. A large pulp-and-paper mill situated on the loch shore and costing £20,000,000, was opened in 1966.

CORRAN, a narrow channel in Loch Linnhe with a car ferry to Ardgour. There is a lighthouse at the entrance to the narrows.

Coylum Bridge.

CORRIE, a seaside hamlet on the east side of Arran at the base of Goatfell.

CORRIESHALLOCH, a canyon-like gorge on the River Broom, 11 miles SE. of Ullapool on the main Ullapool–Garve road, with the Falls of Measach at its head. Despite its name (the "nasty" corrie), it is a grand and impressive sight. The chasm is 250 ft. deep in places, and one of the falls has a sheer drop of 120 ft. Corrieshalloch is the property of the National Trust for Scotland, which has constructed excellent footpaths and vantage points to enable visitors to view the phenomenon.

CORRIEVRECKAN, a strait between Jura and Scarba, with a famous whirlpool in it.

CORRIEYAIRACK, a high pass (2507 ft.) on the hill track from Laggan to Fort Augustus.

CORUISK, a wild loch of Skye to the E. of the Coolins.

COUPAR ANGUS, an agricultural market town 13 miles NE. of Perth. It has some interesting Roman remains and the ruins of a Cistercian abbey.

COWAL, a peninsular district of south-eastern Argyllshire, giving name to the Cowal Games which take place annually near Dunoon.

COWDENBEATH, a mining town of Fife, 7 miles NE. of Dunfermline.

COYLTON, a small colliery town 6 miles E. of Ayr.

COYLUM BRIDGE, a route junction for the Cairngorms, 2 miles E. of Aviemore. Site of the new Rank hotel, including an ice-rink and ski school. It is the largest hotel to be built in Scotland this century.

CRAIGELLACHIE (also called Lower Craigellachie, to distinguish it from a rock of the same name at Aviemore), a village and noted beauty spot at the junction of the Fiddich and the Spey. There is angling for salmon, sea-trout and brown trout in the River Spey.

CRAIGENDORAN, an eastern continuation of Helensburgh, whose amenities it shares. Clyde Coast sailings go from here. The train from Glasgow (Queen Street) runs to the Pierhead.

CRAIGNISH, LOCH, a sea-loch on the west coast of Argyll. The village and castle of Craignish are directly opposite the whirlpool of Corryvreckan, and Craignish Point lies to the S. of them.

CRAIL, a royal burgh and quaint little fishing town, agricultural centre and holiday resort, 4 miles NE. of Anstruther in East Fife. It has angling, golf (18-hole course), tennis and bowls. The town hall dates from the 17th century and in St. Mary's Church, Knox preached. Crail has a delightful harbour. Between Crail and Fife Ness is Balcomie Castle, which gave Mary of Guise, Queen of James V, her first welcome to Scotland.

CRAMOND, a picturesque village at the mouth of the River Almond, *c.* 4 miles W. of Edinburgh and just off the South Queensferry road. It has a well-known inn, yachting and boating. Cramond stands on the site of a Roman Camp. Cramond Island (one-time smugglers' resort) lies off-shore in the Forth and is accessible at low tide. To the E. of the village a fine promenade has been built. Across the river are the beautiful grounds of Dalmeny House (seat of the Earls of Rosebery), with the ancient ruins of Barnbougle Castle. A pleasant path leads up the river towards Old Cramond Bridge. Near here James V was set upon by robbers and rescued by Jock Howieson the miller. In gratitude James bestowed on him the farm or estate of Braehead, on condition that he and his heirs should always provide a ewer and basin for the King's use when he passed.

CRARAE, a village on Loch Fyne, with granite quarries. Afforestation is in progress. The famous gardens of Crarae Lodge are open to the public.

CRATHES CASTLE, a National Trust property (medieval tower, Queen Anne and Victorian wings, both of the latter being virtually destroyed in a recent fire) on Deeside, 15 miles WSW. of Aberdeen, with fine walled gardens.

CRATHIE, a village on Deeside, near Balmoral, with a church attended by the royal family.

CRAWFORD, a village in the upper Clyde Valley, *c.* 15 miles NW. of Moffat on the Glasgow–Dumfries road. It has remains of an ancient tower, once a seat of the Earls of Crawford. There is golf, trout-fishing in the River Clyde, hill-walking and touring.

CRAWFORDJOHN, a village of Lanarkshire, 10 miles S. of Lanark.

CREE, a river of Galloway, flows about 30 miles SSE. to Wigtown Bay at Creetown. There is fishing for salmon and trout.

CREETOWN, a small town and port near the estuary of the Cree in Wigtown Bay.

CRERAN, LOCH, a sea inlet off Loch Linnhe, with Barcaldine Castle near its entrance. The valley above it is Glen Creran, traversed by the River Creran.

CRIANLARICH, a small, pleasantly situated village of western Perthshire on the Fillan Water; an important road junction and fishing, winter sports and mountaineering resort. Ben More, Stobinian, Cruach Ardnan and Ben Lui are in this region.

CRIEFF, a favourite holiday and health resort of Perthshire, 18 miles W. of Perth in the valley of the River Earn, also a market town serving the district of Strathearn. It has a famous hydro, golf, fishing and other attractions. Antiquities include the Cross of the Burgh of Regality of Drummond and the still older (Celtic) Cross of Crieff. At the entrance to the town hall the ancient stocks may

Crieff and The Knock.

still be seen. The Knock (911 ft.), a wooded hill to the N. of the town, offers fine views of Strathearn.

Crieff is a splendid centre for walks, excursions and tours. The road to Gleneagles passes 15th century Drummond Castle. Another favourite walk leads via Glen Turret and Loch Turret to Ben Chonzie (3,048 ft.) a good hill for climbing. Rounding the Knock and bearing N. at Gilmerton, one reaches the Sma' Glen, a steep, narrow glen (not really so small) in the foothills of the Grampians. Near its head is a large, flat stone, and here, according to tradition, sleeps Ossian, the bard of the ancient Celts. Here, too, near the foot of the glen, are remains of a Roman Camp. At Innerpeffray, 4 miles SE., is a castle, a chapel which is the burying ground of the Drummond family, an old-established library and the site of a Roman Camp. Crieff has good bus services to Perth, Stirling, Callander, St. Fillans, and frequent motor coach excursions in the summer.

CRIMOND, a village on the east coast of Aberdeenshire N. of Peterhead, scene of the ballad *Logie o' Buchan,* and giving name to a famous metrical (Scottish) psalm tune.

CRINAN, a pretty little village

Crinan.

on Loch Crinan, at the Atlantic end of the Crinan Canal, one of the beauty spots of mid-Argyll. Across the loch is Duntroon Castle.

The Crinan Canal runs from little Loch Crinan to Ardrishaig, joining Loch Fyne to the Sound of Jura, and cutting out the long passage round Kintyre.

CROMARTY, an ancient small town near the entrance to the Cromarty Firth, royal burgh in the 16th–17th century, birthplace of the geologist Hugh Miller, whose cottage is now a museum. It has boating, bathing and golf (ferry to Nigg, by arrangement), tennis and bowls.

Features of interest are the 16th century Mercat Cross, and the Old Parish Church and Town Hall.

CROMARTY FIRTH, a branch of the Moray Firth, on the east coast of Ross-shire. The entrance is narrow and guarded by the high headlands, both nearly 500 ft. high, called the Sutors of Cromarty. Within it widens to form a great natural harbour, then narrows again to extend inland as far as Dingwall. From the south Sutor one has fine landward and seaward views.

CROMDALE HILLS, a small hill range in Inverness-shire and Moray to the E. of Grantown. It gave name to the ballad *Haughs of Cromdale* from a defeat here of the Jacobites in 1690.

SCOTTISH YOUTH HOSTELS

*National Office—*7 BRUNTSFIELD CRESCENT, EDINBURGH, 10.

*Subscriptions—*Over 5 . . 2s.
Over 16 . . 5s.
Over 21 . . 10s.

Application to District or National Office of the S.Y.H.A., *with photograph.*

Charges for overnight accommodation—
Juveniles . . . . 2s. 0d.
Others . . . . 3s. 6d.

Meals.—Certain hostels provide inexpensive meals.

Hostels are marked as red triangles on the sectional map in this book.

S.Y.H.A. Handbook, price 1s., contains the fullest particulars about the hostels and the association.

CROSSFORD, a Lanarkshire village, delightfully situated among woods and orchards on the banks of the Clyde, 4½ m. WNW. of Lanark.

CROSSRAGUEL. See Maybole.

CRUACHAN, BEN, one of the best-loved of Scottish mountains (3,689 ft.) between Loch Awe and Loch Etive in Argyll. Its twin peaks form a familiar landmark, and its ascent, whether from Taynuilt or Dalmally, is one of the most popular climbs in the West. The Loch Awe (*q.v.*) hydro scheme (the largest in Britain) includes a high-level reservoir (1,315 ft.) in a corrie of Cruachan and a 400-megawatt power station concealed in the body of the mountain.

CRUDEN BAY, a village and resort on Cruden Bay, 23 miles N. of Aberdeen, noted for its golf and its beautiful 2-mile stretch of fine firm sands. Bordering the sands are the sandhills (called the Ward of Cruden), behind and among which are the 18 and 9-hole golf courses. In addition to golf one has tennis and bowls, bathing, boating, and sea-fishing. The coastline has curious and interesting features, caves, pierced rocks, cliff-top "chimneys", while 2 miles N. are the famous Bullers of Buchan. A ridge of skerries runs out from the south point of the Bay.

CUILLIN. See Coolins.

CULBIN SANDS, sandhills of Moray near Forres, which engulfed (1694) the estate of Culbin, now afforested by the Forestry Commission.

CULLEN, a small royal burgh and fishing port, rising from a sandy bay on the Moray Firth, 13 miles W. of Banff. There is boating, bathing, golf, tennis, bowls, fishing in the sea and in the Cullen Burn. Cullen has a fine old Mercat Cross in the Square. 2 miles S. is Cullen House, standing in beautiful grounds. The Church near by, founded by Robert the Bruce, has some notable features. To the E. are the ruins of Findlater Castle.

CULLODEN, Inverness-shire, a ridge forming part of Drummossie Moor, near Inverness, where the Duke of Cumberland routed the clans under Prince Charles Edward (16th April 1746), extinguishing the Jacobite cause. The finely laid out burial place of the Clans is a solemn memorial. Culloden House, near by, the seat of Duncan Forbes, yielded, in 1812, the *Culloden Papers*, correspondence and state documents (1625–1748). To the SE. are the Stones of Clava, remains of three large chambered cairns from the Bronze Age.

CULROSS (koo'ros), a small but fascinating royal burgh situated 5 miles W. of Dunfermline on the Firth of Forth. It is visited for its old Cistercian Abbey, also (by artists and others) for its picturesque air of antiquity. With its steps and stairs, cobbled streets, houses at various levels and at all angles, Culross looks as if it had not greatly changed in several hundred years. There is a

The Tolbooth, Culross.

Tolbooth, and a tall old Mercat Cross, and a number of 17th century houses, some of which are in the hands of the National Trust.

The Abbey dates from 1217. Remains are chiefly of the Choir (now a parish church) and the imposing tower. The 17th century tomb of Sir George Bruce of Camock, with effigies of himself and his children, is of interest. It was this Sir George Bruce who built Culross Palace, a typically Scottish structure of the 16th–17th century, built around a courtyard—the panelled interior richly adorned with mural paintings. Traditionally Culross was the birthplace of St. Mungo (Kentigern), Patron Saint of Glasgow.

Dunimarle Castle (½ mile W.) is famous for its fine art collection, including pictures by Correggio, Van Dyck, Hobbema.

CULZEAN. See Maybole.

CUMBERNAULD, formerly a village, now an industrial "new town", 13 miles NE. of Glasgow, built around an old estate and 18th century laird's house. Near here is a part of the Antonine Wall (called Graham's Dyke) with Roman forts at Westerwood and Castlecary.

CUMBRAES, THE, comprising Great Cumbrae and Little Cumbrae, lie in the Firth of Clyde opposite Fairlie and Largs. Millport on Great Cumbrae is the only town. Near it is the important Scottish Marine Biological Station. Little Cumbrae has a ruined castle, a lighthouse, and associations with the Norwegians who harried these coasts.

CUMNOCK, a pleasant little Ayrshire country town and road junction 6 miles SE. of Mauchline on the Dumfries road, noted for its links with the Covenanters and as the birthplace of Keir Hardie. It has an up-to-date swimming pool and 9-hole golf course, also fishing in the River Lugar and the Afton Reservoir, tennis, putting and bowls. Some interesting relics are contained in the Baird Institute.

CUPAR, a royal burgh and county town of Fife, also a market town, stands on the River Eden in the rich agricultural region called the Howe of Fife. There is a linen industry and a sugar-beet factory. Fishing is available in the Eden and the Ceres Burn, and golf (18 and 9-hole course), tennis and bowls. The town's first charter is said to have been granted in the 12th century by Malcolm IV or his successor William the Lion. Nothing remains of the old castle, but the tower (1415) and 17th century spire of the parish church are still to be seen, also the old Mercat cross.

DAIRSIE, a small Fifeshire village 3 miles E. of Cupar, with a ruined castle and fine church.

DALAVICH, a new village, on the W. shore of Loch Awe, built by the Forestry Commission.

DALBEATTIE, a small pleasant town in south-east Kirkcudbrightshire, built of granite from the nearby quarries, which now produce only granite chips. $2\frac{1}{2}$ miles NNW. is the Mote of Urr, an earthwork of proportions unique in Scotland.

DALCROSS, a parish $6\frac{3}{4}$ miles NE. of Inverness, where there is a restored 17th century castle and the airport for Inverness.

DALKEITH, an industrial and agricultural town on the River Esk, 7 miles SE. of Edinburgh. The chief points of interest are the ancient church of St. Nicholas and Dalkeith Palace, a seat of the Dukes of Buccleuch, dating from early times, but largely rebuilt in 1700. The Palace has historic associations, and its royal visitors include James VI, Charles I and Prince Charles Edward.

Melville Castle (celebrated in song) lies to the W., and is now an hotel. Near Eskbank (S.) is Newbattle

Abbey (presented to the nation by the Marquis of Lothian), a fine mansion in a lovely wooded park, with relics of the ancient abbey which preceded it. Dalhousie Castle (3 miles S.) belonged for centuries to the Ramsay family. It was begun in the 12th century, but much altered.

DALMAHOY, a well-known golfing place, *c.* 7 miles W. of Edinburgh.

DALMALLY, a scattered small village near the mouth of Loch Awe, on the Glasgow–Oban road some 25 miles from Oban. Well-wooded, with the lovely River Orchy running through it, Dalmally is a good place from which to make the ascent of Ben Cruachan.

DALMELLINGTON, a small south Ayrshire colliery town, 15 miles SE. of Ayr. There is a moot or mote hill (seat of an ancient council).

DALMENY, a small West Lothian village situated near the Forth Bridges. It has a beautiful little Norman church, restored, but with much of the glorious stonework of the original unimpaired. Here is the burial vault of the Rosebery family, whose seat of Dalmeny House is about 2 miles away.

DALNASPIDAL, the highest station on British Railways (over 1,450 ft. above sea-level) on the borders of Perthshire and Inverness-shire, a bleak and isolated hamlet among moors and mountains, where once was a hospice.

DALRY (Ayrshire), a town 8 miles N. of Irvine. Once a weaving, then coalmining, area, it produces textiles today.

DALRY (Kirkcudbrightshire), is also known as St. John's Town of Dalry, and is a small place on the Ken Water, *c.* 25 miles N. of Kirkcudbright. Lochinvar Lake (*q.v.*) is within the parish to the NE.

DALWHINNIE, a village standing 1,169 ft. above sea-level near the head of Loch Ericht. Between it and Dalnaspidal (9 miles S.) rail and road reach the highest summit in Britain (1,484).

DANDALEITH, a village of south Morayshire on the River Spey, *c.* 3 miles S. of Rothes.

DARVEL, a small textile manufacturing town of Ayrshire, 7 miles E. of Kilmarnock, the birthplace of Sir Alexander Fleming. At Loudoun Hill, 2 miles E., Bruce defeated the Earl of Pembroke.

DAVAN, LOCH, a small loch, 5 miles W. of Aboyne, with remains of lake dwellings.

DEARG, or DERG, BEN, a mountain (3,547 ft.) in Wester Ross near the head of Loch Broom. (See Ullapool).

DEE, RIVER (Aberdeenshire), rises in the Wells of Dee in the heart of the Cairngorms and runs 87 miles eastwards past Braemar, Balmoral, Ballater, Aboyne and Banchory (*qq.v.*) its valley often referred to here as Royal Deeside, till it enters the North Sea at Aberdeen. It is a good salmon river. The river valley is very beautiful, well-wooded and there is a good motor road from Aberdeen as far as the Linn of Dee, about 65 miles W. At the falls or Linn

Opposite : The River Dee. (Scottish Tourist Board).

of Dee, the river rushes through a deep narrow gorge, and from the bridge above it is a most impressive sight.

DEE, RIVER (Kirkcudbrightshire), flows 38 miles SE. and S. through Loch Dee, past Threave Castle and Kirkcudbright, to Kirkcudbright Bay. Midway it is joined by the Water of Ken, a stream of greater volume than its own. It affords fine fishing.

DEER ABBEY. See Old Deer.

DEERNESS, a peninsula in Orkney on the SE. of the mainland.

DEER SOUND, a large bay on the SE. of the mainland of Orkney.

DENHOLM, a pleasantly situated village in Roxburghshire, 5 miles W. of Jedburgh. It is noteworthy as the birthplace of John Leyden, poet and linguist, and Sir James Murray, the celebrated lexicographer, who worked for many years on the New English Dictionary.

DENNY, a small industrial town in Stirlingshire, 6 miles W. of Falkirk, on the River Carron.

DERRY CAIRNGORM, a mountain (3,788 ft.) of the central Cairngorms.

DERVAIG, a village at the head of Loch Crian, in NW. Mull, a few miles from Tobermory. There is good fishing in loch and river.

DEVERON, RIVER, a river of Banff and Aberdeenshire, 50 miles long, rising in the parish of Cabrach, Aberdeenshire, and entering the sea at Banff. It is a good salmon and trout river.

DEVIL'S BEEF–TUB, 7 miles N. of Moffat, Dumfriesshire, is a steep-sided natural depression in the hills, where the River Annan has its source. It is said to have been used as a pound for the animals stolen by men of Annandale in the days of Border cattle-raids.

DEVIL'S DYKE, Dumfriesshire, is an ancient line of fortifications commencing at Loch Ryan, and once extending to the Solway Firth. It is believed to have been built about the time of the departure of the Romans from Britain. Much has disappeared, but about 2 miles W. of Sanquhar remains of the wall may be seen.

DEVIL'S ELBOW, a high pass with a hairpin bend on the road running between the Cairnwell and Glas Maol, joining Glen Beg and Glen Clunie, c. 10 miles S. of Braemar.

DEVIL'S MILL, a waterfall on the River Devon, Kinross-shire, by Rumbling Bridge, c. 4 miles NE. of Dollar.

DEVIL'S STAIRCASE, a steep track running northward from the head of Glencoe to Kinlochleven, formerly a military road. The name is also applied to a steep incline of tumbled boulders near the road between Lochgoilhead and St. Catherine's, Loch Fyne.

DEVON, a river rising in the Ochils which follows a winding course 75 miles long, and flows into the Forth about 2 miles W. of Alloa. It is dammed in the hills to form Glendevon Reservoir. 3 miles below the reservoir, in the grounds of Glendevon House (hotel), is the ruinous Glendevon Castle Crook of Devon is where the river takes a sharp westward turn, and below at Rumbling Bridge, are famous waterfalls known as the Devil's Mill and Caldron Linn. It is a good fishing river.

DHU HEARTACH, a lonely light-house in the Atlantic, some 15 miles SW. of Iona.

DINGWALL, the county town of Ross and Cromarty at the head of the Cromarty Firth. It is a pleasant market town, first noticed as a settlement of the Culdees in the 8th century, and made a royal burgh in 1226. Its name signifies "Field of the Thing (council or parliament)", and the burgh is linked with Scotland's history and reigning house from early times. Malcolm Canmore found a Norse bride in Dingwall. Macbeth is said to have been born in Dingwall Castle—the *Castrum Dinkual* of the old map-makers. Slight remains of this once-powerful stronghold may still be seen.

The modern town has important marts; distilling and hand-loom weaving; it is a notable touring centre. There are facilities for tennis, putting and bowling.

Ben Wyvis, behind the town, offers magnificent views and is not a difficult climb. Tourists should see also the Falls of Rogie (W.) and (NNE.) the Black Rock of Novar, a deep and narrow gorge through which flows the Ault Graad (ugly burn).

A tower (1907) on a hill to the S. of the town commemorates General Sir Hector Macdonald (1853–1903)—"Fighting Mac" —son of a Highland crofter who enlisted in the Gordon High-landers at the age of 17, and rose from the ranks to major-general, was Knighted, and became A.D.C. to Victoria and Edward V. His conduct as brigade-commander at Omdnoman ensured popular fame, which survived the tragedy of scandal and eventual suicide.

DINNET, a small place on the Dee (Aberdeenshire), 5 miles W. of Aboyne, on Dinnet Moor. Near by are Lochs Kinord and Davan, which are visited for their antiquities —remains of lake dwellings.

DIRLETON, one of the most delightful of Scottish villages 2 miles W. of North Berwick (East Lothian). It has a massive old ruined castle (besieged by the English in Wallace's wars), with a 16th century bowling green and 17th century dovecot, a 17th century church, a village inn and a renowned restaurant and beautiful flower-fringed village green.

DOCHART, a loch, river and glen, W. of Killin. In the loch, which lies to the NW. of Benmore (3,843 ft.), is an islet with a ruined castle of the Campbells of Lochawe. The River Dochart flowing out of the loch and through the glen, is the principal feeder of Loch Tay. Near Killin it forms the famous Falls of Dochart.

DOCHERTY, GLEN, a glen south of Loch Maree, Ross-shire.

Overleaf: Loch Coruisk and the Coolins.

DOLLAR, a small place in Clackmannanshire on the Dollar Burn, 13 miles E. of Stirling. The famous Dollar Academy was founded with a large bequest from John MacNab, a native of Dollar who made his fortune as a sea-captain. On a hill near by are the impressive ruins of Castle Campbell, once known as the Castle of Gloom. The burns which flow on either side of it are called the Water of Care and the Burn of Sorrow. Castle Campbell is said to be one of the first places where John Knox openly dispensed the sacrament of Holy Communion according to reformed practice.

DOLPHINTON, a village in Lanarkshire, 10 miles NW. of Peebles.

DON, a large river in Aberdeenshire, rises close to the Banffshire border, and winds 82 miles east to the North Sea, 1 mile NE. of Old Aberdeen. It is famous for trout fishing.

DOON, a river rising in Kirkcudbrightshire, and forming Loch Doon, now dammed for a hydro-electric scheme. Loch Doon Castle, formerly on an island, has been re-erected near the SW. shore. The river, which flows NW. to the sea about 2 miles S. of Ayr, is made famous by Burns' poem, and the Auld Brig o' Doon is much visited.

DORNADILLA, an ancient broch in Strathmore, Sutherland.

DORNIE, a small place on Loch Duich in Wester Ross, with ferry (pedestrian) to Totaig. The chief feature of interest is the restored castle of Eilean Donan on an island in the loch. An ancient stronghold of the Mackenzies, said to have been built in the reign of Alexander II, it was shattered by English cannon in 1719, after a Jacobite battle at Glenshiel. It is reached from the loch shore by a fine old stone bridge.

DORNOCH, a royal burgh and county town of Sutherland, on the Dornoch Firth, famed for its cathedral, its golf and its magnificent golden sands. The 13th century cathedral, now the parish church, still has some fine arcading and an interesting five-light west window; of the two golf courses, one, the Royal Dornoch, is famous, and the sands are ideal from a holiday point of view.
In addition to golf there is excellent fishing, safe sea-bathing and delightful hill walks. The causeway over Loch Fleet, known as The Mound, carries the road to Dornoch.
Antiquities abound—note the Creich Dun, a vitrified fort, and the Creich Stone monolith. Historical interest ranges from the Norse and Danish invasions to the capture of the town by Jacobite forces in 1746. What remains of Dornoch Castle (the old Bishop's Palace) is now incorporated in a hotel.

Opposite : Dollar : Castle Campbell. (*Scottish Tourist Board*).

Just south of the town is Andrew Carnegie's Castle of Skibo, on the site of an older historic castle.

DOUGLAS, on Douglas Water, Lanarkshire, c. 10 miles S. of Lanark, is an old place formerly of some importance. There is an old church, and Douglas Mill, an old inn of coaching days. Douglas Castle, Scott's Castle Dangerous, lies ¾ mile N.

DOUNE, a picturesque village 3 miles W. of Dunblane in Perthshire, has a 14th century castle (open to the public), which is perhaps the finest remaining mediaeval courtyard castle in Scotland; the iron yett (gate) is noteworthy, as is the early occurrence of machicolation over the postern gate in the west wall. The Mercat Cross seems to have been erected near the present East Church in 1611, and later (between 1700 and 1735) moved to its present site. In the south side of the column may be seen the hole where the "jougs" (iron collar) were fitted. Thomas Caddell's famous pistol factory was in a building (still extant) behind a dairy in the main street. Newton of Doune, on the east boundary of the burgh, is a fine old Scots house dating back before the 16th century.
Another notable feature is the Bridge of Teith, built in 1535 by Robert Spittal, tailor to Margaret, Queen of James IV. He is said to have constructed it to spite a ferryman who refused to ferry him across the river when he had left his purse behind!
Near Doune, the ruins of Old Kilmadock Church stand on the site of the cell of St. Docus, where later arose a monastery of some importance. There is a broch at Coldoch, just outside the parish boundary, and on the Hill of Row some standing stones, remains of a megalithic stone circle.

DOUNREAY, on the extreme N. coast of Caithness, 8 miles W. of Thurso, site of the Experimental Reactor Establishment opened in 1959.

DOURAN, BEN, a mountain (3,523 ft.) to the S. of Rannoch.

DRAINIE, a Morayshire hamlet near Lossiemouth, with a 17th century church.

DREM, an East Lothian village and railway junction near North Berwick.

DROCHIL CASTLE, lies c. 7 miles NW. of Peebles. These ruins are the unfinished palace of Regent Morton, who was executed for his part in the murder of Darnley before the building could be completed.

DRUMCLOG, 14 miles E. of Kilmarnock. An obelisk commemorates the victory of the Covenanters over Claverhouse in 1679.

DRUMELZIER (drum-eel'yer) a village 9 miles SW. of Peebles, the traditional site of Merlin's grave. The ruins of Drumelzier Castle overlook the Tweed. A little to the east is Tinnis Castle, destroyed by James VI in 1592 in reprisal for the murder of Darnley. Dawyck House, once visited by the great botanist Linnaeus, is still notable for its trees and gardens, although no longer for its heronry.

DRUMLANRIG CASTLE, 17 miles NW. of Dumfries, is a fine mansion belonging to the Duke of Buccleuch.

DRUMLITHIE, an old burgh of barony, birthplace of the novelist Lewis Grassic Gibbon, 10 miles SW. of Stonehaven.

DRUMMOND CASTLE, 3 miles S. of Crieff, was originally built in the 15th century, but much damaged by Cromwell, and after the '45. It was rebuilt during the last century and is open occasionally to the public.

DRUMMORE, a small seaside place on Luce Bay, Wigtownshire, 17½ miles S. of Stranraer.

DRUMMOSSIE MOOR. See Culloden.

DRUMNADROCHIT, a picturesque village of Glen Urquhart, near the mouth of the River Enrick as it enters Loch Ness. On a small promontory above the loch stands Castle Urquhart, built by Edward I of England on the site of an earlier stronghold which he had just razed. There is good fishing here.

DRUMOCHTER, PASS OF, connecting Glen Garry and Glen Truim, on the borders of Perthshire and Inverness-shire, over which the main north road and railway to Inverness run. This is the highest point reached by the railway in Britain (1484 ft.).

DRYBURGH, 5 miles SE. of Melrose, in south-west Berwickshire, is one of the most beautiful, though not the largest, of the ruined abbeys for which the Borders are famed. Founded in 1152, it suffered frequently at the hands of the English, by whom it was finally destroyed in 1544. Thereafter, with its lands, it was held successively by various Border families (including ancestors of Scott) until in 1918 it was given to the nation by Lord Glenconner. Ruins of the church are fairly extensive: parts of the nave, choir, transepts and the west front with its fine 13th century doorway. In the north transept is the lovely St. Mary's Aisle, burial place of Sir Walter Scott, his wife, his son and his son-in-law, J. G. Lockhart. Near by is the burial place of the Haigs of Bemersyde, with the tomb of Field-Marshal Earl Haig. There are also considerable remains of the conventual buildings. Points of interest are the beautiful large rose window in the refectory, the fine barrel-vaulting in the (complete) chapter house, the calefactory (central heating of those days), and the little sacristy called St. Modan's Chapel.

DRYHOPE TOWER, a ruined tower near St. Mary's Loch, on the Dryhope Burn and at the foot of Dryhope Rig.

DRYMEN (drim'en), a village and touring centre of Stirlingshire, in the valley of the Endrick Water, *c.* 15 miles S. of Aberfoyle. Near the roofless Buchanan Castle is a fine golf course.

DUART, a bay, point and castle on the east coast of Mull. The 13th century castle was a stronghold of the Macleans who still live in the restored building.

DUFFTOWN, a Banffshire village and resort, 8 miles SW. of Keith, standing high amid pleasant surroundings. It has an important distilling industry. The village is modern (early 19th century), and bears the family name (Duff) of its founder, the 4th Earl of Fife.
Auchindoun Castle (*c.* 2 miles), on the River Fiddich, is a Gordon stronghold of great antiquity, with a moat and other interesting features. Ruins of Balvenie Castle lie to the N. A little to the S. is the ancient Mortlach Church (restored) with a few remnants of the ancient structure. Ben Rinnes (2,755 ft.) and the twin summits of the granite Convals (around 1,800 ft.) may be climbed from here.

DUFFUS, a village 3½ miles NW. of Elgin, with an ancient ruined castle. 1 mile E. is Gordonstoun School. Its main building enjoys the distinction of having been built by a warlock (wizard), a former laird of Gordonstoun. The school, which counts the Duke of Edinburgh and Prince Charles on its distinguished roll, dates from 1934.
Duffus has easy access to the fine expanse of cliff-top between Hopeman and Covesea lighthouse, with steps (precarious) leading down to the small isolated Primrose Bay.

DUICH, LOCH, a wild but strikingly beautiful loch in Wester Ross, a south-east continuation of Loch Alsh, with the Dornie–Totaig ferry at the narrows where they meet. At its head is Ben Attow (3,383 ft.) and the soaring peaks called the Five Sisters of Kintail. Dornie, Inverinate and Kintail are on its shores.

DULL, a small place in the Strath of Appin, near Aberfeldy, Perthshire, with an ancient cross.

DULSIE BRIDGE, 12 miles SE. of Nairn, is a small but beautiful place on the River Findhorn.

DUMBARTON, an industrial town, formerly famous for shipbuilding, an ancient royal burgh, on the Clyde, 14 miles W. of Glasgow. The scanty remains of the castle (supplemented by barracks), now a museum, occupy a dramatic site on Dumbarton Rock (240 ft.), an abrupt two-peaked cone (perhaps once an islet) rising from the Clyde near the mouth of the River Leven. The position is said to have been fortified from prehistoric times, though traditionally the Rock was a piece of Dumbuck Hill which the devil threw after St. Patrick as he sailed for Ireland. Visitors should see the (one-time) Governor's House, Wallace's Guardhouse, the dungeon, and the 12th century Gothic archway above. The higher of the two peaks is called "Wallace's Seat"— Wallace is believed to have been

74

Opposite: *Dryburgh Abbey.*

imprisoned in the castle—taken by the treachery of the governor. From here, too, the six-year old Mary Queen of Scots sailed for France. In later years, when the castle was held in her name, it was captured spectacularly by Thomas Crawford of Jordanhill. Dumbarton, the county town of Dunbartonshire, has playing fields and a pleasant riverside park.

DUMFRIES, the county town of Dumfriesshire, a royal burgh, picturesquely known as "Queen of the South". It stands on the east bank of the River Nith, 7 miles from its mouth at the Solway Firth. On the west bank is Maxwelltown, which has been part of the burgh of Dumfries since 1929.

Originally a strong Border fortress, the name means "a castle surrounded by furze". Devorguilla, mother of John de Baliol, erected a bridge over the Nith in the 13th century. The "Auld Brig" was built in the 15th century and rebuilt in the 17th, but it is said that six of the original nine arches still remain. A Greyfriars monastery was founded by the same lady, and it was in the chapel of that religious house that Bruce slew the Red Comyn. Greyfriars church stands near the site of the old monastery. Several times in its history Dumfries has been devastated, leaving no trace of the castle, and during the '45 the town was heavily plundered by Prince Charles Edward's army. Most visitors, however, are attracted to Dumfries for its close associations with Robert Burns. For three years (1788–91) he farmed Ellisland, 6 miles N. of the town. As a commercial venture it was a failure, but there was written Tam o' Shanter. In 1791 he moved to Dumfries and his house (open to visitors) in Burns Street, off Michael Street, is rich in relics. Here Burns wrote many of his best-known songs. The Globe Tavern which he frequented is in High Street. In 18th century St. Michael's Church is the pew where the poet worshipped. Burns was buried in the north corner of the churchyard beneath a plain stone slab, but in 1815 his remains were removed to the classical mausoleum which was erected by public subscription. Here also lie his wife, Jean Armour, and their sons.

The Mid-Steeple, once the town hall, is in High Street, and was built in 1707. Sir James Barrie was a pupil at the Academy.

Within the Town Hall in Buccleuch Street are portraits of William and Mary and a silver gun presented to the town by James VI.

Over the river in Maxwelltown is an observatory, now a museum. There are golf and fishing facilities near by.

DUMFRIESSHIRE, a Border county. From the Southern Uplands it is drained to the Solway Firth by the rivers Nith, Annan and Esk, whose valleys form the three regions of Nithsdale, Annandale and Eskdale. The first two provide rail and road routes to the NW. (via Sanquhar) and the N. (via Beattock) respectively; the Dalveen and Mennock passes (road) connect these in the N. of the county. Only a small part of the area is arable, the uplands being pastoral or waste. Sheep, cattle and pigs are largely reared, and there are valuable salmon-fisheries. Chapelcross nuclear power station is important. Dumfries is the county town; other towns are Annan, Lockerbie, Langholm, Sanquhar, Moffat, Lochmaben.

DUNADD, a small place near Lochgilphead, Argyllshire, was the ancient capital of the earliest settlement of the Scots. (*Planair*).

DUNBAR, an ancient seaport, royal burgh and popular holiday resort of East Lothian, 29 miles E. of Edinburgh on the London road. It caters for tourists, with two good golf courses, a delightful open-air swimming pond among the rocks; tennis, putting and bowls. Swimming galas, golf and bowls tournaments are held throughout the summer.

Visitors will find interest in the 17th century Town House and the Barracks (formerly Lauderdale House), in the main street, and endless fascination in the Old and New Harbours. On the buildings and rocks around the latter is an almost unique kittiwake colony.

High on a rock above the New (Victoria) Harbour stands the castle, a crumbling but formidable ruin, scene of the famous exploit of Black Agnes, Countess of Dunbar, who in her husband's absence took on herself to defend

Dunbar Harbour.

the castle against the English, and held out bravely for six weeks until help came. In later years Mary Queen of Scots made Bothwell governor of the castle —which proved so useful in his schemes that after Carberry Hill the Scots had it destroyed. Near here, too, is the scene of Cromwell's victory of Dunbar (1650).

To the west are the villages of Belhaven (with lovely sands) and Westbarns, where racehorses are trained on the sands.

DUNBARTONSHIRE, a county of west Scotland lying between the Clyde estuary, Loch Long, and Loch Lomond, with a detached portion NE. of Glasgow between Stirlingshire and Lanarkshire. In the W. is the Rosneath peninsula between Loch Long and Gare Loch. The surface, almost everywhere hilly or mountainous, culminates in Ben Vorlich, S. of which is Loch Sloy with a large hydro-electric undertaking (power-house at Inveruglas on Loch Lomond). The River Leven drains Loch Lomond to the Clyde through the Vale of Leven, where bleaching, dyeing, and printing of textiles are old-established industries. Shipbuilding and heavy engineering are of great importance on the Clyde, with coalmining in the detached portion. Dumbarton is the county town, though Clydebank is more populous; burghs are Kirkintilloch (in detached portion), Helensburgh, Milngavie, Bearsden, Cove, and Kilcreggan.

DUNBEATH, a village in Caithness, 20 miles SW. of Wick, on a stream and a bay of the same name. The castle, on the cliffs south of the village, has an ancient keep.

DUNBLANE, an ancient cathedral and market town of Perthshire, also a holiday place, on the Allan Water, 5 miles N. of Stirling. It owes its distinction largely to its beautiful 12th–13th century cathedral, founded by David I in the mid-12th century, traditionally built on the 6th century church of St. Blane. After the Reformation it fell into disrepair and was completely restored only in modern times. It now has Sunday services and is open daily to visitors. The lovely and dignified interior has some noteworthy features: the stone effigies of the old bishops, the finely carved Bishop's Stalls, and the curious little wall-chamber known as "Katie Ogie's Hole".

Dunblane has a hotel-hydro, and is noted for its beautiful woody walks. Above the town is the high moor of Sheriffmuir, scene of an indecisive battle between Mar and Argyle in the first Jacobite rising (1715). The "Gathering Stone of the Clans" may still be seen.

Duncansby Head. (*Acrofilms Ltd.*).

DUNCANSBY HEAD, a promontory over 200 ft. high at the north-eastern extremity of Caithness, with a lighthouse, remains of an ancient watch-tower and a new coastguard lookout. Rising out of the sea, south of the Head, are two rocky masses known as Duncansby Stacks.

West of the headland is Duncansby village, and just north of it, the Ness of Duncansby.

DUNDARAVE CASTLE, is a 16th century tower on the shores of Loch Fyne, 5 miles NE. of Inveraray, formerly a stronghold of the Macnaughtons. It is the "Doom Castle" in Neil Munro's Novel.

DUNDEE

THE fourth Scottish city, an ancient royal burgh and up-to-date industrial town in Angus, beautifully situated on the north shore of the Firth of Tay (around the twin landmarks of Dundee Law (571 ft.) and Balgay Hill), at the north end of the famous Tay Railway Bridge and the new Tay Road Bridge (1966). There are 18- and 9-hole golf courses, tennis courts and bowling greens.

Despite its extensive docks and large and varied manufactures, Dundee is said to be famous for producing jute, jam and journalists!) it remains a pleasant city.

Buildings to be noted are the City Church (or churches—there are three churches housed here) with its 150 ft. high tower called the Old Steeple, 14th century, restored by Sir Gilbert Scott which abuts upon an extensive

modern commercial centre; the splendid Caird Hall behind its row of Doric pillars, where are the City Chambers and the large City Hall; the Albert Institute (modern, Sir Gilbert Scott), with the library, art gallery and museum. Dundee is now a university city in its own right. The former University College incorporated with the University of St. Andrews has been given the status of Dundee University. Other important

(Scottish Tourist Board).   *Dundee.*

Tay Road Bridge, Dundee. (*Scottish Tourist Board*).

new buildings include the large modern Ninewells hospital (to be completed by 1970), an art college and Kingsway Technical college. The Town Cross (near the city churches) is only a replica, the original being in the Dudhope Museum (16th century Dudhope Castle, standing in the Dudhope Park). In the fine Caird Park are the remains of Claverhouse Castle. The old Howff burial ground is of interest as having been gifted to the townspeople by Mary Queen of Scots (1565). William Wallace went to school in Dundee, and it was an incident here, for which he was outlawed, which started him on his patriotic career. In the War of Independence which followed, Dundee was captured and recaptured, often with disastrous results to the townsfolk; again in 1547 it was taken, sacked and burnt by the English forces. In the 17th century it suffered no less at the hands of Monk and Montrose; in the 18th century, shared in the less harrowing associations of the Jacobite Risings of the '15 and the '45. Among its famous sons was Hector Boece, the mediaeval historian.

4 miles E. is the attractive seaside resort of Broughty Ferry, formerly a separate burgh, now a part of Dundee. The ferry to Tayport which gave it its name no longer operates. Broughty Castle (restored) dates from the 15th century.

DUNFERMLINE

A ROYAL BURGH and ancient royal residence of Fife, 3 miles inland from the Firth of Forth, some 16 miles from Edinburgh via the Forth Bridge. It is noted for its Abbey (burial place of Robert the Bruce) and the slight remains of its palace.

The Abbey, founded in the 11th century by Malcolm Canmore, rebuilt in the 12th, many times restored and now incorporated in the Abbey Church, is still a noble structure, with a splendid Norman nave and some fine carving. Over the choir (rebuilt 19th century and in use as a parish church) rises a great square tower, with the words "King Robert the Bruce" in large letters forming a balustrade. Only the refectory remains of the old monastic buildings.

Historically the Abbey is famous as the burial-place of seven Scottish kings, from Malcolm Canmore to the Bruce. Here, too, is the tomb of Ralph Erskine (d. 1752), a distinguished minister of the Abbey, and leader, with his brother Ebenezer, of the great Secession of 1733–40.

A single wall is all that is left of the palace, where Robert the Bruce spent some time, and later

Bridge Street, Dunfermline.

Dunfermline Abbey.

Mary Queen of Scots. The monastery, not the palace, was the original royal residence, but the later Stuarts chose to occupy the palace, and here Charles I was born, and Elizabeth, the "Winter Queen" of Bohemia, ancestress of our own royal house.

Famous natives of Dunfermline are the early Scots poet Henryson (d. 1502), Sir Noel Paton, the artist, and Andrew Carnegie, noted Scottish philanthropist and millionaire. To his own town he was especially generous, one of his many gifts being the romantic public park of Pittencrieff Glen, with its flower gardens and 17th century mansion, now a museum. The many trusts, both national and local, by which his bequests are administered have their headquarters in the town. His birthplace, an unpretentious little house, is also a museum.

Other places of interest are the Town Buildings, the old Mercat Cross, Malcolm's Tower, traditionally associated with Malcolm Canmore, and the cave said to have been used by St. Margaret, his Queen, as an oratory.

Busy as it is (an ancient "linen" town, with other industries besides), Dunfermline has many attractions for the holiday-maker: three fine 18-hole golf courses (one of which has a very old clubhouse), tennis courts, bowling greens, angling, swimming—and the amenities of "The Glen", which include tearooms, children's pond and band performances.

DUNDONALD CASTLE, 4 miles NE. of Troon, Ayrshire, was an early home of Robert II.

DUNDRENNAN ABBEY, a ruined Cistercian abbey 5 miles SE. of Kirkcudbright. It is said that Mary Queen of Scots fled to Dundrennan after the defeat at Langside, and passed her last night in Scotland there.

DUNGLASS CASTLE, c. 3 miles E. of Dumbarton, on the Clyde, was a stronghold of the Colquhouns. An obelisk (1839) commemorates Henry Bell, of steam navigation fame.

DUNKELD, a charming village built among wooded hills and crags on the Tay, 15 miles N. of Perth. It has a fine old cathedral which stands on the site of a still older Culdee abbey (early 9th century). The existing building is mainly 14th–15th century, although parts of it are considerably older. The choir is still in use as the parish church. Within are some interesting relics, including a recumbent figure said to represent Alexander Earl of Buchan, the notorious Wolf of Badenoch.
Just across the river is Birnam (q.v.), connected with Dunkeld by a Telford bridge. Niel Gow the Fiddler, noted throughout Scotland in the 18th century,

was born at the nearby village of Inver, and is buried in the churchyard of Little Dunkeld Church.

Dunkeld has golf, fishing, touring, tennis and bowling facilities, good walks and vantage points (Craigiebarns). The waterfalls of Hermitage and Rumbling Bridge are near by.

DUNLOP, a small place 2½ miles N. of Stewarton, in Ayrshire, formerly famous for its cheese.

DUNNET, the name of a village, bay and headland in the N. of Caithness. Here are fine bathing sands and the highest lighthouse in Britain.

DUNNIDEER, a ruined castle on a conical hill, in Aberdeenshire, *c.* 10 miles NW. of Inverurie.

DUNNING, a Perthshire village 5 miles ENE. of Auchterarder, 200 ft. above sea-level in rolling hilly country. The parish church with its square Norman tower (*c.* 1200) is of interest. From here a road crosses the Ochil Hills to Rumbling Bridge.

DUNNOTTAR. See Stonehaven.

DUNOLLIE CASTLE. See Oban.

DUNOON

A FAVOURITE holiday resort on the Cowal shores of the Firth of Clyde, headquarters of the Royal Clyde Yacht Club. Here (at the end of August) is held an important Highland Gathering, the Cowal Games, culminating in the spectacular march of a Thousand Pipers, and ending with a fireworks display; also golf and tennis tournaments, sheepdog trials, hill-climbs, etc. Dunoon has magnificent views of the Clyde, especially from its natural vantage point, "Bishop's Seat" (1,651 ft.). Points of interest in the town are Morag's Fairy Glen, the statue of Highland Mary, and the Castle Gardens and Pavilion. Amenities include two good golf courses (one is at Kirn, to the N.), fishing on Loch Eck and the River Echaig, yachting, boating, tennis and bowls; concerts, variety, cinemas and dancing. Tours or cruises run to practically all the Clyde resorts, up the lochs to Arrochar and Lochgoilhead, and to Oban, Inveraray, Glencoe and the Trossachs. There are literally hundreds of boarding houses and hotels. Sir Harry Lauder's former home is now a burned-out ruin.

DUNROBIN CASTLE. See Golspie.

DUNROSSNESS, a parish in the S. of the mainland of Shetland.

DUNS, a small country town, county town of Berwickshire, 16 miles W. of Berwick-upon-Tweed. There is fishing (brown trout) in the Blackadder and Whiteadder.

Duns, rebuilt in the 16th century, is of very ancient foundation, and claims to be the birthplace of the mediaeval scholar Duns Scotus (d. 1308). It has associations also with the Covenanters. The monument crowning Duns Law (700 ft.) which rises behind the town, is known as the Covenanter's Stone. Duns Castle is a modern structure embodying a more ancient tower.

DUNSCORE, a village in Nithsdale, Dumfriesshire, 9 miles NW. of Dumfries. Ellisland, the farm which Burns occupied from 1788–1791 is in this parish, and also Craigenputtoch, the home of Thomas Carlyle (1828–34) where he wrote *Sartor Resartus*. 1½ miles NE. of the village is the ruin of Lag Tower.

DUNSINANE, a hill, 8 miles NE. of Perth, made world-famous in *Macbeth*, still has the ruins of a prehistoric fort on its summit.

DUNSKEY CASTLE. See Portpatrick.

DUNSTAFFNAGE. See Oban.

DUNTOCHER, a village, turned into a housing suburb below the Kilpatrick Hills, *c*. 8 miles NW. from Glasgow.

DUNTULM CASTLE, overlooking Duntulm Bay in the N. of Skye, was once the home of the Macdonalds, Lords of the Isles.

DUNURE, a picturesque little village and resort, 7 miles SW. of Ayr in a niche of the Ayrshire coast. Points of interest are the ruins of Dunure Castle (down by the sea), and the lovely and curious rock garden built by an Ayrshire naturalist.

The castle (a Kennedy stronghold) is very ancient; it probably met the onslaughts of the Norsemen before the Battle of Largs. Mary Queen of Scots took refuge here, and in the Black Vault the Commendator of Crossraguel Abbey was roasted over a slow fire until he agreed to give up the abbey lands.

DUNVEGAN, a village on Loch Dunvegan in north-west Skye. It has golf, fishing and boating. Its chief claim to distinction is Dunvegan Castle, stronghold

Dunvegan Castle.

of the Clan MacLeod, dating reputedly from the 9th century and said to be the oldest inhabited castle in Scotland. It is open to the public in summer, and is well worth a visit, not only for its fascinating relics of the MacLeods (including the Fairy Flag, captured from the Saracens), but also for its relics of Prince Charlie.

Two flat-topped mountains to the south are known as MacLeod's Tables. MacLeod's Maidens are the three large rock-stacks off Idrigill Point, on the southern extremity of the Duirinish peninsula.

DUPPLIN, the name of a loch and a modern castle, *c.* 6 miles SW. of Perth. An old stone cross commemorates the Battle of Dupplin (1332) when Edward Baliol defeated the large army of the Earl of Mar.

DURISDEER, a village in Nithsdale, Dumfriesshire, 18 miles N. of Dumfries. It has an old church with an impressive marble monument to the 2nd Duke of Queensberry and his wife.

DURNESS, on the north coast of Sutherland, a crofting and sheep-farming community on a narrow promontory W. of Loch Eriboll, and E. of the Kyle of Durness. It has excellent fishings. The series of limestone caverns known as the Smoo Cave, visited by Scott in 1814, is still an attraction to tourists. 1 mile NW. on a beautiful sandy bay, is the 17th century church with some noteworthy relics. In its churchyard is a monument to the 18th century Gaelic poet Rob Donn.

DUTHIL, a small place *c.* 7 miles SW. of Grantown-on-Spey in Inverness-shire. Here is the ancient burial ground of Clan Grant.

DWARFIE STONE, on the island of Hoy, Orkney, is a remarkable rock hollowed out into three chambers.

DYCE, an industrial village and airport 6 miles NW. of Aberdeen.

DYSART, a quaint little Fife coast town, included in the burgh of Kirkcaldy.

EARLSFERRY. See Elie and Earlsferry.

EARLSTON, a village of Berwickshire on the Leader Water, 4 miles NE. of Melrose, noted chiefly as the home of the 13th century poet and romance writer Thomas Learmont of Ercildoune (or Earlston). "Thomas the Rhymer" or "True Thomas", as he was also called, was remembered for his seven-year sojourn in Elfinland, even more than for his poems. He was endowed with the "Tongue of Truth", so that his prophecies became famous.

EARN, a river, strath and a picturesque small loch (7 miles) in Perthshire. Ben Vorlich rises on the south shore of the loch. At its extremities are Lochearnhead and St. Fillans. In Glen Ample, on the south shore, are the Falls of Edinample. The

River Earn flows from the east end of the loch, through Strath Earn and joins the Tay *c.* 9 miles below Perth.

EASDALE, a fascinating small place on Easdale Island off the west tip of Seil Island in Argyll. Everywhere is slate, even to the shingle on the beach. Most interesting of all, perhaps, is the forgotten, seaward part on Easdale Island, early in the century a thriving slate-quarrying community.

EASTERHOUSE, a village turned into a housing estate, lying just E. of Glasgow, notable for Provan Hall (*c.* 1 mile N.), country house of the church dignitary whose town house was Glasgow's Provand's Lordship (see Glasgow). Restored, Provan Hall is a perfect example of a 15th century Scottish mansion, crow-stepped and turreted, built on a courtyard, across which it faces a 17th century addition. The mansion is open to visitors in the afternoons.

EAST FORTUNE, an East Lothian village 5 miles S. of North Berwick.

EAST KILBRIDE, a once pleasant pastoral village of north Lanarkshire, 8 miles S. of Glasgow, now almost swallowed up in a "New Town", whose numerous modern industries include the printing of "Radio Times". Among its older features is the Louping Stone beside the old parish church, which has a lantern crown to its tower. To the north are the ruins of 13th century Mains

Castle. Calderwood Glen with its picturesque old tower, and Kittoch Glen, are among the beauty spots in the neighbourhood.

EAST LINTON, a small town of East Lothian, 6 miles W. of Dunbar, picturesquely situated on the River Tyne, with an ancient (16th century) bridge and a linn or waterfall below it. Parts of its church date back to the 13th century. Preston Mill on the River Tyne near by is an ancient monument.

EAST LOTHIAN, formerly Haddingtonshire, is a noted golfing county E. of Midlothian, on the Firth of Forth. It is mainly agricultural, and is also rich in historic and antiquarian interest. The Lammermuirs rise in the south. It has a coastline of rugged rock and sands, with pleasant villages and woods. The various resorts cater for visitors, without losing either dignity or charm. There are three important royal burghs in East Lothian (Haddington, North Berwick and Dunbar), a few industrial towns (Tranent and Prestonpans), and a large number of pretty villages with quaint names, *e.g.* Fortune, Needless, Drem, Traprain. North Berwick, Gullane and Longniddry in the north are especially identified with golf.

Loch Earn.

EAST WEMYSS. See Wemyss.

ECCLEFECHAN, a small town 15 miles E. of Dumfries, birth and death place of Thomas Carlyle (1795–1881). In the "Arched House" rooms and articles associated with him may be seen. To the east is the Roman station of Birrens.

ECK, LOCH, a beautiful loch, 6 miles long, in the Cowal district of Argyllshire. The road from the Holy Loch to Strachur runs along the eastern shore.

ECKFORD, a village of Roxburgh-shire, on the River Teviot, 5 miles NE. of Jedburgh. To the south-east of the village is Cessford Castle.

EDDLESTON, a small place 5 miles N. of Peebles, noted for the prehistoric remains, chiefly hill forts, in the neighbourhood.

EDDRACHILLIS BAY, a rocky indentation of the west coast of Sutherland.

EDEN, a river of Fife which enters the sea to the NW. of St. Andrews and gives name to the Eden golf course there.

SCOTTISH COUNTRY DANCING

THERE has been a spectacular revival of Scottish Country Dancing in recent years. Displays take place in Edinburgh at the time of the Festival, and visitors may by arrangement participate in an evening's dancing.

The Headquarters of the Society are at 12 Coates Crescent, Edinburgh.

EDINBURGH

EDINBURGH the traditional derivation from "Edwin's burgh", in reference to a 7th century Northumbrian king, is now authoritatively discounted). Capital of Scotland, a royal burgh since 1329 (charter from Robert the Bruce), seat of a university and home of the International Festival of Music and Drama, also popularly known as the "Athens of the North" and "Auld Reekie". Turnhouse, the airport which serves the city, is about 7 miles west from the town centre. Edinburgh lies between the Pentland Hills and the Firth of Forth, with the volcanic outcrops of Castle Rock (443 ft.), Arthur's Seat, named after the fabled King Arthur (822 ft.), Calton Hill (355 ft.), Corstorphine (520 ft.), Blackford (500 ft.) and Braid Hills (698 ft.) within the boundary, 9 miles of which lies along the south shore of the Firth of Forth. Industrially Edinburgh has long been associated with printing and brewing.

The High Kirk of St. Giles, Crown Steeple.

Edinburgh International
Festival

THE Edinburgh International Festival was started in 1947 and is under the patronage of the Queen. It opens in the third week in August and lasts until the end of the first week in September.

There are orchestral concerts, chamber concerts, operas, ballet, drama, art exhibitions, and a military tattoo. The finest orchestras and companies in Europe and America are invited to perform.

The Festival Club, the social rendezvous of the Festival, is housed in the Assembly Rooms at 54 George Street. It contains a licensed restaurant, snack bar, lounge, and other facilities for Festival visitors as well as a General Information Bureau. Charges for meals are reasonable. Season tickets 30s., guest cards 2s. 6d. each; daily tickets 5s.

During the Festival the International Film Exhibition takes place in Edinburgh, the Royal Scottish Academy holds its annual exhibition in the Galleries in Princes Street, and there are Highland Games at Murrayfield Rugby Ground.

Tickets and Accommodation: Apply by post to Festival Office, 11 Cambridge Street, Edinburgh. Bookings open at the beginning of April.

Bookings and accommodation can also be arranged through most of the travel agents in London—Dean & Dawson Ltd., Keith Prowse & Co. Ltd., Cook and Son Ltd.—and through British Travel Associations in New York, Los Angeles, Chicago, Toronto, Vancouver, Paris, Rome, Frankfurt, etc.

Late trains are arranged to serve day visitors from Glasgow and Dundee, and special buses run for the nearer surroundings.

The town in earliest times grew up on the mile-long slope from the Castle down to the Palace of Holyroodhouse, aptly called the Royal Mile because so often in its history kings and queens have passed along it on their official occasions. From the Castle Esplanade downhill the Royal Mile is known successively as Castle Hill, the Lawnmarket (once a street market where linen was sold), High Street, Netherbow (site of one of the city gates), and Canongate. In this vicinity are, therefore, the most venerable of Edinburgh's historic buildings.

The Castle Rock, a natural stronghold, is known to have been used as a fortress by primitive tribes, but of the buildings which crown the summit to-day, only the tiny Norman chapel of St. Margaret, originally the private oratory of Queen Margaret, wife of Malcolm Canmore, was constructed before the 15th century. The approach to the Castle is by the Esplanade, a parade ground, once the scene of executions, and where to-day the Military Tattoo is staged during the International Festival. The modern entrance gate, beyond the old dry ditch, is flanked by niched statues of Wallace and Bruce, and is on the site of the ancient outer barrier of the castle. From here the roadway leads to the Portcullis Gate with the portcullis chamber above. Beyond this gate, on the left, are the Lang Steps which lead to the Upper Defence, while on the opposite side of the roadway are the 18th century cannon of the Argyle Battery. Higher up the hill are the Barracks, Hospital and Governor's House (not open

City Observatory, Calton Hill.

(Scottish Tourist Board).

to the public), and the upper part of the rock is reached through the Foggy or Foogs Gate. On the highest point is St. Margaret's Chapel, and near by the famous 15th century cannon known as Mons Meg. Close by the top of the Lang Steps are the Forewall and Half Moon batteries, and the ancient Fore Well. The Half Moon Battery, from which the one o'clock gun is fired, is built over the ruins of David's Tower.

In the square known as the Palace Yard is the strong-room where the Scottish Regalia are kept. The King's Lodging is next to it, in which are many relics, and the room where Mary Queen of Scots gave birth to her son who became James VI of Scotland and subsequently James I of England. In the 16th century Great Hall on the south side is a large display of arms, suits of armour and some gun-carriages. The United Services Museum, containing a vast collection of uniforms and military relics, occupies an 18th century barracks. The impressive Scottish National War Memorial, with a Shrine standing on the exposed rock, was erected after the 1914–18 war. The Navy, the Air Force and every Scottish regiment are represented, together with the ancillary services, and birds and animals (including a mouse and a canary) are shown in the carvings. A Book of Remembrance is open and a page is turned every day.

During the winter months the War Memorial and precincts only are open to the public: December to February, 10–4, Sunday 11–4; March, April, May, October and November 10–5, Sunday 11–5. All apartments are open from 30th May to 10th September 9.30–6, Sunday 11–6, precincts only 6–9 daily; 11th September to 30th September 9.30–6, Sunday 11–6, War Memorial and precincts only. Admission charge to Historical Apartments; War Memorial and precincts free.

On the north side of Castle Hill is the Outlook Tower and Camera Obscura, which is also a museum. Open on weekdays during the summer months 10–6, Sundays 11.30–6. Admission charge.

Lady Stair's House, off the Lawnmarket, now a museum, dates from 1622. It is open daily 10–4, Saturday 10–1, closed on Sunday. Open 10–5 during the Festival period, and 2–5 on Sundays. Small admission fee. Gladstone's Land (17th century house or tenement) is used by the Saltire Society and is often open to visitors, especially at Festival time. On the opposite side is Deacon Brodie's Close and there are other memorials hereabouts of the city personality who was a housebreaker by night and gave Robert Louis

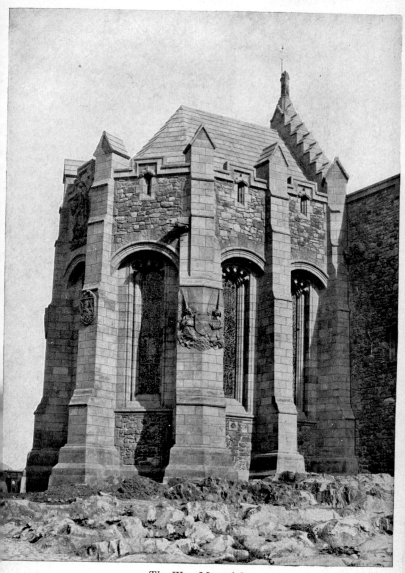

The War Memorial.

Stevenson the idea for "Dr. Jekyll and Mr. Hyde".

The High Kirk of St. Giles is built on the site of an early Christian church which existed before A.D. 854. The present plain gothic structure was commenced in 1387, but was repeatedly altered through the years, at one time, after the Reformation, being partitioned into four churches. In 1829–32 it was so extensively repaired that most of the old fabric, other than the crown steeple, was destroyed. From 1872–83, largely due to the interest and generosity of William Chambers, a former Lord Provost, the restoration was successfully carried out. The modern Thistle Chapel is open to visitors (small admission fee). John Knox was one of the many famous ministers who have occupied the pulpit of St. Giles. It was during the brief period as cathedral of the Diocese of Edinburgh that the celebrated incident occurred, when Jenny Geddes threw the cutty stool at the dean's head, in protest against the introduction of the *Book of Common Prayer*. Services are held on weekdays at 12, Sundays 11 and 6.30. Open weekdays 10–5.

On the south side of St. Giles was formerly the cathedral burying ground, where John Knox and many other notabilities were laid to rest. The supposed grave of the Reformer is marked by a stone in the pavement in Parliament Square. Parliament House, the Law Courts, part of the Scottish National Library, formerly the Advocates' Library, and the Signet Library now stand on the site of the old cemetery. The Great Hall of

Opposite: The Scottish Episcopal Church of St. John and Princes Street from the West End. Below: Chessel's Court, Canongate. ('The Scotsman').   (*Scottish Tourist Board*).

Parliament House, built 1631–40, is often compared with Westminster Hall. It is open Monday to Friday 10–5, Saturday 10–1, free. In it are portraits and statues.

The lead equestrian statue of Charles II in Parliament Square is the oldest in the city, and was cast in Holland towards the end of the 17th century.

To the west of St. Giles, let into the causeway, is the Heart of Midlothian, marking the position of the old Tolbooth, where parliaments assembled prior to the building of Parliament Hall (see above), and which later was used as a prison. The grim old building was demolished in 1817, a new jail on Calton Hill taking its place (now itself demolished).

The Mercat (Market) Cross, from which all Royal Proclamations are read, was erected in 1885. It contains the ancient pillar and occupies the site of the original City Cross.

On the north side of the High Street, near St. Giles, are the City Chambers, commenced in 1753 and completed 1761, headquarters of the Local Administration (not open to the public). At the entrance stands the Cenotaph to commemorate the dead of two World Wars. At the foot of the High Street on the north side stands the picturesque gabled house known as John Knox's House, where the Re-former is believed to have lived while minister of St. Giles. Open 10–5 on weekdays (small admission charge). Opposite is the Museum of Childhood, open Monday to Saturday 10–5, and during the Festival, on Sundays 2–5 (small admission charge), which will interest adults even more than children, since they will see the toys, the games, the magazines and even the medicines they knew when they were very young.

The Canongate, lying beyond the old city walls, E. of the Netherbow gateway, was founded by the canons of the Abbey of Holyrood, hence the name. On the north side of the street, Canongate Tolbooth, built 1591, and once local council offices, is now a museum, open weekdays 10–5 and, during the Festival, on Sundays from 2–5 (small admission charge).

Canongate Church (1688) stands near by. In the crowded churchyard lie the ashes of David Allan, the painter who taught David Wilkie his art, Adam Smith, famed for his "Wealth of Nations", and the poet Robert Fergusson, whose tombstone was erected and epitaph written by his admirer Burns.

Huntly House, built in the lifetime of Mary Queen of Scots, is now a city museum, containing among other exhibits a collection of Burns relics. Open weekdays 10–5; also Wednesday

Canongate Tolbooth. (*W. S. Thomson*).

Edinburgh Castle and Royal Scottish Academy.   (*Scottish Tourist Board*).

evening 6–9, June to September and, during the Festival, on Sundays from 2–5 (small charge). At Acheson House in Canongate is the Scottish Craft Centre for traditional and contemporary crafts. Open Monday to Friday 10–12.30, 2–5.30, Saturday 10–12.30 (Festival period also 2–5.30). Closed on Sunday.

There are many other fine old buildings in the Royal Mile, such as Ramsay Lodge, and Moray House (now part of Moray House College of Education), but they are not generally open to visitors.

The ancient ruins of Holyrood Abbey are all that remain of a rich and powerful Augustinian foundation. Legend tells that when David I was hunting he was attacked by a vicious hart. Suddenly there appeared in the heavens a miraculous shining Cross or "Rood" which scared the angry beast, and the king's life was saved. In gratitude he founded in 1128, at the place where the incident occurred, the Abbey, which he richly endowed and dedicated to the Holy Rood. Special accommodation which was provided for royal visitors was frequently used, and James II was born there. It was James IV who commenced the building of the royal palace beside the old Abbey. The fine gothic chapel was laid in ruins in 1688 by mobs who resented popish worship within its walls. It is the burial place of several kings and queens of Scotland, Darnley, and many other noble and well-known people.

Of the original palace of Holyroodhouse, commenced by James IV in 1501 and enlarged by James V in 1528, only a small part remains. The rest was built in 1671–79 by Charles II, and renovated inside and out in the last century and during the reign of George V. Only the apartments in the 1528 part of the building were left untouched and they are in much the same condition as when Mary Queen of Scots occupied them. It was in these chambers that Rizzio, the Queen's favourite, was murdered (the place is marked by a metal plate in the floor), and John Knox talked with the Queen. The vast picture gallery contains over one hundred portraits of Scottish monarchs, painted from imagination by a Flemish artist, Jacob de Witt. His average payment for each portrait was just over £5, and he worked from 1684 to 1686. A small building near the Palace is known as Queen Mary's Bath. Holyrood is open to visitors except when the Royal Family or the Lord High Commissioner are in residence. Monday to Saturday 9.30–6, Sundays 11–6 from mid-June to September; 9.30–4.30 and 12.30–4.30 for the rest of the year. Admission charge.

The Queen's Park (King's Park when a king is on the throne) includes Salisbury Crags and Arthur's Seat, a wonderful vantage point. On the slopes of the hill are the ruins of St. Anthony's Chapel. High up is Dunsappie Loch and at the foot on the south-east is Duddingston Loch and bird sanctuary. In Duddingston village is an ancient hostelry named the *Sheep's Heid Inn* with some interesting relics. St. Margaret's Loch on the north is a boating pond. A motor road circles the park.

On George IV Bridge, south of the High Street, are the Edinburgh Public Library and the National Library of Scotland.

At the foot of George IV Bridge, on the west side is Greyfriars Bobby, memorial to a faithful dog which, fed by kindly citizens, kept watch for the remainder of its life after its master's death, over the grave in Greyfriars churchyard. It achieved international immortality in the film, "Greyfriars Bobby", made by Walt Disney.

Greyfriars is named after the monastery which preceded it, and after the closing of the cemetery of St. Giles, the garden became the town burial ground. Greyfriars churchyard will be ever memorable as the place of the Signing of the Covenant in 1638, and there also is the mausoleum of Sir George (Bluidy) Mackenzie, the judge who condemned to death so many of its signatories. Among the graves of men of note are those of George Buchanan, historian, and tutor to

Mary Queen of Scots and James VI, and Allan Ramsay of Gentle Shepherd fame. After the rising of Bothwell Bridge in 1679, hundreds of prisoners were interned without shelter in the churchyard, some for as long as five months, until the remnant of 257 were transported to the Barbadoes.

The fine building of Heriot's (Hospital), a large day school, is near by.

The Grassmarket, west of Greyfriars, retains many of its old houses. It was a place of execution during the reigns of Charles II and James II. The actual site of the gallows is marked by a stone St. Andrew's Cross let into the roadway. It was in the West Port and the south-west corner of the Grassmarket that the notorious Burke and Hare committed their murders. Hare escaped but Burke was hanged and his skeleton is to be seen in the Surgeons Hall (see below).

East from the foot of George IV Bridge is Chambers Street, where is the Royal Scottish Museum, open daily 10–5, Sunday 2–5 (free). Here also are the statues of James Watt and William Chambers.

The University Buildings, partly designed by Adam, are near by in the South Bridge, and further south in Nicolson Street is the Surgeons Hall Anatomical Museum, open Monday and Wednesday 12–4, Saturday 10–1 (free). Edinburgh University medical school, the McEwan Hall, and the once fine George Square (in large part now taken over by the University which is rehousing some of its departments in modern buildings such as the David Hume Tower) are close by. Heriot Watt College, in Chambers Street, achieved University status in 1966. Princes Street, which runs parallel to the High Street, is one of the most beautiful streets in Europe, and a famous shopping centre

though some people find its architecture inferior to George Street on its north. On the south side are the well-kept Princes Street Gardens, begun in 1816, after the drainage of the Nor' Loch. The vast Sir Walter Scott Monument, near the east end of the gardens, is open daily (small charge) for climbing. Dwarfed by it is the statue of David Livingstone. John Wilson, Allan Ramsay and Sir James Simpson are all commemorated in stone, and here also are the Scottish American War Memorial and the Royal Scots Memorial. The Floral Clock, at the Mound, is much admired by visitors, and there is a bandstand where out-door concerts and dancing displays are held in fine weather.

Art exhibitions are held at the Royal Scottish Academy at the foot of the Mound, and there is a fine collection of pictures at the National Gallery of Scotland, behind it. The latter is open Monday to Saturday 10–5, (Festival period 10–8). Sunday 2–5 (free).

At the top of the Mound is New College where Church of Scotland ministers are trained, and where the General Assembly is held. It is built on the site of the palace of Mary de Guise, mother of Mary Queen of Scots, and for some years Regent of Scotland.

St. Cuthbert's at the west end of Princes Street is the oldest parish outwith the boundaries of the Old Town. It was once of great extent and was given by David I to Holyrood Abbey. The earliest church of St. Cuthbert is believed to have existed about the time of the Saint's death in 687. The present building was constructed after the old one was demolished in 1775, and stands in a much older churchyard.

North of Princes Street lies the New Town of broad streets, spacious squares, crescents and circuses, of

103

Opposite: The Palace of Holyroodhouse. (*W. S. Thomson*).

handsomely terraced classical buildings, their severity relieved by many tree-filled gardens. Charlotte Square (designed by Adam), Moray Place, Royal Circus, Ainslie Place and Ann Street are among the finest. St. Bernard's Well, Stockbridge, with its classical "temple", a former mineral well with waters similar to those of Harrogate, stands on the Water of Leith, farther up which is the Dean Bridge and Dean Village (below it).

The Episcopalian Cathedral Church of St. Mary in Palmerston Place was consecrated in 1879.

To the west is the fine building of Donaldson's School for the Deaf.

Robert Louis Stevenson's birth-place is at 8 Howard Place. Stevenson's cottage in Swanston village, on the slopes of the Pentlands, is also of interest.

At the east end of Queen Street are the Antiquarian Museum and the Scottish National Portrait Gallery, open weekdays 10–5 (10–8 during Festival). Sundays 2–5 (free). Among the famous exhibits are the Traprain silver and the Naismith portrait of Burns. The Antiquarian Museum also has an exhibition in Shandwick Place (western continuation of Princes Street), and the Transport Museum in Leith Walk is open weekdays from 9–5 (free).

Register House, at the east end of Princes Street, was built from designs by Robert Adam, to house the Scottish Records. It is open 10–4, Saturday 10–1. In front of it is an equestrian statue of the Duke of Wellington.

The G.P.O. is at the corner of Waterloo Place and the North Bridge, opposite Register House.

In Waterloo Place is St. Andrews House, government headquarters for Scotland. The Parliamentary Reformers Monument and the statue of Abraham Lincoln are in the Old Calton Burying Ground, Waterloo Place.

On the Calton Hill is the Nelson Monument, open 8–dusk (small charge), from which a wonderful panorama of the city may be seen. The National Monument, an imitation Parthenon, was intended to be embellished with statues, but remains unfinished. Also on the Calton Hill is an observatory.

There is a monument to Burns in Regent Road, near by (another stands in Constitution Street, Leith), and here too stands the famous Royal High School.

The Assembly Rooms, George Street, originally built in 1787, with subsequent additions, are the oldest of the places of entertainment in Edinburgh (see Edinburgh International Festival). Concerts are given in the Usher Hall and the McEwan Hall (the main University Hall), and there are four theatres, the Lyceum, now Edinburgh's Civic Theatre, the King's, the Gateway, owned by the Church of Scotland, and not in full-time use now, and the 60-seat Traverse, which puts on mainly experimental plays.

Within the city boundaries, near Cramond, is Lauriston Castle (partly 16th century, partly 19th) and gardens. It contains an art collection and is open daily except Friday, the Castle 11–1 and 2–5, the Grounds 11–dusk (admission charge). The ruins of 15th century Craigmillar Castle, near the south-east city limits, are open April to September, weekdays 10–7, Sundays 2–7, October to March weekdays 10–4, Sundays 2–4. Merchiston Tower, in the south-west suburbs, the home of John Napier, inventor of logarithms is now incorporated in Napier College, a modern institution for technical education.

Portobello has a fine open-air swimming pool, amusements, and a promenade which continues along the sea-front to Joppa.

Leith Docks are the second largest

on the east coast of Scotland. There are harbours at Granton and Newhaven, chiefly used by fishing boats. The fisherwomen of Newhaven still wear their traditional costumes and have a much admired choir.

Edinburgh is well provided with parks and gardens in addition to Princes Street Gardens and the Queen's Park which have already been mentioned. Not far from the centre of the city are the Meadows (formerly the South or Borough Loch) and Bruntsfield Links where golf (pitching and putting) has been played since its early days. Leith Links, where the game is said to have originated, is no longer a golf course.

The Arboretum and Royal Botanic Garden were founded in 1670. They have had several moves, being at one time where the G.P.O. stands now, later in Leith Walk, and were finally sited in Inverleith Row (north of Princes Street) early in the 19th century. The gardens today are very extensive and beautifully laid out, with large glass houses, a lily pond, rose garden, rock garden, herbaceous borders and countless trees and shrubs. Inverleith House, now the National Gallery of Modern Art, stands within the Garden. The latter is open daily 9 till sundown, Sunday 11 till sundown (free).

Inverleith Public Park, in which is a boating lake for model yachts, lies west of the Botanic Gardens.

The Scottish National Zoological Park (of over 70 acres) on the southern slope of Corstorphine Hill, west of Princess Street, is rewarding to visit. It houses a very large collection of animals, birds, reptiles and fish. The Zoo is world-famous for its breeding of Antarctic Penguins and there is a Penguin Parade every summer afternoon, conditions permitting. Other features are a Children's Farm and a free flying colony of night herons. There is a car park and restaurant. Open daily, summer 9–7, Sunday 12–7, winter 9 till sundown, Sunday 12 till sundown (admission charge).

Adjoining the Zoological Park is Corstorphine Hill Public Park, in which is Clermiston Tower. The latter is open daily May to September 10–6, October to April 10–3 (small admission charge).

The Royal Highland Show is held at Ingliston, just beyond the Burgh boundary, in the third week of June. Ingliston also has a motor racing circuit opened in 1965.

Blackford Hill, south of the town centre, offers a wonderful panorama of the city. The Royal Observatory and a TV mast are on the hill. At the foot of the hill is a large pond with wild duck, geese and other birds. Skating and sledging are allowed here in hard wintry weather. There is a tree-lined walk along the Braid Burn by the Hermitage of Braid.

The Braid Hills, which lie south of Blackford Hill are famous for golf and are also an excellent place for walking—except of course on the fairways.

Cramond (q.v.) north-west of the town, is a well-known local beauty spot with an attractive promenade extending along the sea-front to Granton.

There are golf courses at Barnton (NW. of city centre), Turnhouse, Murrayfield, Bruntsfield, Carrick Knowe, Silverknowes (W.), Kingsknowe, Baberton (SW.), Lothianburn, Braids and Craigmillar (S.), Liberton (SE.), Duddingston, Prestonfield (E.), and Craigentinny (NE.)

There are short excursions to the Forth Bridge, Dalmeny, Roslin and the Pentland Hills, and inexpensive bus tours of the city run frequently. Day, week-end and weekly tours, covering many parts of Scotland may conveniently be arranged with Scottish Omnibuses Ltd.

SCOTLAND FOR GOLF

There are over 250 first-class courses of which the following are world-famous:

Carnoustie.
Cruden Bay (Aberdeenshire).
Dornoch.
Gullane No. 1.
Gleneagles (Perthshire).
Muirfield (E. Lothian).
Nairn.
North Berwick.
Prestwick.
Royal Burgess (Edinburgh).
St. Andrews: The Old, The New, The Eden.
Troon.
Turnberry.

EDNAM, a village 2 miles NNE. of Kelso, birthplace of James Thomson (*The Seasons*) and H. F. Lyte (*Abide with Me*).

EDROM, a village of central Berwickshire.

EDZELL, a small town or village of Angus and a popular holiday resort in the Grampian foothills, 6 miles N. of Brechin on the North Esk river. There is an excellent golf course, fishing in the North Esk and the West Water. Ruins of Edzell Castle, *c.* 1 mile W., ancestral home of the Lindsays, have much of interest; the Stirling Tower, the bower of Mary Queen of Scots, the garden-enclosure of Sir David Lyndsay, with its uniquely decorated walls.

EIGG, a farming island (4½ miles long) off the coast of Inverness, about 5 miles from Arisaig on the mainland. The distinctive feature is the Sgurr of Eigg (1,289 ft.), a mass of black basaltic columns of volcanic origin.

EIL, a sea loch in Inverness and Argyllshire with Fassifern House, associated with Prince Charles Edward, on its north shore.

EILDON HILLS, a group of three peaks, the highest 1,385 ft., lying south of Melrose, Roxburghshire.

EILEAN DONAN CASTLE, a ruined stronghold on the shore of Loch Duich. See Dornie.

EILT, a small but beautiful loch near Glenfinnan, Inverness-shire.

Opposite: Eilean Donan Castle.

ELGIN

A PLEASANT and prosperous old town on the River Lossie, royal burgh and county town of Moray, also a cathedral city. Though its ancient cathedral has been in ruins for several centuries, the ecclesiastical *motif* is much in evidence, not only in scattered relics and the names of houses, streets, institutions, but in the serene and ordered dignity of the town itself.

Elgin cathedral, called the "Lanthorn of the North", was founded by Bishop Andrew of Moravia (Moray) in 1224. Its history was a troubled one. In 1390 it was burned (along with part of the town) by the outlawed and excommunicated Wolf of Badenoch; another dramatic incident was the "Bloody Vespers" of 1554, a sanguinary clash within its walls between the families of Innes and Dunbar, after whom, respectively, the south and north aisles of the transept are named. Though much despoiled, both before and after the Reformation, it remains one of the most beautiful ruins in the country. The familiar distinctive outline of its west front—the two great towers flanking the deep, round-headed doorway surmounted by the Alpha window, lacking its tracery—may be seen to advantage from the east walk of the Cooper Park, near the Library. Little remains of the interior.

The piers of the nave are gone, but a single exquisite clustered column (9 ft. in circumference) supports the groined roof of the Chapter House.

In the High Street history and antiquity blend with the bustle of modern commerce. At the top (east) end, is the Little Cross (where the Wolf of Badenoch did penance after his act of sacrilege), in the centre the parish church, and (rebuilt) Muckle Cross. Just north of the lower end is Lady Hill (site of an ancient castle) bearing a tall column commemorating the last Duke of Gordon. This with South Street and the connecting thoroughfares forms the business and shopping centre of the town.

Sporting facilities include fishing (salmon, sea and brown trout) in the River Lossie, golf and bowls. The well-wooded Cooper Park (40 acres) has a children's pond and stretches to the banks of the Lossie.

Elie Bay.

ELGOL, a village on the east coast of Loch Scavaig in Skye. Boats may be hired here to take one to Loch Coruisk.

ELIE AND EARLSFERRY, a royal burgh and favourite resort, at the east end of Largo Bay in south-east Fife. There is bathing from the excellent sandy beach, golf (18 and 9-hole courses), tennis, bowls and angling. Some search the beaches here for the so-called rubies which are to be found. They are really a kind of garnet. Earlsferry is traditionally associated with MacDuff, who was ferried here across the Forth. MacDuff's Cave is a mile to the west.

ELLON, a village on the Ythan, 13 miles N. of Aberdeen. There is fishing in the Ythan, golf in the beautiful MacDonald Park (9-hole course), tennis, putting, bowls, and a children's paddling pool in the six-acre Gordon Park within the town.

ELPHINSTONE, a village 10 miles E. of Edinburgh with a ruined tower near by, and associations with the family of the name.

ELVANFOOT, a small place at the junction of Clyde and Elvan, 12 miles NW. of Moffat.

ENARD BAY, a deep bay between Lochinver and Rhu Coigach, the north-west point of Ross-shire.

ENTERKIN, a stream and village (Enterkinfoot) and pass 15 miles NNW. of Dumfries.

ERIBOLL, a fine sea-inlet on the north coast of Sutherland. Cran Stackie (2,630 ft.) is to the south-west of the loch.

ERICHT, a river of Perthshire joining the Isla to the north of Coupar Angus.

ERICHT, LOCH, a deep loch (15 miles long) in Inverness-shire and Perthshire among wild scenery, is richly stocked with trout. It is one of the main reservoirs of the Tummel-Garry hydroelectric scheme. On the west shore is Ben Alder.

ERISKAY, a small island off the southern tip of South Uist, where Prince Charlie landed in 1745; it is famous for its songs and legends, notably the "Eriskay Love Lilt" of the Kennedy-Fraser *Songs of the Hebrides*.

ERROL, a village in the fertile Carse of Gowrie, 11 miles E. of Perth, on the Tay, gives name to the hereditary High Constableship of Scotland.

ESK (1), a river of Dumfries flows south into England to the head of the Solway Firth. (2) A river of Midlothian flowing to the Firth of Forth at Musselburgh. (3) Two rivers of Angus, the one (North Esk) flowing from the hills through Glen Esk south-east past Edzell to the sea north of Montrose, the other (South Esk) flowing from Glen Clova past Brechin to enter Montrose Basin.

ESKDALEMUIR, on the White Esk, 14 miles NW. of Langholm.

ETIVE, a river and sea-loch of Argyll. The sea loch opens on Loch Linnhe just north of Oban. Near its mouth at Connel, it narrows to the Falls of Lora. Ben Starav and Ben Cruachan are on its shores. Villages and hamlets include Connel, Achna-cloich, Taynuilt, Bonawe and Kinlochetive. The river flows through Glen Etive to the north end of the loch.

ETTRICK, a river of Selkirk-shire, tributary to the Tweed, gives name to Ettrick Bridge an angling village on it, Ettrick Pen (2,269 ft.) a mountain near its source, and Ettrick Forest, a popular and historic name often applied to the whole or part of Selkirkshire. James Hogg, the "Ettrick Shepherd", is buried in Ettrick churchyard.

EVANTON, a village of Ross-shire, 7 miles NNE. of Dingwall.

EWE, LOCH. See Poolewe.

EYEMOUTH, a fishing town of Berwickshire, at the mouth of the Eye, c. 8 miles NNW. of Berwick-upon-Tweed. It was noted in the past for its smuggling propensities (it was said that there was as much of it under as above the ground!) and in the present for its attractions as an unspoiled holiday resort. It has sea-fishing, trout-fishing in local waters, golf, bathing and boating.

FAIR ISLE, a small island between Shetland and Orkney, a bird-watching station of great importance. It has a hostel for visitors, and gives name to characteristic woollen patterns.

FAIRLIE, a famous yacht-building village and resort, 2½

miles S. of Largs on the Ayrshire coast. It has a harbour and pier, and sailings to Millport and Arran. In Fairlie Glen are the ruins of Fairlie Castle (16th century). Kelburn Castle, seat of the Earl of Glasgow, stands about a mile to the N., an imposing structure in the Scottish baronial style. Its beautiful grounds include a 9-hole golf course. Some of the world's most famous racing yachts (among them *Shamrock* and *White Heather*) have been built at Fairlie.

FALKIRK, a busy iron-working town of east Stirlingshire, scene of two major battles, formerly noted for its great cattle fairs, called the Falkirk Trysts. It has an old Market Cross.

The first Battle of Falkirk (1298) was a defeat for Wallace, the second (1746) a victory for Prince Charles Edward. A room is shown in which Prince Charles slept on the night before the battle. To the SE. is Callander House—in its grounds substantial fragments of Antonine's Wall.

FALKLAND, an ancient royal burgh of Fife, *c.* 10 miles SW. of Cupar, chiefly notable for its palace, a former royal residence. The Covenanter Richard Cameron was a native of Falkland. The little town is delight-fully situated at the foot of the Lomond Hills.

Falkland palace (open to visitors) dates from the 15th century, is a graceful Renaissance structure with a still usable south wing and a massive but decorative gatehouse. From the first it was a favourite residence and hunting lodge of the Stuarts. Here James V came to die after his defeat at Solway Moss. Later visitors were Charles I, Charles II and Cromwell. During the '15 Rob Roy and his men were for a time in possession of the palace, which figures in Scott's *Fair Maid of Perth*. Especially interesting is the chapel (old banqueting hall) which has a beautiful oak rood screen and a richly tapestried gallery.

Falkland Palace is now in the care of the National Trust. The former castle on the site has practically disappeared.

FALLOCH, a stream flowing into the head of Loch Lomond, giving name to the romantic Glen Falloch which it traverses and the Falls of Falloch.

FANNICH, a loch of central Ross and Cromarty, a hydroelectric scheme reservoir.

FARR, a village to the NE. of Betty-hill (Sutherland) with a fine Celtic sculptured stone in its churchyard.

FARRAGON, a Perthshire mountain (2,559 ft.) to the N. of Aberfeldy.

FASKALLY, LOCH. See Pitlochry.

FASLANE, a former shipbreaking port at the head of the Gare Loch, Dunbartonshire.

FEARN (properly HILL OF FEARN), a village of Easter Ross. It has an ancient historic abbey, part of which is still in use, and offers excellent fishing in Loch Eye.

FENWICK, a trim little village on the edge of the Fenwick Moors, 4 miles NNE. of Kilmarnock.

FESHIE, an affluent of the Spey, giving name to the magnificent Glen Feshie which it traverses.

FETLAR, a north-eastern island of Shetland.

FETTERCAIRN, a pleasant village, one-time burgh of barony, 4½ miles WNW. of Laurencekirk (Kincardine). There is fishing in local waters for salmon, sea-trout and finnock. The centre of interest for visitors is the Market Cross, formerly the Town Cross of the vanished burgh of Kincardine. In Fettercairn House numerous letters and other papers of James Boswell came to light in 1930.

FIDDICH, a river in the south of Banff, giving name to a famous whisky (Glenfiddich) distilled here.

FIFE, a peninsular eastern county between the Firths of Forth and Tay. The "Kingdom of Fife", formerly of greater extent, is fertile, with cultivated vales, and some hills, of which the Lomonds (West Lomond, 1,713 ft.) are the chief. The Eden, which flows into the North Sea near St. Andrews, is the chief river. Though some of the characteristic industries (coal-mining, linoleum) have declined, there is still much else (engineering, aluminium, whisky, paper, and some ship-building), and fisheries are important. Many of the coast towns, including St. Andrews, Elie, Crail and Leven, are holiday resorts. Cupar is the county town; Kirkcaldy and Dunfermline the largest centres.

FIFE KEITH, a village of Banff-shire, on the River Isla opposite Keith.

FIFE NESS, the eastern promontory of Fife.

FINDHORN, a picturesque angling river flowing almost 70 miles NE. to the Moray Firth and the village of Findhorn on Findhorn Bay.

FINDOCHTY, a fishing village on the Moray Firth.

FINDON, or FINNAN, a small coastal village of Kincardineshire, 9 miles NNE. of Stonehaven, noted for having been the place where Findon or Finnan haddocks were first prepared.

FINGAL'S CAVE. See Staffa.

FINGLAS. See Trossachs.

FINNART, on the E. shore of Loch Long, in Dumbartonshire, an import depot for crude oil, which is then sent by pipeline to Grangemouth (q.v.).

FINTRY, a village and hill range of Stirlingshire. The Loup of Fintry is a spectacular 100 ft. waterfall on the Endrick Water.

FLANDERS MOSS, a low tract of Stirlingshire on the north bank of the Forth.

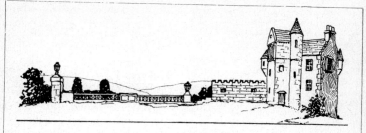

SCOTLAND'S COUNTRY HOUSES
open to the Public

Name	Location	Approximate Dates Open
ABBOTSFORD	near Melrose	April—October
ACHAMORE (garden, house by written appointment)	Gigha, off Kintyre	March—October
BALMORAL CASTLE (grounds only)	near Ballater	May—July
BINNS, THE	near Bo'ness	mid-June—mid-September
BLAIR CASTLE	near Blair Atholl	April—early October
BRODICK CASTLE	Arran	May—September
CRARAE LODGE (garden only)	near Inveraray	April—October
CRATHES CASTLE	near Banchory	All year round
CULZEAN CASTLE	near Maybole	March—November
DUNVEGAN CASTLE	Skye	May—mid-October
FALKLAND PALACE	near Cupar	April—October
GLAMIS CASTLE	near Kirriemuir	May—September
HOPETOUN HOUSE	near S. Queensferry	May—October
INVERARAY CASTLE	Inveraray	Easter—September.
INVEREWE (garden only)	near Gairloch	All year round
KILLOCHAN CASTLE	near Girvan	June—Spetember
KILORAN (garden only)	Colonsay	April—October
LEITH HALL	near Huntly	May—September
LENNOXLOVE	near Haddington	April—September
LOCHINCH CASTLE (gardens only)	near Stranraer	Summer months
MELLERSTAIN	near Gordon	June—September
THIRLESTANE CASTLE	near Lauder	May—September
TRAQUAIR	near Innerleithen	May—September

Further information from National Trust of Scotland, 5 Charlotte Square, Edinburgh.

FLEET, a river and its landlocked estuary (Loch Fleet—noted for bird life) in Sutherland, N. of Dornoch.

FOCHABERS, a neat and pleasant village on the River Spey, 8 miles E. of Elgin, formerly a ducal village centred in Gordon Castle, in recent years a notable centre of the food canning industry. It was rebuilt in the 18th century, but retains its old Market Cross. The Castle (now Crown property) was until 1937 the seat of the Dukes of Richmond and Gordon. It stands in a magnificently wooded park, and is one of the most imposing mansions in Scotland. The oldest part is the 15th century Tower of Gight.

FORD, a small village at the S. end of Loch Awe (Argyllshire) with good fishing in Loch Awe.

FORDOUN, a small place 12 miles SW. of Stonehaven, a burgh of barony in the reign of Mary Queen of Scots, is said to be the birthplace of the early historian John of Fordoun. There was a shrine of St. Palladius here to which, traditionally, Kenneth II was making pilgrimage when he was slain by Fenella, wife of the Mormaor. (See Auchenblae).

FORDYCE, a village SW. of Portsoy on the Moray Firth.

FORFAR, an ancient royal burgh and county town of Angus at the east end of little Loch Forfar, 12 miles SW. of Brechin; noted for its witches, and the succulent pasties called "Forfar bridies". Forfar is a route centre and a good touring base. The Town Hall has some interesting features, including the "Forfar Bridle". The former Town Cross presented to the town by Charles I in acknowledgment of its loyalty, now marks the site of the old castle, where Malcolm Canmore held a parliament. In Loch Forfar the slayers of Malcolm II were drowned while escaping after the crime.

FORRES, a pleasant town near the mouth of the Findhorn in Morayshire, 10 miles E. of Nairn. Forres is very old, reputedly the Varris of Ptolemy. Here Duncan held court. Sueno's Stone (23 ft. high, intricately carved) commemorated a battle—perhaps the last battle on this coast—with the Danes. Beyond it is the Witches' Stone, where formerly witches were burned.

FORT AUGUSTUS, a quiet little town at the head of Loch Ness in the Great Glen, with good fishing, golf and boating. The name is derived from the fort (called after William Augustus, Duke of Cumberland) erected for the suppression of rebellious clansmen after the '15. During the '45 it was occupied by Jacobites, and afterwards again by Hanoverians. Later (19th century) it was bought by Lord Lovat and given to the Benedictine Order for a monastery (now an abbey and school).

FORTEVIOT, 7 miles SW. of Perth; formerly a Pictish capital—now a model village. Has associations also with Kenneth Macalpin and Malcolm Canmore.

FORT GEORGE, a fortress (1748) on a promontory 10 miles NE. of Inverness, whose grey walls dominate the entrance to the Inverness Firth.

FORTH, a large river rising from two head-streams which join near Aberfoyle, flows E. with many windings, via Stirling and Alloa to the Firth of Forth, which latter separates the Lothians and Fife, and merges with the North Sea. The total length is 116½ miles, of which 53 miles are tidal. East of Stirling, it is bridged thrice— by a road bridge (1936) at Kincardine-on-Forth, a railway bridge (the Forth Bridge, 1882–90—see below), and the new Forth Road Bridge (opened 1964), at Queensferry.

FORTH BRIDGES. (1) The fine bridge carrying the railway across the Forth some 9 miles W. of Edinburgh, a spectacular landmark and a notable triumph of Scots engineering. Built (1882–90) on the cantilever principle to the designs of Sir John Fowler and Sir Benjamin Baker, it is 450 ft. high and more than a mile long. From shore to shore the only "foothold" is

Overleaf: Loch Drumbeg, near Lochinver.
Forth Rail Bridge.

the tiny islet of Inchgarvie (once fortified against Paul Jones) which supports the central pier. The bridge cost £3,250,000; and no tourist escapes being told that it takes 35 men $3\frac{1}{2}$ years to paint it, and when it is finished it is time to start all over again! (2) To the west is the Forth Road Bridge, opened by the Queen in 1964. It cost £16,000,000 and is 1.56 miles long. It was the first long-span suspension bridge to be built in Scotland. On the south side it is approached by motorway from Cramond Bridge (outside Edinburgh). The motor car toll of 2s. 6d. is payable at the south entrance. An elevated and spacious car park (leave motorway $\frac{1}{2}$ mile before bridge) with restaurant facilities affords splendid views of both bridges and the Firth.

FORTINGALL, a village on the N. shore of Loch Tay, 7 miles W. of Aberfeldy with a famous Yew Tree said to be 3,000 years old.

FORTROSE, a village in the Black Isle on the Moray Firth nearly opposite Fort George. It is a royal burgh and formerly was a centre of learning. Only fragments remain of its once famous 15th century cathedral (chapter house, south aisle of chancel and nave, and a bell inscribed with the name of Thomas Tulloch, Bishop of Ross in 1460). It was not merely a religious house; like the great mediaeval universities it had its schools of law and divinity known far beyond its borders. Practically continuous with Fortrose is Rosemarkie, also ancient, dating from the 7th century, when St. Moluag, Bishop of Lismore, founded a monastery here. Fortrose has good sailing facilities, and there is a golf course on Chanonry Peninsula and a caravan site at Rosemarkie.

FORT WILLIAM, a picturesque market town and tourist resort on Loch Linnhe, with a view up Loch Eil, an important road and rail centre, with steamer services to Oban and the Hebrides. Ben Nevis may be climbed from here. The town is a gateway to the north and north-west Highlands, and also (via the Great Glen and Inverness) to the NE. It takes name from the fort built by General Monk and called after William III. Fort William has a West Highland Museum. There is an important aluminium factory, powered by hydro-electricity derived from the harnessed waters of Lochs Laggan and Treig. The pipe-lines emerging from the shoulder of the Nevis massif are a familiar landmark. The large new pulp- and paper-mill at nearby

Corpach is providing further prosperity for the town.

FOULA (fool'a), a remote outlying island of the Shetland Islands, 27 miles W. of Scalloway. The island is notable for its variegated bird colonies, including kittiwakes red-throated divers, and the fierce great skua or bonxie birds.

FOWLIS EASTER, 6 miles NW. of Dundee, has a 15th century church with quaint carvings, paintings on oak, and other curious features.

FOYERS, a village, with aluminium works nearby, and a stream falling into Loch Ness from the E., having on its course the famous Falls of Foyer.

FRASERBURGH, an old town and port at the NE. point of Aberdeenshire, almost entirely taken up with herring and white fisheries. It has a good harbour and a few evidences of its antiquity, including the 16th century castle or keep (topped by a lighthouse) on lofty Kinnaird's Head, and the riddling Wine Tower nearby. The castle was built by an ancestor of the Saltoun family, Sir Alexander Fraser (who also formed the town) in the mid-16th century. The Wine Tower (15th century) is built over a large (100 ft.) cave, and has no entrance to the lower story save through an opening in the floor of the upper. It is 25 ft. high.

In Saltoun Square is the Town Cross, and the Town Hall, adorned with a statue of the 16th Lord Saltoun.

Fraserburgh has several hotels and two municipally owned caravan sites. Its unobstructed outlook on the North Sea, and its nearness to Fraserburgh Bay with its excellent sands draws many visitors.

FRUIN, a stream of west Dunbartonshire. Glen Fruin, through which it flows into Loch Lomond, is sometimes called the Glen of Sorrow from an affray here between MacGregors and Colquhouns (1603).

FUINARY. See Lochaline.

FURNACE, a village on Loch Fyne (Argyllshire), site of old powder mills, a granite quarry and a smelting furnace.

FYNE, LOCH, a long sea-loch running from the Clyde estuary into the heart of Argyllshire. Glen Fyne, traversed by the River Fyne, lies at the head of the loch. The loch has some very good scenery. The fishing industry has several stations here, and angling is a popular sport. Inveraray, chief town of Argyll, stands on the north shore near the head of the loch, and there are a number of interesting villages and hamlets (see Tarbert, Lochgilphead, Ardrishaig, Strachur).

FYVIE, a village and castle 15 miles N. of Inverurie (Aberdeenshire). The village was once a royal burgh. The castle (formerly a royal possession) is one of the finest examples of its kind in Scotland, rich and dignified, with four massive turreted towers, built by the Preston, Meldrum, Seton, and Gordon families, the earliest of which dates from the 15th century. A fifth has been added in modern times by the family of Leith. The romantic old ballad of the Trumpeter of Fyvie has its setting here, and a stone effigy of the Trumpeter stands on one of the towers. The beautifully wooded policies are extensive and charming.

In the village centre behind the market cross is the Buchan Stone, marking the division between the Buchan earldom and the Formartine thanage. Near the village is the Priory Cross (1868), on the site of the 12th-century Priory of St. Mary. There is a Fyvie Angling Association, and some excellent salmon and sea-trout fishing in the Ythan.

GAIRLOCH, a favourite holiday place at the head of the Gair Loch on the west coast of Ross-shire. There is much fine scenery and magnificent western seascapes as well as fishing, boating, bathing, stalking, bird-watching, rough shooting, and a 9-hole golf course. This is the region of the golden eagle and the red-throated diver, one of the few mainland districts where the grey lag goose nests. Tourists should visit Flowerdale House, former seat of the Mackenzies of Gairloch and Kerrysdale.

GAIRLOCHY, a small place near the foot of Loch Lochy (Inverness-shire).

GALASHIELS, an ancient settlement and busy modern town on the Tweed and the Gala Water, 6 miles N. of Selkirk. A burgh of barony since 1599, "Gala" takes its name from the shiels or huts (on Gala Water) where pilgrims on their way to Melrose were hospitably entertained. Modern Gala is famed for its tweed and hosiery manufactures. There are facilities for golf, fishing, swimming, tennis, putting and bowls. The big event of the holiday season is the "Braw Lads' Gathering" in June, when the "Braw Lad" and "Lass" and their company ride round the town and visit Scott's house, Abbotsford, nearby. Their tour includes the Old Town Cross, where Margaret Tudor was given her dowry of Ettrick Forest on her marriage in 1503 to James IV of Scotland. Here the Braw Lass mixes the red and white roses of the Houses of Lancaster and York. The Gala motto is "Soor Plums". The story goes that in 1337 a band of English marauders were surprised and vanquished by the lads of Gala while raiding a plum orchard. The town has an ancient Mercat Cross, and in Corn Mill Square a modern War Memorial—a mounted mosstrooper against a background of Peel Tower. The

Scottish Woollen Technical College is an important institution for research and the practical training of men and women in all branches of the tweed and woollen industry.

GALA WATER, a small river rising in the Moorfoot Hills in Midlothian, and joining the Tweed a mile below Galashiels.

GALLOWAY, or "the country of the Gael", is a district of south-west Scotland now comprising the counties of Wigtown and Kirkcudbright, but formerly much more extensive. It is noted for its horses, cattle, and dairy produce. Here, based on Loch Doon and Rivers Dee, Ken, etc., is the Galloway hydro-electric scheme (1935). The Mull of Galloway, a bold headland (210 ft.) at the south end of the Rhinns of Galloway (the double peninsula in the SW. of the county) is the most southerly point of Scotland.

GALSTON, lace-making town of Ayrshire, 5 miles E. of Kilmarnock. To the NE. is Loudon Castle, once seat of Ayrshire's hereditary sheriffs, badly damaged by fire in 1941. There is a golf course nearby.

GANNOCHY BRIDGE, a picturesque spot on the North Esk, 1½ miles N. of Edzell.

GARDENSTOWN, a fishing village to the E. of Macduff.

GARE LOCH, an arm of the Firth of Clyde, projected into Dunbartonshire opposite Greenock in a northwesterly direction, to the length of 12 miles. It does not exceed 1 mile in breadth and forms the east side of Rosneath peninsula. It has been used as an anchorage by many ocean-going vessels. Helensburgh and Rhu (*qq.v.*) are on its east shore.

GARELOCHHEAD, a peaceful village at the head of the Gare Loch, popular as a holiday resort and yachting centre.

GARLETON, name of a village, 15th century castle and hills, 2 miles N. of Haddington. On Garleton Hill is a monument to the 4th Earl of Hopetoun, a distinguished soldier of the Peninsular War.

GARLIESTOWN, a small pleasant seaside place in Wigtownshire, 8 miles S. of Wigtown on Garliestown Bay. There is a harbour, and to the N. on the cliffs is Eggeness Castle.

GARMOUTH, a small Morayshire village at the mouth of the Spey.

GARRY, a glen, river and loch in north Perthshire. The Falls of Garry are on the upper course of the river. See Tummel.

GARRY, a glen, river and loch in Inverness-shire, SW. of Fort Augustus. The river falls into Loch Oich near Invergarry. It gives name (Glengarry) to a cap worn by Highlanders. Lochs Garry and Quoich are both hydroelectric reservoirs.

GARTEN, LOCH, a loch on Speyside, famous as the breeding place of migrant ospreys. They can be watched from a specially built "hide".

GARTH CASTLE, a ruin in the Strath of Appin, Perthshire, was a stronghold of the Wolf of Badenoch.

GARTLY, a small village of Aberdeenshire, on the Huntly–Kildrummy road.

GARVALD, a retiring little hamlet in the Lammermuir Hills, *c.* 6 miles SE. of Haddington. Nearby is the fascinating old house of Nunraw, now a monastery, where the new Cistercian Abbey of Sancta Maria is being built by the monks.

GARVE, a village 13 miles WNW. of Dingwall, near Lochs Garve and Luichart. The main road from Inverness to Kyle of Lochalsh here sends off a branch (33 m.) to Ullapool, skirting the Wyvis range and, beyond Altguish, the spectacular Loch Glascarnoch, a hydroelectric reservoir.

GATEHOUSE - OF - FLEET, a small town and angling resort in Kirkcudbrightshire, picturesquely situated on the River Fleet, 7 miles NW. of Kirkcudbright. Burns wrote "Scots wha hae" in the Murray Arms Hotel.

GATTONSIDE. See Melrose.

GIFFORD, a trim delightful village in the Lammermuirs, *c.* 5 miles S. of Haddington. One of its hotels is called after the famous Goblin Ha' in nearby Yester Castle—but Gifford itself has many points of interest: a quaint village green, village cross and a fine 9-hole golf course, the graceful Adam mansion of Yester House (seat of the Marquis of Tweeddale), standing in beautiful grounds on Gifford Water, and the 15th century church of Bothans, with a Dutch spire and a long association with the Tweeddale family.

Beyond Yester House and higher up the stream is Yester Castle, a picturesque ruin with all the interest centred in the large underground vault known as Goblin Ha', built, if one will credit it, by a wizard, Sir Hugo de Gifford, in 1268. The Hall is 37 ft. long, 19 ft. high, with a ribbed stone vaulted roof and certain intriguing features suggestive — to the quick

Galloway: Glen Trool.

imagination—of the dark secrets of wizardly practice.

To balance the ghostly influence, Gifford disputes the claims of Haddington and Morham to be the birthplace of John Knox.

GIGHA, an island near the mouth of West Loch Tarbert (Argyll) separated from the mainland by the Sound of Gigha, noted for its prehistoric remains. A ferry plies to Tayinloan on the mainland.

GILNOCKIE, 4 miles S. of Langholm in Eskdale, Dumfriesshire, is notable for its connections with Johnnie Armstrong, most famous of Border freebooters, who was treacherously summoned by James V and hanged. Hollows Tower, ruins of which still stand, is sometimes said to have been Johnnie Armstrong's fortress, but it was more likely nearby on a rocky promontory above the Esk.

GIRVAN, a small port and golfing and holiday resort on the Ayrshire coast 21 miles SSW. of Ayr. It has a splendid safe bathing beach equipped with diving-stage and gymnasium, facilities for sunbathing, golf on a sporting 18-hole course laid out by James Braid, tennis, bowls and putting. There is angling (salmon, sea trout, brown trout) on the Rivers Girvan, Stinchar and Cree, also sea-fishing, motor-boat trips to places on the coast; day and evening cruises round bird-haunted Ailsa Craig. Girvan is sunny and dry, sheltered on the E. by the hills which rise behind it—opening on a wonderful seaward prospect which includes Arran, Ailsa Craig and Kintyre.

GLAMAIG, a mountain in Skye (2,537 ft.).

GLAMIS (glams), a village of Angus, 5 miles SW. of Forfar, noted chiefly for Glamis Castle, seat of the Earls of Strathmore and childhood home of Queen Elizabeth the Queen Mother, daughter of the 14th Earl. The oldest parts of the Castle date back to antiquity, notably the Square Tower with its tremendously thick walls; but mostly it is 17th century—a splendidly picturesque baronial castle with many closely-grouped pepper-pot turrets. In the reign of James V, a Lady of Glamis was burned for using witchcraft against the King's life. When (too late) her innocence was established, the forfeited castle was restored to her son, Patrick, ancestor of the Earls of Strathmore. In the 18th century it was used as headquarters by both James (called the Old Pretender) and Prince Charles Edward. In 1930 Princess Margaret was born in Glamis.

Within, Glamis has everything one would look for—fine vaulted ceilings, huge fireplaces, winding stairs, a crypt, a secret chamber, and a wonderful outlook over wooded Strathmore to the Grampians. Parts of the castle and grounds are open to visitors at certain hours.

Glamis Castle

Glasgow Cathedral.   (*A. D. S. MacPherson*).

GLASGOW

SOME 45 miles W. of Edinburgh, on the River Clyde, is Scotland's largest city (population *c.* 1,000,000) and her business and commercial capital, a royal burgh since 1454. Uniquely situated between Highlands and Lowlands, within the rich industrial belt, yet close to the borders of agricultural Ayrshire and the fertile fruit-growing regions of the Upper Clyde.

Glasgow is primarily a seaport and a birthplace of ships, cradle of the *Queen Mary*, the *Queen Elizabeth*, *H.M.S. Hood* and so many more. Ships and shipping have been her concern since the days of sail—but shipbuilding now seems to be declining and there are not as many active yards on the Clyde as there were during the Second World War, when more ships were built and rebuilt on the Clyde than in all the shipyards of the U.S.A. put together.

The most romantic approach to the city is by sea. First you have the long winding sail up the Firth of Clyde, past Ailsa Craig ("Paddy's Milestone") and the Wagnerian backdrop of the Arran Alps, by the Greater and Lesser Cumbraes and the Isle of Bute, past the comely Clyde resorts and the peaks of Argyll, by the ports of Greenock and Port Glasgow, all amid scenery of great beauty. Then there is the slow progress up the river from Dumbarton Rock, passing Old Kilpatrick and Bowling. Then come the large ship-building yards and marine engineering works of Glasgow itself.

Glasgow University. *(Scottish Tourist Board).*

What lies behind those rather drab-looking 14 miles of docks and quays? The tourist is agreeably surprised to find a city handsomely laid out with large, imposing Victorian buildings, and a sprinkling of skyscrapers among them, fine shopping streets and many parks and gardens. George Square is the civic centre, with 12 statues, the Cenotaph, an information kiosk and the City Chambers, seat of local government for the County of the City of Glasgow. It was opened in 1888 and is in the Italian Renaissance style (open Monday, Tuesday, Wednesday and Friday, admission free). The halls are largely marble and mosaics and the Chambers include the Council Room, reception salons and a Banqueting Hall. The sculptured frieze over the main doorway illustrates the original form of today's motto of the city, "Let Glasgow Flourish". The full motto is "Let Glasgow Flourish by the Preaching of the Word".

Westwards from here is the business and shopping part of the town. Eastwards is the University of Strathclyde (1964: formerly Royal College of Science and Technology) with its ancillary modern buildings towering over George Square.

The old centre of the city was Glasgow Cross, where stands the Tolbooth tower, built in 1626 and a relic of the former Town House and Jail. The High Street leads from the Tolbooth to Glasgow Cathedral, passing the site of the first

Provan Hall, near Glasgow (see Easterhouse).

university. Glasgow's most notable building is St. Mungo's Cathedral. This beautiful and dignified 12th century gothic church arose on the site of a little chapel built in the 6th century by Glasgow's founder and patron saint, St. Kentigern (better known as Mungo, "the beloved"). There is much to see in the Cathedral—the impressive nave, the (stone) rood screen depicting the Seven Deadly Sins, the beautiful East Chapel, the well in which Mungo baptised his converts and his own tomb; best of all, the lovely vaulted crypt or Laigh Kirk, said to be the most perfect example of its kind in Europe (open daily, admission free). Nearby is Provand's Lordship, built about 1471 and the oldest house in Glasgow. Originally it was the Preceptor's House of the Hospital of St. Nicholas, and it seems probable that both James II and James IV stayed here. Mary Queen of Scots is supposed to have lived here when the famous "Casket Letters" were written. The house is now a museum furnished with some fine period pieces. It is maintained by the Provand's Lordship Society (open daily except Thursday and Sunday, small admission charge).

Near this tiny "hospital" and

Opposite: Glasgow. (The Scotsman).

The Tolbooth.

behind the Cathedral looms the vast beneficent bulk of the Royal Infirmary (founded in 1792) where Lister made his earliest experiments in antisepsis.

Glasgow University now stands on one of Glasgow's many hills, Gilmorehill, overlooking the Kelvingrove Park. Founded in 1451, it was moved from the High Street in the second half of the 19th century. A massive stone gateway, known as Pearce Lodge, at its south-east entrance is a relic of the old university. It was moved from the High Street.

Close by in the Kelvingrove Park stands the handsome red-sandstone structure of the Art Gallery and Museum. Glasgow is said to have the finest municipally owned art collection in Britain. At Kelvingrove (open every day, admission free) the art collection includes a long series of Old Masters, Rembrandt ("Man in Armour"), Rubens, Velasquez, Titian, Giorgione, Botticelli. Here, too, is Whistler's "Portrait of Carlyle", Turner's "Modern Italy": the "Pifferari" and Millais' "Forerunner". A more recent notable acquisition is the "Christ of St.

John of the Cross", by Salvador Dali. In February, 1944, Sir William Burrell gave Glasgow his vast collection of objets d'art. A suitable place has not yet been found for the entire collection, but parts of it are always on display. The Museum, in addition to a wealth of artistic and antiquarian exhibits, has sections devoted to armour, shipping, engineering and natural history. Other museums are the People's Palace, Glasgow Green, which houses the "Old Glasgow" exhibits, a children's museum in Tollcross Park, the Camphill Museum in Queen's Park, showing part of the Burrell Collection, and the Museum of Transport, Eglinton Toll, which includes a comprehensive collection of tram cars showing this form of transport over its whole history. All these museums are open daily and admission is free.

Across the way from Kelvingrove Art Gallery is the Kelvin Hall, the largest exhibition centre in Scotland and holder of many exhibition records. Its four acres house a succession of shows and exhibitions throughout the year, a circus and carnival every Christmas, and Promenade Concerts by the Scottish National Orchestra in early summer.

Cultural interests are represented by the Glasgow School of Art, designed by Charles Rennie Mackintosh, and the Royal Scottish Academy of Music, to which is attached the College of Drama with its own theatre and television studio. The Scottish National Orchestra has its headquarters in the city. Glasgow has made no mean contribution to Scotland's cultural progress; the "Glasgow School" of painting is renowned and in music and literature also she is well abreast of contemporary thought. The St. Andrew's Halls in North Street were destroyed by fire in 1962 and a new cultural centre is to be built where Buchanan Street Station now stands. In the meantime concerts and political meetings are held in the Glasgow Concert Hall, Argyle Street.

Visitors should see Stirling's Library in Royal Exchange Place, formerly the Royal Exchange and embodying the "country" mansion of a Glasgow Tobacco Lord of the 18th century.

The Kelvingrove Park is but one of Glasgow's open spaces. There are 58 public parks and many gardens and squares. A short distance from Kelvingrove are the Royal Botanic Gardens, also on the banks of the Kelvin, colourfully laid out around the huge domed conservatory of the Kibble Palace, which contains palms, tree-ferns, banana trees and remarkable orchid houses and tropical ferneries.

Glasgow Green is said to be the oldest public park in

Overleaf: Dumbarton Rock.

Britain. It is on the banks of the Clyde, and opposite it the sky-scrapers of the new Gorbals make a fascinating contrast. Another favourite resort is the Zoo at Calderpark, which has a large collection of wild animals and birds, in something like their natural surroundings. The polar bears' den is the largest in Europe.

There are eight public golf courses and many private ones in and near Glasgow. There are many more within easy travelling distance, including the championship links at Prestwick and Troon. Glasgow has fourteen swimming pools, an ice-rink (for skating, curling, and ice-hockey) at Crossmyloof; several bowling alleys; dance-halls and cinemas without number and several excellent theatres—King's, Alhambra, Pavilion, Metropole and the Citizens', with its famous repertory company.

One of Glasgow's attractions is her lovely hinterland. Beyond her immediate environs and yet within day-touring distance are (1) the Ayrshire Coast — Troon and Prestwick, Ardrossan and Saltcoats, Ayr and the Burns Country; (2) Aberfoyle and the Trossachs; (3) Loch Lomond via Balloch with its houseboats and charming lochside park (which also belongs to Glasgow); (4) Helensburgh and the Gareloch (a favourite tour is round the Three Lochs, Gareloch, Loch Long and Loch Lomond, returning by Balloch); (5) Greenock, Gourock and Inverkip along the south shores of the Clyde. There are Class A roads in most directions from Glasgow, and some broad boulevards for the motorist. But the favourite tours are sailings down the Firth to the famous Clyde resorts, Cove and Kilcreggan, Dunoon, Rothesay, Millport and the Arran coast, Tighnabruaich, and Campbeltown.

Opposite: *George Square.*   (*Scottish Tourist Board*).

Provand's Lordship.   (*Scottish Tourist Board*).

GLAS MAOL, a mountain in Perthshire (3,502 ft.) *c.* 10 miles S. of Braemar.

GLASS, a river of Inverness-shire, below its confluence with the Affric flowing through the beautiful Strathglass to the Beauly.

GLEN AFFRIC. See Affric, Glen.

GLENALADALE, a glen to the west of Loch Shiel (Inverness-shire).

GLENALMOND, the beautiful valley of the Almond to the N. of Crieff (Perthshire) in part called the Sma' Glen, with Trinity College (1847; often known as "Glenalmond"), a famous public school on its middle course.

GLENBERVIE, 7 miles SW. of Stonehaven, in Kincardineshire, has an interesting church. Robert Burns's father was a native of this village and Burns's ancestors are buried in the churchyard.

GLENBRITTLE, a climbing resort in Skye, a centre for the Cuillins.

GLENCAPLE, a small bathing-place to the S. of Dumfries.

GLENCOE, runs inland from Loch Leven, an arm of Loch Linnhe, about 1½ miles from Ballachulish; one of the wildest and most desolate of Scottish glens, and one of the most rewarding for the tourist, traversed by the Coe. Over the glen hangs the tragic memory of the Massacre of Glencoe. Clan chiefs were required to swear allegiance to William III before the end of December 1691. MacDonald of Glencoe was a few days late. Early in February some 120 Campbell troopers, under Campbell of Glenlyon, visited Glencoe ostensibly in friendship and were hospitably received. Then in the early morning of the 13th they fell on their sleeping hosts, slaughtering men, women and children indiscriminately, turning the rest out to perish in the snow, and burning their houses to the ground.

Scene of the Massacre is indicated by a monument, and near by is the Signal Rock, from which, traditionally, the signal for the Massacre was given. A hotel stands at the mouth of the glen, which is guarded by the Pap of Glencoe (2,430 ft.). A few miles farther up is the Clachaig Hotel, last outpost of civilisation. From here the glen grows wilder and wilder, with the towering "Three Sisters" facing the Black Rock across Loch Triochatan, near which the Celtic bard Ossian is said to have been born. "Ossian's Cave" may be seen high upon one of the "Three Sisters"— Aonach Dubh—and behind them rises lofty Bidean nam Bian.

The first ski lift in Scotland was built in Glencoe.

GLEN CROE. See Rest-and-be-Thankful.

GLENDARUEL, a beautiful valley, traversed by the Ruel, in Argyllshire running north from Loch Riddon.

GLENEAGLES, a golfing place, scarcely less famous than St. Andrews, 1 mile W. of Auchterarder in Perthshire. It has three fine golf courses, the "King's" (championship standard), the "Queen's" (for the fairly proficient) and the "Wee" (for the novice), all among heather and gorse, in splendid open country facing the Ochils. There is a large and excellent hotel. Fishing, squash and tennis are available—but golf is the order of the day.

GLENELG, a village on the west coast of Inverness-shire with prehistoric remains in Glen Beg near by.

GLENFARG, a village and picturesque wooded defile in which is the Bein Hotel, about 8 miles SSE. of Perth.

GLENFINNAN, a small place at the head of Loch Shiel and the foot of Glen Finnan. Here Prince Charles Edward set up his standard on 19th August, 1745. A commemorative monument bears an inscription in Gaelic, English and Latin.

GLENGYLE, birthplace of Rob Roy, at the head of Loch Katrine.

GLENISLA, See Isla.

GLENKINDIE, an angling village of west Aberdeenshire.

GLENLIVET, the basin of the Livet Water in southern Banffshire, giving name to a famous whisky.

GLENLUCE, a village near the mouth of the Water of Luce, on Luce Bay, Wigtownshire. To the N. is Luce Abbey (q.v.).

GLENMORE. See Great Glen.

GLENMORE LODGE, a lodge on the ascent of the Cairngorms from Aviemore, a national centre for physical recreation.

GLENROTHES a new development town of central Fife, between Leslie and Markinch, built near the experimental Rothes collieries.

GLENSHEE, a glen in Perthshire N. of Blairgowrie, with the River Shee running through it. The Spittal of Glenshee at the top of the Glen, was once a hospice and a tumulus a little off the road is known as Dairmid's tomb. It is a principal skiing resort.

GLOE, BEN-y-, a mountain (3,671 ft.) NE. of Blair Atholl (Perthshire).

GLOMACH, on the Ault a Ghlomach in the district of Kintail (Ross-shire), believed to be the highest waterfall in Britain (270 ft. to 300 ft. sheer descent), impressive, but a long way off the beaten track.

GOATFELL, a mountain (2,866 ft.) in Arran, of which it is the highest point, ascended best from Brodick (path). There are magnificent and extensive views from the summit.

GOIL, LOCH, a picturesque arm of Loch Long. Its lower slopes are well wooded and very charming in spring and early summer. The village of Lochgoilhead has an hotel, and is a good base for climbing and hiking, also for fishermen. From here a road leads through Hell's Glen to St. Catherine's, thence down the east shore of Loch Fyne.

GOLDIELANDS, a ruined keep 2 miles SW. of Hawick.

GOLSPIE, 7 miles N. of Dornoch, a pleasantly situated resort, backed by woods, on a wide sandy bay. There are fine fishing waters, a golf course and bathing beaches, good hotels, shops, and a cinema. Of topical interest is the modern Technical School. St. Andrew's Church has some good features, including an 18th century canopied pulpit. A little to the NE. is the imposing bulk of Dunrobin Castle, recently the seat of the Dukes of Sutherland, and now being turned into Scotland's newest public school, with the Countess of Sutherland on its board. Here and in the vicinity are evidences of prehistoric occupation—brochs and earth houses.

GORDON, a small place in Berwickshire, 8 miles NW. of Kelso, was the original seat of the Gordon family (afterwards Dukes of Richmond and Gordon).

GORDONSTOUN. See Duffus.

GOURDON, a small fishing port 10 miles S. of Stonehaven, with a picturesque harbour in the lee of Doolie Ness (hotel).

Glenfinnan Jacobite Memorial.   *(Scottish Tourist Board).*

Gourock from Lyle Hill. (*Scottish Tourist Board*).

GOUROCK, adjoining Greenock on the Firth of Clyde, is a residential and holiday place and a yachting centre, headquarters of the Royal Gourock Yacht Club. It stands on a woody promontory with excellent views of the Firth and is a good cruising centre with sailings to most of the Clyde resorts. Round the Point is the Cloch Lighthouse. On the hillside above Gourock is the Cross of Lorraine, a memorial to the Free French Naval Forces in the Second World War.

GOWRIE, CARSE OF, a fertile tract in Perthshire, SW of Dundee, noted for its fruit-growing.

GRAMISDALE, a small place on the island of Benbecula.

GRAMPIANS, a great mountain range running across Scotland from Argyll in the W., through northern Perthshire, Inverness-shire, southern Aberdeen and northern Angus, almost to the sea. It has many high summits, including Schiehallion, (3,547 ft.), Ben Lui (3,708 ft.), and Ben Lawers (3,984 ft.).

GRANGEMOUTH, an industrial town and seaport in Stirlingshire, on the Firth of Forth, at the east end

Overleaf: A view of the Grampians. (*W. S. Thomson*).

ATLAS OF SCOTLAND

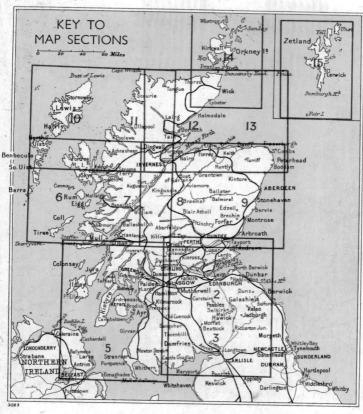

KEY TO
MAP SECTIONS

0   20   40   60 Miles

3023

NOTE TO MAP SECTIONS

Motorways   Access Point

Main Roads — 20	Motor Ferries ============
Secondary Roads — 16	Youth Hostels ▲ Y.H.
Other Roads —	Altitudes in Feet 1357
Red Figures give distances in miles between black dots	*Adjoining Map Section Numbers* 13

SCALE OF MAP SECTIONS   1:1,000,000

0   5   10   20   30   40 Miles

0   5 10   20   30   40   50   60 Kilometres

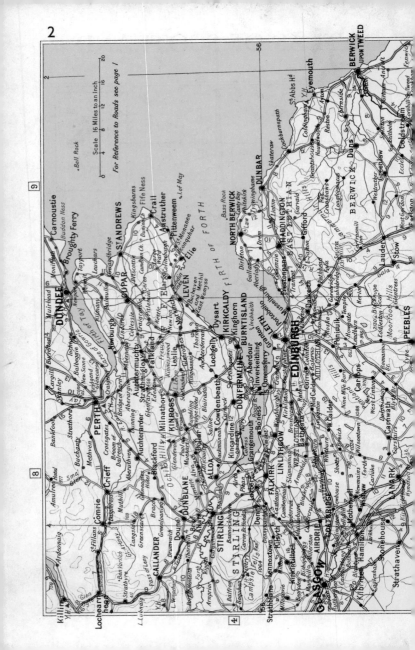

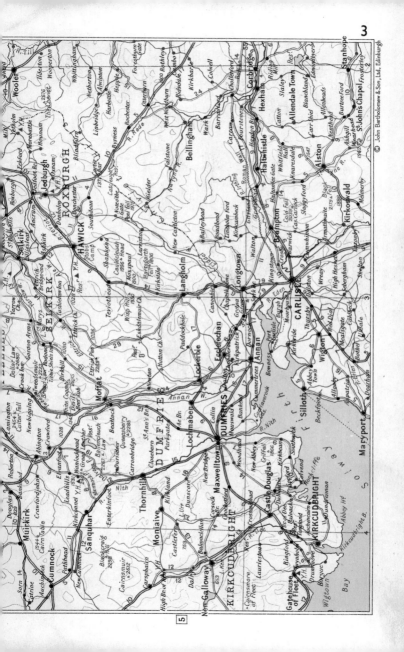

Scale 16 Miles to an Inch

For Reference to Roads see page 1

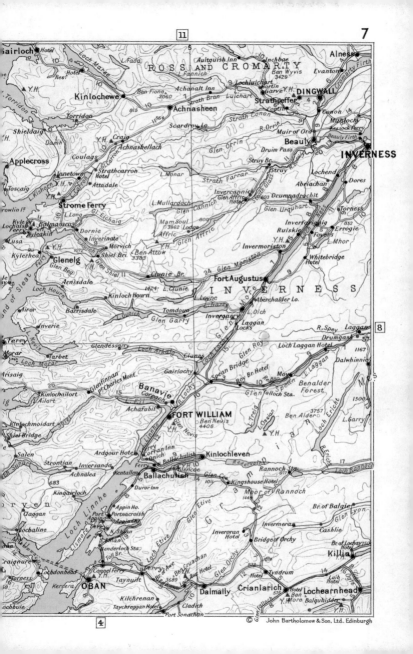

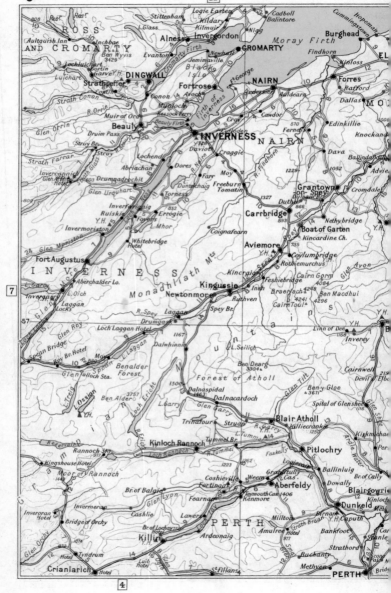

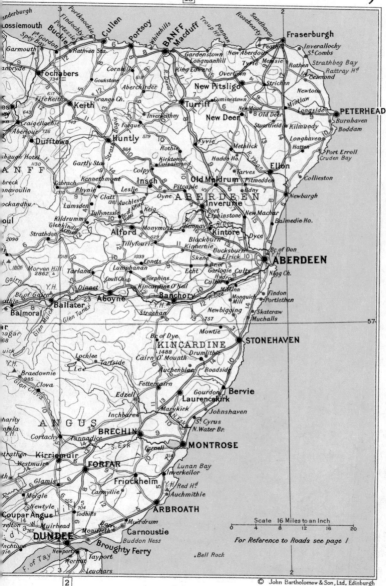

Scale 16 Miles to an Inch

0   4   8   12   16   20

For Reference to Roads see page 1

© John Bartholomew & Son, Ltd., Edinburgh

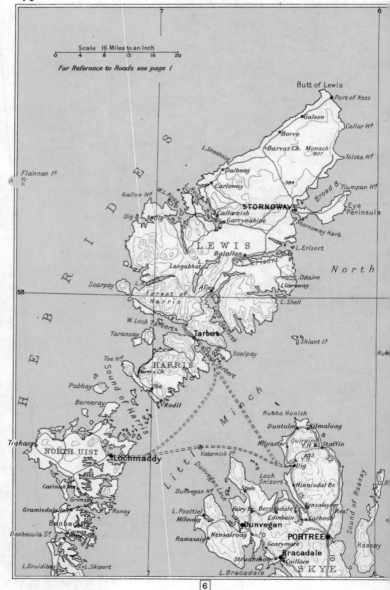

Scale   16 Miles to an Inch

0   4   8   12   16   20

For Reference to Roads see page 1

Butt of Lewis

Port of Ness

Galson

Cellar H⁴

Borve

L. Sheaboie

Barvas Ch.   Monach
807

Tolsta H⁴

Dalbeag

384

Broad B.

Tiumpan H⁴

Carloway

Eye
Peninsula

STORNOWAY

Callarnish
Garrynahine

Stornoway Harb.

Uig B.

W.L.Roags

L.Road

L E W I S

Gallon H⁴

Balallan

L. Erisort

Langabhat

Erisort

L.Odairn

Scarpay

Alne

Limreway

Forest of
Harris

North

L. Shell

W. Loch Tarbert

Taransay

Tarbert

Shiant Is

Scalpay

Toe H⁴

HARRIS

Pabbay

Obe

Berneray

Rodil

Rubha Hunish

Duntulm   Kilmaluag

NORTH UIST

Tighary

Sound of Harris

Quiraing

Staffin

Kilvaxter

Lochmaddy

Vaternish Pt.

Uig

Carinish

Grimsay

Loch
Snizort

Hinnisdal Br.

Ronay

Dunvegan Hd

Loch

Kensaleyre

Gramisdale

Stein

Res⁴

Benbecula

Dunvegan

Loch

Fairy Br.

Bernisdale

Benbecula S⁴

Iarnan

L. Pooltiel

Milovaig

Edinbain

Carbost

Dunvegan

PORTREE

Ramasaig

Kensalroag

Gearymore

Bracadale

L. Druidibeg

L. Skiport

Struanmore

Coillore

L. Bracadale

S K Y E

Sound of Raasay

Raasay

H E B R I D E S

Flannan Is

Little   Minch

5

C. Wrath
Kyle of Durness
Kearvaig
Sandwood L.
Durness
Rhiconich Hotel
Melness
13
Bettyhill
Heilim
L. Eriboll
Oldshoremore
Kinlochbervie
14
Eriboll
Tongue
Kyle of Tongue
Badcall
Achriesgill
L. Hope
Loch Inchard
Rhiconich
Ben Hope 3040
Ben Loyal 2504
Loch Laxford
Foinaven 2980
L. an Deire
Laxford Br.
Laxford Br.
3
Reay Deer Forest
L. Loyal
Scourie
Y.H.
Edrachillisch.
Achfarry
More
Meadie
732
Edrachillis Bay
Kylestrome
Hotel
Altnaharra
Kylesku Inn
SUTHERLAND
Pt. of Stoer
Unapool
Oldany
Drumbeg
Ben Klibreck
The Crask 828
Ben Armine
Clashnessie
Stoer Ch.
813
Skiag Br.
Overscaig Hotel
Lochinver
ASSYNT
Inchnadamph
Inverkirkaig
2779
Canisp
3273 Ben More Assynt
Loch Shin
Enard Bay
Suilven
542
Rubha Coigeach
inch
Knockan
Altnacealgach Hotel
R. Cassley
Laig
15
Achiltibuie
Y.H.
Cam Loch
Elphin
536
R. Oykel
Strath Fleet
12
Summer Is.
G. Rosehall 502
7
Strathcanaird
Oykel Bridge
Invershin
Y.H.
3
Ardmuir
Greenstone Pt.
Bonar Bridge
Loch Broom
Ullapool
Strath Carron
Ardgay
Kincardine
10
Gruinard Bay
Laid
Y.H.
Gruinard Ho.
Ardcharnich
Glen More
Aultnamain Inn
Melvaig
Loch Ewe
Aultbea
Dundonnell
Y.H.
Inverlael
1110
Stittenham
Poolewe
Turnaig
Sheallag
L. Glass
Gairloch
Hotel
Flonn Loch
Braemore Lo.
Rest.
Rest.
Alness
L. Fada
10
ROSS AND CROMALTY
Cromarty Firth
Res.
Inchbae
Evanton
Hotel
Aultguish Inn
Ben Wyvis 3429
Pt.
L. Fannich
Lochluichart
Garve Y.H.
DINGWALL
Kinlochewe
Ben Fionn 3060
Achanalt Inn
Luichart
Strathpeffer
Conon
Loch Maree
Strath Bran
Contin
4
Mulrochie
Achnasheen
815
1564
Strath Conon
R. Orrin
Kessock Ferry
Scardroy Lo.
Muir of Ord
Shieldaig
Y.H.
Craig
Glen Orrin
Beauly
Beauly Firth
Y.H.
Achnashellach
Druim Pass
INVERNESS
Applecross
Coulags
L. Monar
Struy Br.
Loscaig
Lannetown
Strathcarron Hotel
Y.H.
Attadale
Strath Farrar
Lochend
Abriachan
Dores
L. Kishorn
Invercannich
Glen Affric Hotel
Drumnadrochit
L. Mullardoch
Glen
Torness
Crowlin Is.
Strome Ferry
Glen Cannich
Glen Urquhart

© John Bartholomew & Son, Ltd., Edinburgh

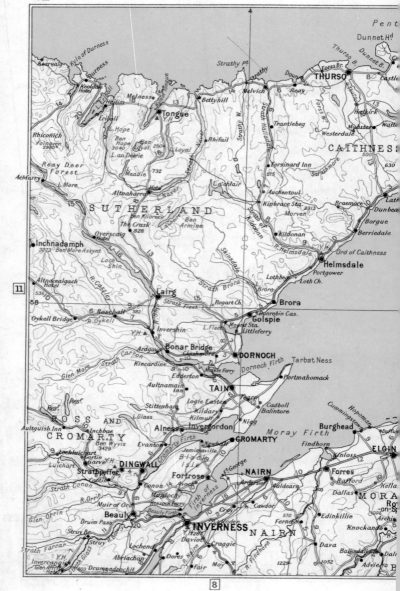

13

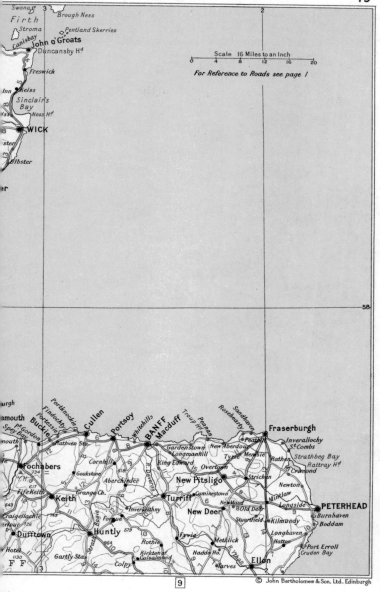

Scale 16 Miles to an Inch

For Reference to Roads see page 1

58

Firth

Swona
Brough Ness
Stroma
Pentland Skerries
Canisbay
John o'Groats
Duncansby Hd
Freswick
Inn
Keiss
Sinclair's
Bay
Noss Hd
WICK
ster
Ulbster
er

urgh
emouth
Findochty
Portknockie
Portessie
Buckie
Cullen
Portsoy
Whitehills
BANFF
Macduff
Troup Hd
Pennan
Gardenstown
New Aberdour
Rosehearty
Sandhaven
Fraserburgh
Inverallochy
St Combs
Pt Gordon
Spey Bay
mouth
Rathven Stn
Cornhill
Longmanhill
King Edward
Is
Tyrie
Pennan
Memsie
Rathen
Strathbeg Bay
Rattray Hd
Crimond
Fochabers
Y.H.
734
Goukstone
Aberchirder
Overtown
New Pitsligo
Strichen
Newton
617
Grange Ch.
Cuminestown
New Maud
Mintlaw
Longside
PETERHEAD
Fife Keith
Keith
Inverkeithny
Turriff
New Deer
Old Deer
Kilmundy
Burnhaven
Boddam
Craigellachie
126
Forgue
Fyvie
Stuartfield
Longhaven
Hatten
Dufftown
Huntly
879
Rothie
964
Methlick
Haddo Ho.
Ryban
Port Erroll
Cruden Bay
Hotel
1130
Gartly Stn
Kirkton of
Culsalmond
Colpy
Tarves
Ellon
F F

9

© John Bartholomew & Son, Ltd. Edinburgh

14

North
Ronaldsay

Papa
Westray
Noup Hd
North Ronaldsay Firth

Pierowall
Kenbister   *Start Pt*
Westray   *Sanday*

The North Sound

Westray Firth   Calf Sound   *Sanday Sound*

Wasbister   *Egilsay*   Eday
Eynhallow Sd   *Rousay*

Birsay   *Wyre*   *Lower Whitehall*
          Gairsay   Stronsay Firth   Stronsay
P O M O N A   *Wide   Shapinsay*
   OR   *Firth   Bal Iou*
L. of Stenness   *Shapinsay Sd*   ○ Auskerry

59   M A I N L A N D   ● KIRKWALL   O R K N E Y   59

Stromness   18   Mull Hd

Graemsay   Skaill
Old Man of Hoy   St Marys
Rora Hd   Scapa   ○ Copinsay
          Cava   Flow
     H O Y   *Fara*   Burray
          Flotta
          St Margaret's
Hurliness   Hope
          S. Walls   South
               Ronaldsay
          Swona
               Brough Ness

Pentland   Firth

     Dunnet Hd   Stroma   *Pentland Skerries*
          Canisbay
Thurso   Mey   John o'Groats
     Dunnet B.   Duncansby Hd
THURSO   Dunnet   Freswick
     8   Castletown
     21   *Thura Inn*   Reiss
Halkirk   *Watten   Ph*   *Reiss*   Sinclair's
     13   Watten   Bilbster   Bay
Mybster   8   Noss Hd
Westerdale   *Thrumster*   ● WICK
C A I T H N E S S   500
          630   *Ulbster*

          Scale   16 Miles to an Inch
          0   4   8   12   16   20

     For Reference to Roads see page 1
Lybster
Latheron

© John Bartholomew & Son, Ltd., Edinburgh

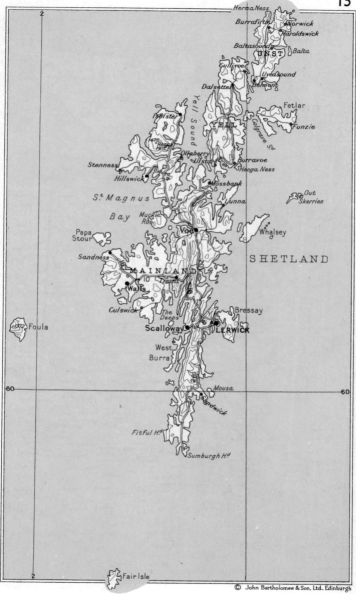

15

Herma Ness
Burrafirth Norwick
Haroldswick
Baltasound
UNST Balta
Saxavoe
Uyea Sound
Dalsetter Belmont

Fetlar

YELL Funzie

Isbister
Colgrave Sd.

Ollaberry Burravoe
Stenness Ulsta Heoga Ness
Hillswick

Mossbank
St. Magnus
Lunna

Bay Out
Muckle Skerries
Roe
Papa Voe
Stour Whalsey

Sandness
SHETLAND
MAINLAND
Walls Tresta

Culswick Bressay

The
Deeps
Scalloway LERWICK

Foula
West
Burra

60 60

Mousa
Sandwick

Fitful Hd.

Sumburgh Hd.

Fair Isle

© John Bartholomew & Son, Ltd., Edinburgh

HIGHLAND CLANS

Scale of English Miles

Orkney I?

Pentland Firth
Dunnet Hd. Stroma Duncansby Hd.
Thurso Wick Sinclair Bay

C.Wrath Strathy Pt. Dunnet Hd.

Butt of Lewis
L.Inchard Loch Eriboll Kyle of Tongue

MACKAYS SINCLAIRS

L.More L.Naver R.Brora R.Halladale Wick

Eddrachillis B. Lairg Helmsdale Latheron

Stornoway Broad Bay
Eye Peninsula
Lewis
MACKENZIES
Erisort
Seaforth
MACLEODS

North Minch

SUTHERLANDS

Ullapool Lochinver Brora
Golspie Dunrobin Cas.

Shiant I? ROSSES Dornoch
Tain Dornoch Firth Tarbat Ness

Dundee Cas.
MACDONALD OF SLEAT
MACLEODS
Skye

Gair Loch Poolewe
L.Maree
L.Fannich

MACKENZIES
Cromarty Lossiemouth
Moray Firth

Elgin
Gordon Cas.
Fochabers

L.Broom

L.Glass
Invergordon
Forres
Nairn
Keith

Beauly
Dingwall Fortrose
Inverness Castle Grant Rothes

Beldornie
Lumsden Cas.

MACINTOSHES
VARIOUS

FRASERS
GRANTS GORDONS
Abernethy STEWARTS & FORBES Kildrummy Cas.
Grantown Cairn

MACPHERSONS
Kingussie Braemar Balmoral
Aberdeen

CAMERONS
MACDONELL OF GLENGARRY
Fort Augustus
GRANTS
Dalwhinnie

FARQUHARSONS

MACDONELL OF KEPPOCH
LINDSAYS
ATHOLL OGILVIES
ROBERTSONS Pitlochry Airlie Cas.
Kirriemuir
Glamis

CAMERONS
MENZIES
STEWARTS Dunkeld
Forfar Montrose

STEWARTS
MACNABS MURRAYS Scone
Perth
Dundee
Broughty Cas.
BETHUNS

Mull
Iona
Staffa
Oban

ARGYLL
LORN

GRAHAMS STEWARTS & DRUMMONDS
Aberfoyle
Dunblane
Stirling
Crieff
Clackmannan
SETONS

Colonsay MACNEIL
Oronsay

STEWARTS Kilsyth HAMILTONS
Dumbarton
Greenock Renfrew Kirkintilloch Linlithgow EDINBURGH Dalkeith

Jura

Glasgow HAMILTONS
Rothesay
Paisley

CAMPBELLS
Islay

Bute
Arran Brodick

Cunningham
CUNNINGHAMS
Kyle
Lanark Peebles
SCOTTS

KINTYRE
Campbeltown

Ayr
DOUGLAS

Rathlin I.

Carrick
GORDONS
DOUGLAS

Coleraine

Ailsa Craig
Girvan
Ballantrae
Dumfries
Lockerbie

of the Forth and Clyde Canal (closed to navigation in 1963), with a large crude-oil refinery, chemical, plastic, timber and engineering works, growing dock and ship-building yards. Grangemouth is called the "boom town" of Scotland because it has grown so fast. It is now the second most important port in Scotland, due mainly to the oil pipe line from Finnart on Loch Long which crosses Scotland to Grangemouth and serves the oil tankers there.

GRANTOWN-ON-SPEY, a

delightful and popular tourist resort of Morayshire, on the River Spey near the Inverness-shire border. It is sometimes referred to as the "Capital of Strathspey". Grantown is renowned for its picturesque situation and its beautiful woods of pine and fir.

As a town it is less than two hundred years old, though as a "township" centred on Castle Grant it goes back for five centuries or more. The Castle (seat of the Earls of Seafield) has been largely rebuilt, but still boasts a fragment of the original structure in Babbie's Tower. Until the close of the 17th century it was known as Frenchie, and the village as the Castletown of Frenchie.

Grantown today is a fine holiday and sporting centre. There is fishing (salmon, sea-trout, brown trout) in the Spey and other waters, golf, tennis and bowls. In winter, there is curling and skating, climbing, skiing and other winter sports in the Cairngorms, and on the lower Cromdale Hills, and there are modern hotels, a ski school and sports

Overleaf: A view of the Great Glen. (*W. S. Thomson*).

Grantown-on-Spey

shop to cater for these. Highland Gatherings, Sheep Dog Trials and the Annual Show of the Strathspey Farmers' Club are among the seasonal events.

GRANTSHOUSE, a Berwickshire village on the Great North Road near the south end of the Pease Dene.

GREAT GLEN, THE (or GLENMORE), a large glen traversed by the Caledonian Canal which strikes across Scotland from Inverness on the east coast to Fort William in the W. The road from Inverness follows the north-west shore of Loch Ness (Glen Urquhart, Castle Urquhart, Glen Moriston), the north-west shore of Loch Oich (Glen Garry) and south-east shore of Loch Lochy to Spean Bridge, thence to Fort William, this latter part, in spring, between masses of flowering rhododendrons.

GREENLAW, a small Berwickshire town picturesquely situated on the River Blackadder, 8 miles SW. of Duns. The 18th century church has points of interest. To the S. is 13th century Hume Castle (ruins), once the seat of the Home family. There is some angling.

GREENOCK, *c.* 23 miles SW. from Glasgow, on the south shore of the Firth of Clyde, is a busy seaport with a considerable shipbuilding industry. It also has sugar refineries and distilleries. It has literary and piratical associations as the home of John Galt (*Annals of the Parish*) and the birthplace of Captain Kidd. It is also the birthplace of James Watt. The oldest shipbuilding yard in the world is Scott's of Greenock (18th century). The newest dry dock in Scotland was opened in 1964. Greenock also houses the Gourock Ropework Co. which made the ropes for the Queen Mary and the Queen Elizabeth and the "big tops" for some of the most important European circuses.

GRESS, a small place near Stornoway on the River Gress. Nearby on the coast are famous seal caverns.

GRETNA GREEN, a village in Dumfriesshire on the border of England and Scotland, 10 miles N. of Carlisle, famed for runaway marriages. Until one hundred years ago Scottish law allowed immediate marriage after couples crossed the Border, simply by a declaration before witnesses. After 1856 residential qualifications were enforced, and now marriages by declaration are illegal, though a number of young couples still cross the Border to Scotland where parental consent for under-21's to wed is not required. The famous smithy where so many marriages were solemnised, is open to visitors.

GREY MARE'S TAIL, a cataract 10 miles NE. of Moffat, Dumfriesshire. It is formed by a small stream, which, running from Loch Skene to the Moffat Water, falls over a rock about 200 ft. high.

GRUINARD, the name of a large bay, island and two rivers (Gruinard and Little Gruinard) on the west coast of Ross-shire.

GUARDBRIDGE, Fifeshire village 4 miles NW. of St. Andrews with a 15th century bridge over the River Eden.

GULLANE, a village and favourite golfing resort on the Firth of Forth, 18 miles E. of Edinburgh. It has several fine golf courses including Muirfield (headquarters of the Honourable Company of Edinburgh Golfers) over which many championships have been played. There are also facilities for putting, tennis, bowls; a children's playground at Goose Green; and a magnificent sandy beach, safe for bathing, with extensive sand dunes. There was a time, indeed, when Gullane suffered from too much sand; in one of the great sandstorms of the 17th century the village was nearly engulfed. The ruined old church and Saltcoats Castle are survivors of these days. Gullane has associations with R. L. Stevenson's *Catriona*.

HADDINGTON, a historic royal burgh, county town of East Lothian, on the River Tyne, 17 miles E. of Edinburgh. It has an electrical engineering plant, malting and market-gardening, woollen, hosiery and flour mills, cattle and sheep and corn markets. The town has been enlarged by a number of Glasgow's overspill families. The chief building is the 12th or 13th century Abbey Church of St. Mary, called the "Lamp of Lothian" (though the title is also claimed for an earlier, vanished church), from the "lantern" which is said to have adorned its 90 ft. tower. Though partly in ruins, its nave is still in use as a parish church. Another ancient church is St. Martin's in the Nungate. The county buildings in Court Street occupy the site of the Palace where Alexander II was born; the Town Buildings are in High Street, as is the Corn Exchange (scene of the weekly markets) and the Town Cross.

Haddington was the birthplace not only of Alexander II, but of John Knox, Samuel Smiles and Jane Welsh Carlyle. Carlyle House may still be seen, and the site of Knox's house. Bothwell Castle in the Hardgate was a residence of the Earl of Bothwell, husband of Mary Queen of Scots, and the Queen herself stayed here on at least one occasion. A mile or so south is the mansion of Lennoxlove (formerly Lethington) once home of Mary's secretary of state, Lord Lethington. William Dunbar (best known of Scotland's early poets) was a pupil in the school where later Knox, and—later still—Jane Welsh, were also pupils, and where Edward Irving, celebrated divine and friend of Thomas Carlyle, was a youthful teacher.

Burns enthusiasts may note that Burns's mother, sister and brother lived at Bolton, a little way along the Gifford road, in a house called Grant's Braes, and some of the family are buried in the nearby churchyard. A monument marks the site of the house.

HADDINGTONSHIRE, the former name of East Lothian.

HAILES CASTLE, a considerable ruin, 4 miles E. of Haddington, on the banks of the Tyne. An ancient monument, Hailes was once a stronghold of the Earl of Bothwell, and here he brought Mary Queen of Scots in April 1567.

HALIDON HILL. See Berwick-upon-Tweed.

HALKIRK, a village in Caithness on the River Thurso, 8 miles S. of Thurso. There are angling facilities here.

HALLADALE, a river of east Sutherland flowing through Strath Halladale to the north coast.

HAMILTON, a pleasant old Lanarkshire town, on the River Clyde, 11 miles SE. of Glasgow, noted for the ancient royal residence of Cadzow Castle, and the wide and beautifully-timbered parks of the now-demolished Hamilton Palace; also for its long and fascinating history. Despite coal-mining interests, Hamilton is neat and trim, with a long, wide main street and handsome town buildings including the modern multi-storeyed County Buildings. There is also a racecourse.

Historical associations (too numerous to detail) go back to Roman times and link the town with Alexander II, Alexander III, Mary Queen of Scots, Cromwell and many lesser notabilities; and of course, with the ducal house of Hamilton.

In the Low Parks is preserved the beautiful Hamilton Mausoleum; here, too, is the original site of Netherton, the ancient village from which Hamilton sprang. The mote hill is all that remains.

The River Avon runs through the High Parks; on its banks (c. 1 mile) are the picturesque ruins of Cadzow Castle, royal residence of the Alexanders, and visited by other later monarchs. This was the seat of the Hamiltons before the erection of the magnificent palace, pulled down in 1925 because of coal-mine subsidence. Visitors should see the famous Cadzow Oaks (some around one thousand years old), and the equally famous herd of white cattle, last descendants (in Scotland) of the wild white cattle of early Britain; also the pretty 16th century Dutch gardens of Barncluith, and the French-looking Castle of Châtelherault, an 18th century replica of its French namesake, from which the Duke of Hamilton takes one of his titles.

HANDA ISLAND, a bird sanctuary off the west coast of Sutherland.

HARDMUIR, 5 miles SW. of Forres, Morayshire, is said to be the "blasted heath" where Macbeth met the weird sisters, though it is now largely woodland.

HAROLDSWICK, a hamlet and bay in Unst, Shetland.

HARRAY, a loch on the mainland of Orkney.

HARRIS, the south part of the island of Lewis and Harris in the Outer Hebrides, bare and hilly but delightfully unspoilt and typically Hebridean in character. It is divided into North and South Harris by the sealochs of East and West Loch Tarbert, between which on a narrow isthmus (one-third mile) stands the principal village, Tarbert. Other places are Leverburgh, on the west coast, and Rodel, near the south point of the island, where is the restored 15th century church of St. Clement, formerly a priory. Industries are restricted. Formerly there was a whaling station on West Loch Tarbert. In modern times Lord Leverhulme tried unsuccessfully to establish a fishing station at Leverburgh (before his advent, Obbe). But Harris is still concerned with the production of the famous handwoven Harris tweeds, an industry which now it shares with Lewis.

There is excellent trout, seatrout and salmon fishing throughout the region. The ascent of Clisham (2,622 ft.), the highest mountain in the Outer Hebrides, is made from Tarbert. An extensive deer forest, the Forest of Harris, lies to the north-west. Motoring is possible, and excursions may be made to the satellite islands, Scarpa (NW., reached by ferry from the delightful Husinish Bay), Taransay and Scalpa. The smaller Shiant Isles lie off the mouth of Loch Seaforth, around which was the mustering ground of the Seaforth Highlanders.

HARRIS, SOUND OF, a sea channel separating North Uist from Harris.

HAWICK, the largest town in Roxburghshire, standing among wooded hills where Slitrig and Teviot meet, 50 miles SSE. of Edinburgh. It is noted for its beautiful tweeds, woollens and hosiery (or "knitwear"—with Dior among the designers), also for its sheep and lamb sales.

Hawick is a fine holiday centre, with good shops and cinemas. One of its hotels, Tower Hotel, incorporates the 12th century Drumlanrig Tower which sheltered the Jacobite forces in 1715, and became an inn nearly two hundred years ago. Several public parks include the beautiful Wilton Lodge Park with its mansion-museum, and pretty glen and waterfall. There are also facilities for sport, 18-hole and 9-hole (Minto) golf courses, excellent angling, tennis, bowls and putting, as well as racing on Hawick Common. The stirring traditional festival of the Common Riding takes place on the Friday and Saturday after the first Monday in June. On the Friday the "Cornet" and his men ride the town's marches and afterwards "buss" the Colours on the "Teribus" Memorial in the High Street. Early next morning they climb the Moat (Moot) Hill to sing their ancient song "Teribus ye Tery Odin", supposed to be an invocation of Thor and Odin.

The "Teribus" Memorial is a bronze equestrian statue commemorating the "callants" who captured the English colours at Hornshole in 1514—the event celebrated in "the Riding". Hawick had its full share in Border warfare and was several times burned by the English.

The handsome Town House with its pinnacled clock tower, the old parish church of St. Mary, James Hogg's house and the cottage of "Old Mortality" are other interesting features.

Two miles SW. is the old keep of Goldielands, 4 miles SW., Branxholm Tower. Four miles W. is Harden House, formerly the seat of the Scotts of Harden, among whom was the redoubtable Border reiver, "Auld Wat" who married Mary Scott, the "Flower of Yarrow", and was an ancestor of Sir Walter.

HAWTHORNDEN, a mansion 11 miles SE. of Edinburgh, the seat of the Drummond family, largely rebuilt in the 17th century by the poet William Drummond.

HEBRIDES, THE, or **WESTERN ISLES,** a much-scattered group of *c.* 500 islands, off the west coast, comprising the Outer Hebrides (Lewis with Harris, North and South Uist, Benbecula, Barra, etc.) and Inner Hebrides (Skye, Eigg, Coll, Tiree, Mull, Iona, Staffa, Jura, Islay, etc.). They belong administratively to the counties of Ross and Cromarty, Inverness and Argyll. In the centuries of Norwegian domination the term Sudreyar (Southern Isles) applied to them and was extended as far as the Isle of Man. About one-fifth of the islands are inhabited, for the most part sparsely, and little of the land is arable. Stock-rearing, fishing, crofting and tweed-making (in places) are the only industries.

HEE, BEN, a mountain (2,864 ft.) of north-west Scotland, N. of Loch Shin.

HELENSBURGH, on the Firth of Clyde, near the entrance to the Gareloch, is a trim residential and holiday town. It has good shops and cinemas, a golf course, open-air swimming pool, fishing in the River Fruin, tennis courts and putting greens. Some of its streets, intersecting at right angles, are lined with flowering trees. There is an obelisk in memory of Henry Bell, who launched the *Comet*, the first steam passenger vessel in Europe (his house is now the Queen's Hotel); and another famous native is John L. Baird, the British pioneer of television. Delightful walks are over the hill to Loch Lomond, through Glen Fruin, and along the Gareloch, past Rhu and Shandon to the head of the loch.

Helensburgh has a pier, but Clyde Coast sailings are mostly from its eastern continuation, Craigendoran.

HELL'S GLEN, a beautiful glen in Argyllshire, through which a road runs connecting Loch Fyne with the main road at Rest-and-Be-Thankful, near Arrochar.

HELMSDALE, a fishing village with a good harbour, on the east coast of Sutherland, at the mouth of the River Helmsdale. There is salmon and trout fishing, sea-bathing and golf for the visitor.

Helmsdale Castle (15th century, now a ruin) was the scene of a classic drama in 1567, when a Countess of Caithness, planning to poison the Earl and Countess of Sutherland so that her son could become heir, accidentally poisoned her son as well.

HERIOT, a small place in Midlothian, on the Heriot Water, 16 miles SE. of Edinburgh.

HERMITAGE CASTLE, *c.* 15 miles S. of Hawick in south Roxburghshire, on the banks of a stream of the same name, was a Border stronghold held in turn by the Monteiths, Grahams, Douglases and Earls of Bothwell. It is one of the largest and finest fortresses in the Borders and is open to visitors.

HIGHLANDS, THE, mountainous regions lying N. and NW. of a line drawn (on geological considerations) from Stonehaven to Dumbarton, especially those portions within this area in which the Celtic language (Gaelic) and manners have more or less lingered until modern times; thus Caithness, Orkney and Shetland are customarily excluded.

HILLSWICK, a township on the west coast of the mainland of Shetland, with angling facilities.

HOLLOWS TOWER, 4 miles S. of Langholm, Eskdale, Dumfriesshire, is one of Johnnie Armstrong of Gilnockie's fortresses. (See Gilnockie.)

HOLY ISLAND, an island in Lamlash Bay, Arran. A cave is said to have been the retreat of St. Molaise, and nearby is his holy well.

HOLY LOCH, an inlet of the Firth of Clyde, a few miles N. of Dunoon. There are several small places round its shores—Hunter's Quay, Ardnadam, Sandbank and Kilmun. A road from the head of the loch leads past the beautiful wild park of Puck's Glen. On the way are extensive forests from which a Scottish firm makes matches. The Holy Loch takes its name from Kilmun Church, allegedly built on some Palestinian soil salvaged from a wreck. It was intended for St. Mungo's Church in Glasgow. It is the anchorage of a U.S. depot ship for missile-carrying submarines.

HOLYWOOD, a village 3 miles N. of Dumfries. An ancient stone circle is known as the Twelve Apostles, though only 11 stones remain.

HOPE, a river, mountain and loch of Sutherland. The river flows northward past the mountain (Ben Hope; 3,040 ft.) into the loch, and thence to Loch Eriboll.

HOPEMAN, a fishing village 7 miles W. of Lossiemouth, with a golf course and good sands.

HOPETOUN HOUSE. See South Queensferry.

HOURN, LOCH (Loch of Hell), a sea-loch on the west coast of Inverness-shire opposite Isleornsay in Skye, noted for its wild and gloomy aspect. Ben Screel (3,196 ft.) and Lairven (3,343 ft.) are on its shores.

HOWNHAM, a village and favourite angling resort of Roxburghshire, on the Kale Water, 10 miles S. of Kelso. Hownam Law rises above it.

HOY, an island in the south of the Orkneys, separated from the mainland by Hoy Sound and Scapa Flow. It is the highest of the islands and has fine cliffs, over 1,100 ft. high in places, on the west, where, too, is the Old Man of Hoy, an immense pillar-like rock, 450 ft. high.

HUNTER'S QUAY, a sailing resort at the mouth of the Holy Loch, with a pier.

HUNTERSTON, near W. Kilbride, ancient seat of the Hunter family (13th century castle still in use), and site of Scotland's first civil nuclear generating station.

HUNTINGTOWER, a castle 3 miles W. of Perth, open to visitors.

HUNTLY, a handsome, well-built market town, business and agricultural hub and route centre of north-west Aberdeenshire, in the fork of the Rivers Deveron and Bogie. Though a burgh of barony in 1545, the town is mainly of the last two centuries. Huntly Castle, however, seat of the Gordon family, dates from the 15th century and still shows the dungeons of an earlier castle, not called Huntly in those days but Strathbogie. It occupies a beautiful site on the wooded Deveron, and in its heyday, when Lady Catherine Gordon married Perkin Warbeck, was magnificent indeed.
Other buildings of note are mainly 18th and 19th century: the Gordon schools founded by a Duchess of Gordon in 1839, the one hundred-year-old Scott Institute (home for the aged) on the banks of the Bogie, the Brander Library with its plaque and museum commemorating George MacDonald, poet and novelist of the last century, born here in 1824. One of Huntly's hotels was the "Boar's Head"

of MacDonald's novel *Robert Falconer*, another the 18th century dower-house of Huntly Castle.

For visitors there is fishing (salmon and trout) in Deveron, Bogie, Isla, golf (9-hole course) in beautiful surroundings, tennis bowls, and even bathing from a sandy river beach at Hill of Haugh. Huntly is conveniently situated for touring Deeside, Donside and the Moray Firth to Inverness.

IME, BEN, a mountain (3,318 ft.) near the head of Loch Long, Argyll.

INCHCAPE ROCK. See Bell Rock.

INCHCOLM, a small island in the Firth of Forth, off Aberdour, famous for its ruined abbey. It has been called the "Iona of the East".

The abbey (dedicated to St. Columba) was founded by Alexander I in the 12th century. Considerable ruins include a 13th century church (in which wall paintings were discovered in 1926) and an octagonal chapter house with a stone roof, also some fine cloistral remains. Nearby is a small ruined oratory of the 9th century.

INCHINNAN, a small place 1 mile W. of Renfrew with a church built on the site of a 12th century edifice. In the churchyard are some old tombstones known as Templars' Graves.

INCHKEITH, a small rocky island (¾ mile long) in the Firth of Forth, 2½ miles SE. of Burntisland, c. 4 miles NE. of Leith. It has a lighthouse. In the 16th century wars it was garrisoned successively by the English (enemy) and the French (allies); it was fortified also in two world wars.

James IV marooned two young children here with a dumb nurse. They were alleged to have later evolved "a very guid Ebrew" tongue.

INCHMAHOME (ISLAND). See Menteith, Lake of.

INCHMARNOCK, an island off the west side of Bute, separated from Kintyre by Inchmarnock Water.

INCHNACARDOCH, a new village, 1 mile W. of Fort William, founded by the Forestry Commission.

INCHNADAMPH, a picturesque village at the head of Loch Assynt in Sutherland, 10 miles E. of Lochinver. It is a good sporting base and the loch is famous for its brown trout, and game is plentiful. Ben More Assynt is only 4 miles away, and Suilven and Quinag are within easy reach. To the south at Allt-nan-Uamh are prehistoric caves where remains of Ice Age animals have been found.

INCHTURE, a village 14 miles NE. of Perth with interesting Roman antiquities in the grounds of Rossie Priory, above it.

INNELLAN, 4 miles S. of Dunoon, a peaceful little holiday place with a sandy beach (Dunoon's is shingle).

INNERLEITHEN, a pleasant little town, formerly a noted spa, standing where Tweed and

Traquair House, near Innerleithen.

Leithen meet, *c*. 6 miles E. of Peebles. There is fishing in the Tweed and local lochs, an 18-hole golf course, and motor coach touring. Innerleithen is generally accepted as the setting of Scott's novel *St. Ronan's Well.* There is still a St. Ronan's Well in the town, housed in a decorative pavilion, very picturesquely placed. The Cuddy Bridge over the Leithen is a charming survival. The ancient church was bestowed by Malcolm IV on the monks of Kelso, and acquired the privilege of sanctuary. Older still are the prehistoric forts on neighbouring hills, and the curious terracing on Purvis Hill to the east.

The modern town has an important woollen-spinning and knitwear industry, which (unlike most industries) actually attracts the tourist.

The big event of the season is the Border Games, embodying the Cleikum ceremony and its gay pageantry.

INNERPEFFREY. See Crieff.

INNERWICK, a Lammermuir village of East Lothian, 4 miles S. of Dunbar, with ruins of a small tower and an 18th century church.

INSCH, a small agricultural town, 27 miles NW. of Aberdeen. Interesting features include an ancient inscribed sonte (inscription in Gaelic and Ogham) in Newton House to the north-east. The Hills of Dunnideer and Christ's Kirk are notable, the former for a prehistoric hill fort, the latter as the scene of the poem *Christ's Kirk on the Green,* attributed to James I, and the site of a vanished village, remembered for its fairy-tale fantasy of a night-fair, called the "Sleepy Market".

INSH, a small place on Loch Insh, 6 miles NE. of Kingussie, Inverness-shire, with an old church.

INVERALLOCHY, a coastal village of north-east Aberdeenshire, 4 miles SE. of Fraserburgh, with ruins of an old castle.

INVERARAY, a small picturesque royal burgh and county town of Argyll, on Loch Fyne near the mouth of the River Aray. The dominant feature is Inveraray Castle, seat of the Dukes of Argyll. From the remote past, town and castle have been linked together, and both were rebuilt in the 18th century. In recent years a restoration scheme has been carried out on old tenements. Under the regime of the present Duke the castle is open to the public.

Inveraray is renowned for its beautiful woods, and for the fine peal of bells installed by the 10th Duke, Niall Diarmid, in the early part of this century. A tall Celtic Cross stands at the head of the quay. From the great gateway beside the Argyll Arms a shady beech avenue extends to Essachosan Glen, one of the local beauty spots. A little to the north is the pretty wooded hill of Duniquoich, a vantage point offering charming views. On the brink of the loch towards its head is Dundarave Castle (the "Doom Castle" of Neil Munro's novel), restored and modernised, and sharing with several other Scottish castles the reputation of being "the oldest inhabited castle in Scotland".

Inveraray Castle.

Mary Queen of Scots (dressed in Highland garb) visited Inveraray in 1563.

The visitor finds excellent salmon and sea and brown trout fishing in the Aray and other streams, and in little Loch Dubh, on the Shira about 1 mile beyond the town, also sea fishing, boating, bathing, golf, tennis and bowls.

INVERBERVIE, or **BERVIE,** an ancient royal burgh of Kincardineshire, on a wide bay at the mouth of the Bervie Water, *c.* 10 miles S. of Stonehaven. Its charter has a romantic history. David II, returning with his queen from exile—chased by an English fleet, driven by a storm—came ashore here, at the rock called "The King's Step", and was so impressed by his welcome, and the hospitality he received, that he raised the town to its royal status. A later charter was granted by James VI.

The old market cross still stands. Inverbervie has linen and rayon industries, and for the tourist, fishing in the Bervie water and boating.

INVERCANNICH, a village at the entrance to Glen Cannich, Glen Affric and Strath Glass in north-west Inverness-shire. There is hill-walking and fine scenery. The level of the neighbouring Loch Benevean has been raised by a dam as part of the Glen Affric hydroelectric scheme, and there is a power station at Fasnakyle nearby.

INVERCAULD, 3 miles E. of Braemar, Aberdeenshire. Invercauld Castle is the home of the Farquharsons of Invercauld, closely associated with the Braemar Gathering.

INVEREWE. See Poolewe.

INVERFARIGAIG, a small place on the east shore of Loch Ness, at the mouth of the lovely glen traversed by the River Farigaig.

INVERGARRY, a small place with angling facilities, on the River Garry near its confluence with Loch Oich, 7 miles SW. of Fort Augustus (Inverness-shire). On a headland are the ruins of the old castle which once sheltered Bonnie Prince Charlie. To the west are Loch Garry and Glen Garry (q.v.)

INVERGORDON, on the Cromarty Firth, has a fine harbour, was an important naval base in World War I, and still has naval depots and numerous oil tanks. A grain distillery was recently built. There is a very fine swimming pool, facilities for golf (9-hole course), tennis and bowls, sea-fishing and boating. The woods around Invergordon make a pleasant background to a trim little town.

INVERGOWRIE, village, 4 miles W. of Dundee, with ruined 15th century church.

INVERINATE, a small place on the north shore of Loch Duich, Ross-shire.

INVERKEITHING, an ancient royal burgh of Fife, on the Firth of Forth, just north of North Queensferry and the Forth Bridges, with an interesting old church and a 15th century friary, housing the public library. David I had a residence in Inverkeithing. In 1651 a battle was fought here between Cromwell and Scottish Royalists. Quarrying, papermaking and shipbreaking are industries. Rosyth naval dockyard adjoins.

INVERKIP, a small place on the Clyde coast, 5 miles SW. of Greenock, popular with visitors, especially campers.

INVERKIRKAIG, a hamlet on the River Kirkaig, noted for angling, 3 miles S. of Lochinver, Sutherland.

INVERLOCHY, a ruined castle 2 miles NE. of Fort William on the banks of the River Lochy, Inverness-shire. Montrose's forces defeated Argyle here in 1645. The modern castle nearby is part of a cattle-ranching scheme started in the 1950s.

INVERMAY, a small place 7 miles SW. of Perth, which gave name to the ballad *The Birks of Invermay*.

INVERMORISTON, a small place on the River Moriston at the foot of Glen Moriston, near Loch Ness.

Inverness and the River Ness. (*Scottish Tourist Board*).

INVERNESS

THE largest town in the Highlands, an historic royal burgh, county town of Inverness-shire, stands on the River Ness at the north-east end of the Great Glen, and of the Caledonian Canal which runs through it. It is a fine holiday place and the best of all bases for touring in the North and the North-West. The route between Inverness and Kyle of Lochalsh is one of the most beautiful in Britain.

The modern town is famous for tweeds. Sports include shooting, fishing, golf, tennis and bowls. Shinty, the oldest ball game in the world, is worth watching. Motor-coach day or afternoon tours run to John o' Groats, Durness, Lochinver, Ullapool, Skye; to Aberdeen, Deeside and Balmoral, Speyside and Grantown; to Nairn, Elgin and Lossiemouth; to Strathpeffer, Falls of Rogie and Cromarty; to Glen Affric, Kilmorack; to Falls of Foyers, Glen Uurqhant and through the Great Glen to Fort William.

Except in the handsome business and shopping centre there is little or no evidence of "planning", yet with its old houses, stairs, wynds, its bridges, wooded riverbanks and islets, it creates a good impression.

Landmarks are plentiful. On a hill above the river stands the "Castle", housing the law courts and the county offices. Though not really old (*c.* 120 years), it has an honourable ancestry: successive Inverness castles have figured in history for more than thirteen centuries. One was the stronghold of the Pictish King Brude, one the castle of Macbeth, others were associated with Bruce and the Stuart kings, while one sheltered Prince Charlie before Culloden. Mary Queen of Scots, denied admission, promptly set about reprisals—the castle was taken and the governor hanged. Meanwhile she lodged in Queen Mary's House in Bridge Street. On a site nearer the river Cromwell built himself a fort, of which nothing now remains but the clock tower.

Across the river rise the twin towers of the Cathedral of St. Andrew, surrounded by trees. Other landmarks are the bronze statue of Flora Macdonald, heroine of the '45, in the castle grounds, the Town Steeple, and the old Mercat Cross with its Clachnacudainn, "Stone of the Tubs", where women rested their washtubs as they came up from the river. Traditionally it was the coronation stone of the early kings.

Open spaces include Bellfield Park and the Ness Islands, linked with footbridges and beautifully wooded, enlivened in the summer with concerts, bands and open-air dancing. Beyond the Cathedral is the hill-cemetery of Tomnahurich (220 ft.).

Around Inverness itself are some places of interest. Clachnaharry (1¾ miles) stands on the Beauly Firth, at the north-east outlet of the Caledonian Canal. A ferry to the Black Isle plies from South Kessock near the mouth of the river. Culloden Moor is 5 miles east.

INVERNESS–SHIRE, the largest county of Scotland, including both a great area of the Highlands and part of the Outer and Inner Hebrides. The mountain mass includes many peaks of over 3,000 ft.; Ben Nevis (4,406 ft.) is the highest mountain in the British Isles. Glenmore (the Great Glen), in which lochs Ness, Oich, and Lochy are linked to form part of the Caledonian Canal, runs south-west from the Beauly Firth to Loch Linnhe on the west coast (Argyllshire). The rivers Spey, Findhorn and Nairn flow north-east to adjacent counties. Rough grazing, deer-forest and grouse-moor form a large part of the land mass; cattle-ranching is carried out in Glenmore, and considerable afforestation is being undertaken. Hydro-electric schemes are in operation in Strath Glass, Glen Cannich, Lochaber and elsewhere; and a Perthshire scheme uses Loch Ericht. Tourism is a growing industry, especially on Speyside, an important winter sports area.

Inverness is the county town; Fort William is the only other important centre.

INVERSHIEL, a small place on Loch Duich in Wester Ross. The ascent of Scour Ouran (3,505 ft.) can be made from here.

INVERSHIN, a hamlet 4 miles S. of Lairg, where the Shin and Oykell meet. There is excellent fishing in the Kyle of Sutherland and the River Shin. The picturesque Falls of Shin are 2½ miles to the north.

INVERSNAID, a hamlet of the east shore of Loch Lomond (*q.v.*), 3 miles NNE. of Tarbet, with a steamer pier. From here a road runs E. to connect with Loch Katrine about 5 miles away. On the Arklet Water nearby is a pretty waterfall.

INVERURIE, a royal burgh, agricultural hub and holiday place, scene of two famous battles, in the fork of the rivers Don and Urie, 16 miles NW. of Aberdeen. Both Don and Urie offer good trout fishing in spring and summer; later in the season salmon are plentiful. There is golf on the 9-hole burgh golf course, or at Kintore (3 miles) or Kemnay (5 miles), also tennis and bowls, touring and excursions in the wooded Don valley or around the east coast.

Inverurie is very old. Though the earliest charters extant are those of Mary Queen of Scots and James VI, traditionally the first burgh charter was granted by Robert the Bruce in 1308. In that year he won a victory at Inverurie (Barra Hill) which broke the domination of his rivals the Comyns. A century later (1411) came the equally decisive battle of

Harlow, fought between the Highlands (under Donald of the Isles) and the Lowlands (led by the Earl of Mar), which finally established Aberdeenshire or the greater part of it, as Lowland territory. Other historic monuments are the large, once-fortified mound called the Bass, and the Cuninghill mound said to be the burial-place of King Aodh (d. 878). Older still are the prehistoric relics found here in profusion—barrows, cairns, monoliths and sculptured stones. There is a prehistoric fort on Barra Hill (634 ft.), and half-a-dozen stone circles in the neighbourhood, one of them close to the town.

Inverurie today is a pleasant, modern-looking town. Port Elphinstone, one hundred years ago the terminus of a busy Aberdeen–Inverurie canal, is now included in the burgh.

IONA, a small island (3 miles by 1½ miles) off the Ross of Mull, its importance greater than its size. This is the cradle of Scottish Christianity, the spot where St. Columba landed and founded his church in 563. The site is now occupied by St. Oran's Chapel, said to have been built by Scotland's Queen, St. Margaret, in the 11th century. The abbey dates from the 12th century, and although not large is a singularly beautiful relic. It has been largely restored in recent years by the Iona Community (Church of Scotland) and is now a centre of worship and a focus for the manifold activities of the Community, so that its religous life is once more a distinctive feature of the island.

Iona Abbey.   (*Scottish Tourist Board*).

The Street of the Dead leads to Reilig Oran, which contains the tombs of 48 Scottish kings besides rulers of Norway, France and Ireland. The last Scottish king to be buried here was Macbeth, and the last but one, King Duncan.

Holidaymakers will find interest also in the Spouting Cave, the Granite Quarries, and the golf course. Dun-I (332 ft.) should be climbed. Accommodation in summer is severely taxed.

Steamer cruises from Oban enable one to see the island under very comfortable conditions. It may also be reached from Fionphort in Mull.

IRONGRAY, a village in east Kirkcudbrightshire, 6 miles NW. of Dumfries. In the churchyard is buried Helen Walker, on whom Scott modelled Jeannie Deans. To the west of the village is a Covenanters monument.

IRVINE, an engineering and industrial town and port at the mouth of the River Irvine, 11 miles N. of Ayr. It has a good harbour and a fine bathing beach. Marymass, a local celebration late in August, is well worth seeing and includes processions and the racing of Clydesdale horses.

The town has literary associations with John Galt and James Montgomery, who were born here. Burns worked here as a flax-dresser for a year or two and relics of his stay are preserved by the local Burns Club. Edgar Allan Poe went to school in Irvine.

ISLA, a beautiful river rising in the Grampians, *c.* 10 miles S. of Braemar, and running south through Glenisla, then winding down to the Tay 4 miles W. of Coupar Angus, a course about 45 miles long. There are waterfalls at Reekie Linn and the Slug of Auchrannie.

ISLAY, after Mull, the largest of the Argyllshire islands, lying to the south-west of Jura, from which it is separated by the narrow Sound of Islay. Islay has considerable natural beauty. There are high hills in the east and in the west fine coastal scenery with wide bays, rocky headlands and smooth sandy beaches; trout lochs like Finlaggan, Lossit, Gorm, salmon rivers like the Laggan. Loch Indaal in the south cuts so deeply into the island as to give it roughly a horseshoe shape, the Rhinns peninsula to the west, and to the east the Oa, terminating in the Mull of Oa (the most southerly point). Villages are mainly on the coast, and among them are scattered standing stones, beehive houses, Celtic crosses and other relics of antiquity; also the ruined castles of Finlaggan and Dunyveg, once held by the Lords of the Isles. Islay was once the hub of a Norse settlement ranging all up and down the Western Isles. Later it was a battleground for the clans.

Port Ellen: Islay.

Distilling is important, but Islay is also increasingly known as a holiday place. There is a fine 18-hole golf course at Machrie. Of the excellent fishing on the island, a fair proportion is available for visitors. Some hotels also offer riding and rough shooting. Highlights of the season are the Highland Games and the Gaelic Mod at Bowmore There is a B.E.A. air service from Abbotsinch to Glenegedale on Laggan Bay; also a ferry to Jura (Feolin Ferry) at Port Askaig.

ISLE OF WHITHORN, a seaside village 3 miles SE. of Whithorn, Wigtownshire, built on what was once a little island, hence its name. It has a harbour and ruins of an old church.

ISLE ORNSAY, a village 8 miles SE. of Broadford (Skye). The little island of Ornsay off the coast has a lighthouse and a ruined chapel. To the north is the small Loch na Dal, to the south ruined Knock Castle.

ISLES OF THE SEA (or HOLY ISLES), small but picturesque uninhabited isles to the south of Mull. Cruises run from Oban in the summer months.

JAMESTOWN, a small place 5 miles N. of Dumbarton, on the River Leven, now in the centre of large new housing schemes.

JARLSHOF, near Sumburgh Head on the mainland of Shetland, is an ancient settlement, with Bronze Age, Early Iron Age and Viking remains (see p. 249).

JEANTOWN (also called LOCH-CARRON), a fishing village on Loch Carron.

FAMOUS MOUNTAINS

over 4,000 Feet

Ben Nevis .	. 4,406
Ben Macdhui .	. 4,296
Braeriach .	. 4,248
Cairntoul .	. 4,241
Cairngorm .	. 4,084

JEDBURGH, a royal burgh and county town of Roxburghshire, 10 miles N. of the Border on the Edinburgh – Newcastle road; visited for its famous abbey, long history and delightful situation on the banks of the Jed Water. On the practical side it manufactures tweeds and rayons, and there is engineering and electric goods manufacture. There is fishing in the Teviot, Jed, Oxnam and Kale; golf (9-hole course), tennis and bowls. The "Redeswire Ride" (commemorating the last Border battle), the Callants' Festival Day and the Border Games are highlights of the Festival Week in July. The town is centrally placed, and is an excellent centre for touring the Border abbeys, with Dryburgh, Melrose, Kelso, all within easy reach.

Jedburgh Abbey.

Jedburgh Abbey is the ecclesiastical counterpart of a great Border castle; its massive Norman tower (86 ft. high, restored), long nave and triple ranks of windows giving an effect of power as well as of beauty. The walls of the nave are practically intact. The best features are the fine Norman west doorway, another Norman doorway opening on the cloisters from the south wall of the church the graceful 3-tiered arcading of the 9-bay nave and some beautiful window tracery in the north transept. The abbey suffered severely in the Border wars, and was finally sacked by the Earl of Hertford. Only the church remains; the cloistral buildings towards the river have long since vanished.

The history of the town goes back for 1,000 years, is mainly a record of Border clashes, but covers also the dramatic ride of Mary Queen of Scots to visit Bothwell, lying wounded in Hermitage Castle, and her subsequent illness from exhaustion and the rigours of the long, rough, hill-moor-and-bog ride to Liddesdale. "Queen Mary's House", a fine old Scottish mansion, now belongs to the town and has some fascinating relics of Queen Mary and her times. A tablet marks the house when Prince Charles Edward stayed (for one night) in 1745. Other distinguished visitors were Burns (who lived in the Canongate), Scott and Wordsworth. Sir David Brewster, founder of the British Association, was a native of Jedburgh.

The prefix "Jethart" or "Jeddart" (Jedburgh) is applied to a number of things. "Jethart justice" was the summary kind that hanged first and tried afterwards! The "Jethart staff" was a lethal weapon of the old days, a kind of halberd. "Jethart pears" were far-renowned when the town lived off its orchards. To-day "Jethart snails" vie with "Berwick cockles" as the distinctive sweet of their respective localities.

A little to the north is the Waterloo Monument of Penielheugh, a favourite viewpoint. To the south of the town is Ferniehurst Castle (*c.* 3 miles), a 16th century mansion, now a Youth Hostel.

JOHN O' GROATS, an octagonal house, now gone but leaving its name to what is now a hamlet, marking, except for the slight natural advantage of Dunnet Head, the most northerly point of the Scottish mainland. It offers spectacular seascapes, magnificent views of Hoy, South Ronaldsay and Stroma. Strewn along its shores are the curious little cowrie shells called Groatie Buckies.

Both name and fame are derived from John de Groot, a 16th century Dutch settler, who, harassed by strife among his eight sons, built for them here an octagonal house with eight windows, eight doors and an eight-sided dining-table, so that, as they entered and sat down to meat, all (or none!) took precedence. Its site is still shown and the nearby hotel has an octagonal tower to commemorate the legend.

Two miles E. is Duncansby Head and 7 miles W. is the Castle of Mey (*q.v.*).

JOHNSHAVEN, a small fishing village 9 miles N. of Montrose in Kincardineshire. Its name is derived from an early association with the Knights of St. John of Jerusalem.

JOHNSTONE, a village in Annandale, Dumfriesshire, 6 miles N. of Lockerbie.

JOHNSTONE, an industrial town in Renfrewshire, 3 miles W. of Paisley.

JURA, an island of Argyllshire to the NE. of Islay, separated from the mainland by the Sound of Jura. It is *c.* 30 miles long by 7 miles broad, mountainous and splendidly picturesque, but rugged and isolated. The population is sparse and scattered mainly over the east (landward) side of the island, which is almost cut in two by Loch Tarbert leaving only a narrow eastern "portage" joining north and south. In the south Feolin Ferry connects with Port Askaig in Islay. At the north end the island is separated from Scarba by the Strait of Corrievreckin, famous for its whirlpool. Around the coast are many caves and raised beaches. Craighouse, chief village on the island, has a good harbour and a modern pier.

The island is most suitable for campers. Large herds of red deer roam the high ground; game (grouse, pheasants, woodcock, snipe, etc.) is plentiful. Here are splendid yachting harbours and fine sandy beaches, boating and sea-fishing. The three fine summits in the south are called the Paps of Jura (all around 2,500 ft.), and may be reached from Feolin Ferry.

KAMES, a small resort, 1½ miles S. of Tighnabruaich, Argyll.

KAMES CASTLE. See Port Bannatyne.

KATRINE, LOCH, a freshwater loch 8 miles long, in Perthshire and Stirlingshire, its SE. end in the Trossachs. It is the chief source of Glasgow's water supply, and the main scene of Scott's *Lady of the Lake*.

KEEN, MOUNT, a mountain (3,077 ft.) on the Aberdeen–Angus border.

KEIR, a small village 2½ miles SW. of Thornhill (Dumfries), the birth-place (Courthill Smithy) of Kirk-patrick Macmillan, inventor (1839) of the bicycle.

KEITH, a trim country town and route centre in Banffshire, 10 miles NW. of Huntly on the Elgin road. Other roads run to Dufftown and Craigellachie, Banff, Portsoy and Cullen. Keith has remains of an old castle, a Roman Catholic church with huge statues of St. Peter and St. Paul, and the oldest (1786) working distillery in Scotland. There is trout fishing in the River Isla, which here flows between Keith and Fife-Keith, the two connected by an ancient bridge (1609) and a more modern one. Witches in the old days were drowned in a pool in the Isla. The Balloch (1,199 ft.), 2½ miles E. is an excellent viewpoint.

Loch Katrine, Trossachs.

(*Scottish Tourist Board*).

*Kelso
Abbey*

KELSO is a prosperous little market town of Roxburghshire, on the River Tweed where it joins the Teviot, and according to Scott "the most beautiful if not the most romantic village in Scotland". It is chiefly notable for its Abbey, and some old coaching inns still remain. Ednam House (1761), now a hotel, has famous Italian ceilings. There are facilities for fishing and golf, and race meetings are held in March, May and October. Civic Week, and the Agricultural Show take place in July.

Kelso Abbey (1128) was the largest and one of the most important of the Border abbeys, until, in 1545—fortified and with the monks mingling with the soldiers in its defence—it was taken and destroyed by the Earl of Hertford, and its garrison slain. The ruins, mainly late Norman, were presented to the nation by the late Duke of Roxburghe in 1919.

Other features of the town are the Market Square of Flemish design; the fine Rennie bridge (1803); Shedden Park and Playing Fields; and the racecourse at Berrymoss, 1 mile away. Burgh School stands on the site of the old Grammar School, at which Scott was a pupil, along with his future publishers, the Ballantynes. Also associated with Scott are the house called Rosebank (property of his uncle) and Garden Cottage (now Waverley Lodge), home of a favourite aunt. To the north of the Town stands Floors Castle (1718), remodelled by Playfair in the 19th century. A holly tree in its grounds is said to mark the spot where James II was killed in 1460.

KEMNAY, a village 15 miles WNW. of Aberdeen. There is fishing in the River Don, golf (9-hole course), tennis and bowls. A spectacular item for the sightseer is the huge 400-ft. deep quarry of light-grey Aberdeen granite, fabric of many famous structures, including the Town House and Marischal College of Aberdeen, the piers of the Forth and Tay bridges, and the Thames Embankment in London. Down by the river is the cave where Bruce spent the night before the Battle of Barra (or Inverurie).

KEN, a river and loch of Kirkcudbrightshire. The river rises in the hills S. of New Cumnock and in its southward course forms two reservoirs and Loch Ken. S. of the entry of the Dee the loch is named Loch Dee.

KENMORE, an attractive Perthshire village at the foot of the wooded Drummond Hill (1,500 ft.), at the east end of Loch Tay. There is a golf course and facilities for climbing and skiing. Taymouth Castle (now used as a clubhouse by the local golf club) stands on the site of a 16th century castle built by Colin Campbell of Glenorchy. A rough but scenically charming hill-road runs to Glen Quaich and Amulree, and others follow

166

Overleaf: The Tweed some distance above Kelso.

the numerous mountain glens on both shores of Loch Tay.

KERRERA, an agricultural island, 4 miles by 2 miles, sheltering Oban Bay and extending to the S., separated from the mainland by Kerrera Sound. It is hilly, with fine views of Mull, Loch Linnhe and the Firth of Lorne. Alexander II of Scotland died here in 1249, while preparing to do battle with the (Norse) Western Isles. The field in which he died is still called Dalrigh ("The King's Field") and the King's Well is here also. At the south end of the island is ruined Gylen Castle, formerly a stronghold of the MacDougalls of Lorne. Farming, boatbuilding, lobster-fishing, are the main industries. Horseshoe Bay has a good anchorage for small yachts.

KESSOCK, NORTH AND SOUTH, two villages on the opposite shores of the narrows at junction of the Beauly and the Inner Moray Firths. They are connected by a car-ferry ($\frac{1}{2}$ mile), quickest means of access to the Black Isle (q.v.) from Inverness. Behind North Kessock is Ord Hill, with remains of a vitrified fort. South Kessock, $1\frac{1}{4}$ miles N. of Inverness, lies on the River Ness estuary.

KILBARCHAN, a tartan-weaving town 5 miles W. of Paisley. A statue of a local 17th century piper is on the church steeple.

KILBIRNIE, village, 10 miles N. of Irvine, which forms, with the adjacent village of Glengarnock, a small industrial and engineering area, with a large steelworks. Its mid-17th century church has good features—some fine carving and a gallery emblazoned with colourful coats of arms. Kilbirnie Place—a ruin for 200 years—dates from the 14th century and was the seat of the

Earls of Crawford. Kilbirnie Loch, E. of the village, is a popular venue for water-skiing.

KILCHATTAN BAY, a quiet dairying village and resort on Bute, 8 miles S. of Rothesay.

KILCHRENAN, a hamlet near Loch Awe.

KILCONQUHAR (kin-yu´car), an attractive village to the N. of Elie (Fife), with, near it, Balcarres, seat of the Earls of Crawford and Balcarres.

KILCREGGAN, a small but dignified coast resort, on the Rosneath peninsula opposite Gourock, has a rocky shore and a magnificent outlook. It shares a pier and is contiguous with Cove, another small place with similar advantages. Knockderry Castle is $2\frac{1}{2}$ miles N.; it figures in Scott's *Heart of Midlothian* as "Knock Dunder".

KILDONAN, a hamlet on the River Helmsdale (Sutherland), site of an early Christian church, scene of a "gold rush" in 1869—gold is found here, though apparently not enough to make its working profitable. On the north–south road and the railway, Kildonan is 8 miles inland from Helmsdale. It is interesting here to note that Winnipeg—settled from this district—was originally called New Kildonan.

KILDRUMMY, a village 6 miles W. of Alford in the Don Valley, with angling facilities. Interest centres on Kildrummy Castle (now an Ancient Monument), one of the largest old castles in the country, and a seat of the early Scottish kings. Built in the 13th and 14th centuries, it sheltered Wallace and the family of Bruce, was taken by the English and burnt on seven different occasions, later held by the Erskines of Mar, who played their part in the '15 Rising—and lost Kildrummy in consequence. Formidable despite its hoary antiquity, it still has features of interest: remains of the old towers, the dungeon, massive gatehouse and especially the chapel.

KILLEARN, a village 16 miles N. of Glasgow, in pleasant surroundings NW. of the Campsie Fells. It was the birthplace of George Buchanan, humanist and reformer, commemorated here by an obelisk.

KILLIECRANKIE, PASS OF,
a rugged and romantic wooded pass on the River Garry, 4 miles N. of Pitlochry, famous in history as the scene of a battle between "King and Covenant" in 1689 in which "Bonnie Dundee" (Graham of Claverhouse—the victor) was slain. At the top of the pass is the Soldier's Leap, where a pursued Royalist is said to have cleared the river in one bound. Ben Vrackie rises to the NE.

KILLIN, a picturesque village resort of Breadalbane (Perthshire) at the west end of Loch Tay, with Ben Lawers in the background. This is a notable area for winter sports—skiing, mountaineering—as also for fishing. There is a good golf course. Near Killin are the famous Falls of Dochart. On an island in the River Dochart is the burialplace of the Clan MacNab.

KILMACOLM (kil-ma-coam´), a pleasant resort with a hydro, among low hills with good viewpoints, in Strath Gryfe (Renfrewshire), 4 miles SE. of Port Glasgow.

KILMARNOCK, an ancient burgh (1591) and important industrial town of Ayrshire, 12 miles NE. of Ayr, with which it is comparable in size. It gave its name to the Kilmarnock bonnet and the famous First Edition of Burns's poems, printed at John Wilson's Press in 1786. The town has a large variety of manufactures (including locomotives, hydroelectric equipment, carpets, boots and shoes, lace and whisky), but does not lack amenities. Besides a number of public parks one has the charming and extensive Bellfield Estate (240 acres) with its gardens, rock-gardens, and playing fields, also facilities for golf (18-hole municipal course, and the Kilmarnock Golf Club's fine course at Barassie), tennis, bowls and (in winter) curling.

Burns Monument in the Kay Park takes the form of a classical temple enshrining relics of the poet; it has an 80-foot-high tower which is both a landmark and a first-rate viewpoint. Other features of interest are Tam Samson's house (Burns wrote Tam's epitaph), the Masonic Temple, Laigh Kirk, and the small but interesting museum of the Dick Institute. There is a fine Technical College.

Craufurdland Castle (2 miles

NE.) and Dean Castle (nearer the town) have lovely and extensive grounds.

KILMARTIN, a small village 8 miles NW. of Lochgilphead (Argyll). There are prehistoric remains here, and fragments of a church dedicated to the pre-Columban missionary, St. Martin. Nearby is Carnassarie Castle.

KILMAURS, a small town, 3 miles NW. of Kilmarnock, with a Tolbooth (jougs still to be seen) and Mercat Cross. Rowallan Castle is 1½ miles E.

KILMELFORT, an angler's resort, with loch and sea fishing, as well as sea-bathing, on Loch Melfort, 14 miles S. of Oban.

KILMORACK (Falls). See Beauly.

KILMORIE, 4 miles S. of Oban, a scattered hamlet, once the ecclesiastical centre of the district, with good loch and stream fishing. 2 miles away is Kilbride old churchyard with remains of a fine Celtic cross.

KILMUIR, the burialplace (Celtic cross; inscription by Dr. Johnson) of Flora Macdonald, 5 miles N. of Uig, Skye.

KILMUN, a sheltered resort on the Holy Loch.

KILPATRICK HILLS, a range of hills NE. of Dumbarton, rising to 1,313 ft. There are several small lochs and reservoirs, and some interesting hill walks. On the north side of Auchineden Hill (1,170 ft.) is the curious cleft called The Whangie.

KILSPINDIE, a golf course (East Lothian) near Aberlady.

KILSYTH, a small mining town of Stirlingshire, at the foot of the Kilsyth Hills, scene in 1645 of one of Montrose's battles, when the Covenanters were defeated with heavy loss. The small industrial town of Lennoxtown, and Campsie (ancient ruined church), with picturesque Campsie Glen, are to the W.

KILSYTH HILLS, a range of hills in Stirlingshire, S. of the River Carron, its highest summit Meiklebin (1,870 ft.). The range is an eastern continuation of the Campsie Fells.

KILWINNING, an industrial town and railway junction of Ayrshire, 3½ miles NNW. of Irvine. It has slight remains of a beautiful 12th century priory, built on the site of the little (8th century) Church of St. Winnen—from which Kilwinning takes its name. The town is also distinguished as the earliest Scottish home of Freemasonry, introduced from the continent by the masons at work on the Priory. "Mother Lodge Kilwinning" (dating from 1107) is therefore the Matriarch of Scottish Lodges, root from which the others have sprung. Industries include iron founding and other heavy industries and the manufacture of worsted, while, in a waste of sandhills, the huge Ardeer Chemical and Explosives factory lies between Kilwinning and the sea.

To the SE. (1½ miles) is Eglinton Castle, late 18th century, memorable as the scene, in 1839, of a great tournament on mediaeval lines, designed to bring about a revival of the Age of Chivalry. Napoleon III was one of the "Knights" who took part in it.

KINCARDINE (also Kincardine-on-Forth) a small town of west Fife, at the north end of Kincardine Road Bridge (centre swing span) over the Forth. It has an 18-hole golf course and is noted for its 17th century church, for Tulliallan Castle (now a police college) and Kincardine Power Station. The Forestry Commission have large plantations here.

KINCARDINE O'NEIL, a small village on the Dee, with Auld Kirk remains.

KINCARDINESHIRE (also "the Mearns"), an eastern county between Aberdeen and Angus, with a rocky North Sea coast. In the W. and NW. are the Grampians, but in the fertile Howe and elsewhere agriculture is actively pursued. The Dee forms the north boundary of the county, which includes part of the city of Aberdeen. Stonehaven is the county town.

KINCRAIG, a village on the Great North Road, 5 miles NE. of Kingussie, with a golf course.

KINGHORN, a royal burgh and small resort 2½ miles E. of Burntisland. Golf-club making is an industry. For the visitor there is a popular beach, golf (18-hole course with fine views over the Forth), tennis, bowls and angling. The spot where Alexander III was thrown from his horse and killed is marked by a monument.

KINGSBURGH HOUSE, 5 miles S. of Uig, Skye, on the site of that in which Prince Charlie sheltered in 1746.

KINGSHOUSE, a climbing centre (inn) for Glencoe peaks, including Buachaille Etive Mor, and Mealla Bhuiridh. It figures in Neil Munro's *John Splendid*.

KINGUSSIE, (king-yu'si), a pleasant village and summer and winter resort of Inverness-shire, at the foot of the Monadhliath in the Spey Valley. Standing high (760 ft. above sea-level), surrounded by tall pinewoods and sheltered by the mountains, Kingussie is notably healthy. Across the river rise the foothills of the Grampians, with the Cairngorms to the E. Nearly opposite the village are the remains of Ruthven Castle, built as a Government barracks in 1718, burnt by the Jacobites after Culloden to prevent its being retaken by the Hanoverian forces. Here in a fold of the hills are faint traces of the little village of Ruthven, birthplace of James MacPherson, "translator" of the Ossianic poems. Mac-Pherson's handsome house of Belleville (Balavil) stands empty on the Kingussie side of the valley.

In Glen Gynack to the N. is a fine 18-hole golf course laid out by

Falls of Dochart, Killin. (*W. S. Thomson*).

Vardon and Braid and shinty is much played.

For the angler there is fishing in the Spey (salmon and trout) and in many little lochs and streams. Visitors will appreciate Dr. Grant's small but delightful museum of *Am Fasgadh*, with its fascinating collection of Highland antiquities, and specimens of old crafts and "ways of life".

Creag Dhubh (2,581 ft.), Creag Bheag (1,593 ft. and Cruadh-la (2,099 ft.), all in the vicinity, are worth climbing for the sake of the magnificent views from their summits. Motor coach tours run to Braemar, Loch Ness, Glen Affric and other places of interest. A favourite hike leads through Glen Feshie, from which a path through Glen Geldie takes one to Braemar.

KINLOCHBERVIE, a village on the north shore of Loch Inchard (west coast of Sutherland) with good fishing waters for anglers.

KINLOCHEWE, a hamlet (with hotel) near the head of Loch Maree in Wester Ross, with fishing, boating and climbing. It is a good starting point for the ascent of Slioch (3,260 ft.) and Ben Eighe (3,309 ft.), a Nature Reserve, distinguished by its white quartzite peaks; the latter summit for practised climbers only. Kinlochewe Deer Forest is to the E.

KINLOCHLEVEN, a small town in Argyllshire, unexpectedly industrial (aluminium works and hydroelectric scheme on the River Blackwater), at the head of Loch Leven. Access is by scenic roads on each side of the loch.

KINLOCH RANNOCH, a small trout-fishing resort at the east end of Loch Rannoch, 22 miles W. of Pitlochry. Rannoch School (1959, formerly Dall House) is similar to Gordonstoun.

KINLOSS, a small village 3 miles NE. of Forres, with remains of a 12th century abbey.

KINNAIRD'S HEAD. See Fraserburgh.

KINNEFF, a small coastal village, 6 miles S. of Stonehaven, in whose church the Scottish Regalia were hidden (1652–1660).

KINORD, LOCH, a small loch 6 miles W. of Aboyne, with relics of lake-dwellings.

KINROSS, the county town of Kinross-shire, situated W. of Loch Leven, renowned for angling. Kinross House (17th century) was designed by Sir William Bruce, famous for his work on the Palace of Holyroodhouse, Edinburgh. Balcado airfield, headquarters of the Scottish Gliding Union is 2¼ miles E. Mary, Queen of Scots, was imprisoned in Loch Leven Castle (1567–1568).

KINROSS, OR KINROSS–SHIRE, is a small inland county between Perth and Fife shires. The county town is Kinross. Milnathort is an agricultural market town.

KINTAIL, a district round Loch Duich, with impressive mountain scenery (Five Sisters of Kintail—highest 3,505 ft.— and others). Much of the district is Scottish National Trust property.

KINTORE, an old town on the River Don, 12 miles NW. of Aberdeen, a royal burgh with a quaint 18th century town hall. Hallforest Castle (1½ miles; ruins) is said to have been a hunting tower of Robert the Bruce.

KINTYRE, a peninsula (40 miles long) of Argyll, stretching from Tarbert in the NE. to the Mull of Kintyre in the SW. From the west coast road may be seen Islay, Jura, and, in the distance, Ireland, while that along the east coast provides fine views over Kilbrennan Sound towards Arran.

KIPPEN, a small village 10 miles W. of Stirling, whose vine, claimed to be the largest in the world, has now been cut down.

KIPPFORD, a yachting resort on Rough Firth, 4½ miles S. of Dalbeattie (Kirkcudbrightshire).

KIRKCALDY (kir-kaw'di), a manufacturing town and seaport on the Firth of Forth, a royal burgh since 1450 and the largest town in Fife. Known as the "lang toun" because of its 4-mile-long main street, Kirkcaldy is well laid out, with handsome gardens, Museum, Art Gallery—and here and there the picturesque red-tiled roofs and crow-step gables of the best east coast towns. There is an 18-hole golf course at Balwearie (1½ miles W.); good sandy beaches, putting, tennis and bowls.

Distinguished natives include Adam Smith (*Wealth of Nations*), the brothers Adam, architects, and the "Wondrous Wizard", Michael Scott of Balwearie. Thomas Carlyle taught in the burgh school, as did his friend Edward Irving. Here, too, is the tomb of Sir Walter Scott's "Pet Marjorie".

There are some good features in the ancient church, and near by are Ravenscraig Castle, built by James II—depicted in Scott's *Rosabelle*, Seafield Tower by the sea, and the still formidable ruin of Michael Scott's castle of Balwearie.

KIRKCONNELL, a churchyard, 4 miles NE. of Ecclefechan, in which are buried "Fair Helen of Kirkconnell Lee" and her lover.

KIRKCUDBRIGHT (kir-koo´ bri), county town of Kirkcudbrightshire, royal burgh and market town, a favourite artist's place of residence, on the estuary of the River Dee at the head of Kirkcudbright Bay. The ruined MacLellan's Castle, the Tolbooth (both 16th century), and the 17th century Mercat Cross (jougs still retained) are all within the town. In the churchyard of St. Cuthbert are buried three Covenanting martyrs. On the peninsula of St. Mary's Isle, 1½ miles S., there is an old heronry (private), while at the mouth of Kirkcudbright Bay is Little Ross lighthouse, built by R. L. Stevenson's father. Kirkcudbright has a harbour, suitable for small vessels.

KIRKCUDBRIGHTSHIRE, an agricultural county, mainly concerned with cattle and dairy farming, in the SW. of Scotland. Popularly called The Stewartry, having been governed by a steward from the 14th to the 18th century, the county forms part of Galloway.

Many streams and rivers (Dee, Fleet, Ken, Cree and Urr) water the county, the Dee and its headstreams being utilised in the Galloway hydroelectric schemes. The visitor will find, both inland and on the coast, numerous attractive towns and villages, such as Castle Douglas, Gatehouse-of-Fleet, Creetown, Kirkbean and Auchencairn, while in the W. is Glen Trool National Forest Park, with its many beautiful lochs and lofty heights—Merrick, highest point in the Southern Uplands, Rhinns of Kells. Loch Trool is one of Scotland's beauty spots. Of interest are Threave Castle, on an island in the Dee, Sweetheart Abbey (New Abbey), Dundrennan Abbey (4 miles SE. of Kirkcudbright), and Lincluden College (3 miles NW. of Dumfries).

KIRKINTILLOCH, a small, hilly old town of Dunbartonshire, 7 to 8 miles NW. of Glasgow, with ironworks as well as some new industry. There was a Roman fort near here.

KIRKLISTON, a village 8½ miles W. of Edinburgh, with an interesting Romanesque church.

KIRKMAIDEN, near the Mull of Galloway, the most southerly parish in Scotland.

KIRK O' SHOTTS, the site of B.B.C. and I.T.V. television transmitters, on Edinburgh–Glasgow road, 4 miles W. of Harthill.

KIRKOSWALD, an attractive village 4 miles SW. of Maybole, in the churchyard of which are the graves of Burns's "Tam o' Shanter" and "Soutar Johnnie". The cottage of the latter has Burns relics, and in its garden, life-size figures from the poem *Tam o' Shanter*.

KIRKWALL, a seaport and royal burgh, capital of Orkney. It has a golf course. The town is picturesque, with many houses gable-on to the streets, and narrow alleys running between. Of interest are the 12th century St. Magnus Cathedral (resting-place of King Haco's body; desecrated by Cromwell's soldiers; restorations early 20th century), the ruined Bishop's Palace (where King Haco died while returning to Norway after the Battle of Largs), and the remains of the 17th century Earl's Palace. The airport is to the SE. of the the town.

KIRN, a resort on the Clyde, NE. of and linked by promenade to, Dunoon. It has a lido, pier and golf course, and is a yachting base.

KIRRIEMUIR, a jute-manufacturing town on the Braes of Angus, 6 miles NW. of Forfar, birthplace of Sir J. M. Barrie, and the "Thrums" of his novels (Thrums: weavers' "loose ends" —the town was once noted for its handweaving). There is excellent trout-fishing and an 18-hole golf course.
Associations with Barrie are everywhere: the house where he was born, part of it a museum with relics of both Barrie and "Thrums"; the "Auld Licht Kirk", "Auld Licht Manse", and "Window in Thrums". Favourite excursions from here take one up Glen Clova and Glen Prosen.

KNAPDALE, a district N. of Kintyre, with low hills and attractive coast roads. The Crinan Canal forms its north boundary, and the Point of Knap is on its west coast.

KNOCKANDO, Morayshire village picturesquely situated above the River Spey, 8 miles SW. of Craigellachie.

KNOIDART, a mountainous peninsula of west Inverness-shire bounded by Loch Hourn on the N. and Loch Nevis on the S.

KYLE. See Ayrshire.

KYLEAKIN, a coastal village of Skye, landing point of the Kyle of Lochalsh ferry, with the ruined Castle Moil overlooking it. The name is derived from King Haco of Norway, who sailed through the narrows on his way to Largs.

KYLE OF LOCHALSH, or Kyle, a village, railway terminus and steamer port, with ferry to Kyleakin in Skye at the west end of the deep sea-inlet of Loch Alsh. In summer it is much frequented by tourists, both because of its position as the "Gateway to Skye", and because of the beauty of its surroundings.

KYLES OF BUTE, the picturesque narrow straits which separate the north of Bute from the

Cowal district of the Argyll mainland. Near Colintraive are the low, rocky Burnt Islands, and on the north point of Bute may be seen the two standing stones, the "Maids of Bute" painted to represent—no-one knows why—Welsh ladies. At South House, on Cowal, are the remains of woods planted to represent the positions of the French and British armies at Waterloo. The classic sail down the Clyde is from Bridge Wharf, Glasgow, to Tighnabruaich in the Kyles of Bute. This lasts from 11 a.m. to about 7.30 p.m. and includes time ashore at Tighnabruaich. It is the ideal way to see almost the whole of the Firth of Clyde.

KYLESKU, a hamlet on narrows of Loch Cairnbawn (Sutherland) with car-ferry N. to Kyle Strome.

LADY ISLE, a rocky island with lighthouse off the Ayrshire coast, 3 miles from Troon. A well-known bird breeding-ground.

LADYBANK, a small industrial burgh of Fife, 6 miles SW. of Cupar.

LADYKIRK, a small place on the banks of the Tweed, 6 miles NE. of Coldstream where James IV built a church in gratitude after being saved from drowning in the river.

LAGGAN, LOCH, a high freshwater loch in central Inverness-shire. It is included in the Lochaber Power Scheme with a dam which increased the loch's length from 7 to $11\frac{1}{2}$ miles. There is good trout fishing.

LAIDE, a village on the shores of Gruinard Bay (Wester Ross). It has interesting rocks and caves and the remains of a ruined chapel (Sands of Udrigle) of the early Christian church.

LAIRG, a small but important township of Sutherland, at the southern extremity of Loch Shin, from which the River Shin flows to join the Oykell at Invershin. Lairg itself is an important route-junction for north and north-west Sutherland, and is an ideal touring base for country of wild, often desolate, grandeur. There is excellent fishing on the River Shin (salmon) and on Loch Shin (trout); the Falls of Shin are noted for their salmon-leaping spectacle. Lairg is well-known for its lamb-sales, the surrounding hills and moorlands being ideal sheep-rearing terrain; it was here that the "Sutherland Clearances" (for sheep-farming) began early in the 19th century. Today Lairg is the centre of very considerable hydroelectric development, involving the whole basin (250 sq. miles) of Loch Shin, across the foot of which stands a dam 1,400 feet long.

LAMANCHA, an estate 20 miles SW. of Edinburgh, formerly Grange of Romanno, with a partly 17th century mansion house.

LAMBERTON TOLL, a tiny place on the Scottish border, 3 miles N. of Berwick, once almost as popular with eloping couples as Gretna Green.

LAMINGTON, a village 12 miles SE. of Lanark, picturesquely laid out during the last century by Lord Lamington. Near the mansion-house are the ruins of the 16th century tower. Sir William Wallace married a lady of Lamington and relics of the patriot are preserved in Lamington House. The church has a fine Norman doorway and exhibits the jougs and stool of repentance of former days.

LAMLASH, a resort on the east side of Arran on Lamlash Bay, in which lies the bold Holy Isle (over 1,000 ft. high) with the cave of St. Molaise. There are golf, bowling, tennis and sea-fishing, and it is the head-quarters of the Arran Yacht Club.

LAMMER LAW, the highest point (1,733 ft.) in the Lammermuir Hills, lies 9 miles S. of Haddington.

LAMMERMUIR HILLS, a range of hills on the borders of East Lothian and Berwickshire—highest summit Lammer Law. This is a delightful region for walking, rambling, motor touring, among hills and valleys, with old castles and towers and rich in the romance of the Borders. The Whiteadder, Faseny and Gifford Water were once famous trout streams.

LANARK, county town of Lanarkshire, a royal burgh of David I, 24 miles SE. of Glasgow, visited for its historical associations, and for the picturesque Falls of Clyde nearby. There is fishing on the upper Clyde, golf (18- and 9-hole courses), tennis and bowls, boating in the little loch on Lanark Moor. Here too is the racecourse. "Lanark Races" have a long history: the Silver Bell competed for annually was given to the town by William the Lion in 1100, as a racing trophy. Lanimer Day, the Lanark equivalent of the Border Ridings, is a festive occasion with processions and the crowning of the Lanimer Queen.

The old castle, near which Wallace lived in the Castlegate, has vanished, but there are still slight remains of the 12th century church of St. Kentigern, in which, according to tradition, he was married. About 1 mile W. are the Cartland Crags, where he took refuge after killing a soldier of the garrison; they tower above a deep wooded gorge of the Mouse Water, here crossed by a graceful Telford Bridge, said to be the highest road bridge in Scotland.

To the south is the textile community of New Lanark (founded 1784; flourished under the aegis of Robert Owen); to the west, the pretty village of Kirkfieldbank.

LANARKSHIRE, an inland county traversed by the Clyde, hence often called Clydesdale. In the north are Glasgow, Rutherglen, Hamilton, Airdrie,

Opposite: *Lamlash*.

Coatbridge, Motherwell and Wishaw—a heavily industrialised area (steel, heavy engineering, textiles, coal-mining) which contains nearly one-third of Scotland's population. This industrial predominance has owed much to the valuable coal and iron deposits, the latter no longer worked and the former now rapidly reaching exhaustion. To the south the uplands rise to Green Lowther (2,403 ft.) and Tinto (2,335 ft.). After Wanlockhead (Dumfries), Leadhills, in the Lowthers, is the highest village (c. 1,400 ft.) in Scotland. In the centre the orchards of the Vale of Clyde have long been famous, though now small fruits (especially tomatoes) and vegetables for the industrial areas are the chief products. Much of the county is adapted to stock-raising and dairy-farming; Clydesdale horses are a famous breed.

LANGHOLM, a small town (burgh of barony in 1621) and popular angling resort of Dumfriesshire, rising from the River Esk near its junction with the Ewes Water and the Wauchope Burn, c. 20 miles N. of Carlisle. It has 5 tweed mills. There is fishing in the Esk, Ewes, Liddel and other streams, golf, tennis, riding, bowls and hill-walking. The traditional Festival of the Common Riding (last Friday in July) is carried through with spirit and verve.

Historical interest centres on the exploits of Johnny Armstrong of Gilnockie, famous freebooter and, north of the Border, popular hero. Johnny Armstrong did his reiving in style, went always attended by 24 "able gentlemen well-horsed"; but in the end he and his men were hanged at Caerlanrig Castle by James V, who had invited them thither to a "hunting party".

LARBERT, a large Stirlingshire village and railway junction comprising the formerly separate villages of Larbert and Stenhousemuir, with several iron foundries. There is an attractive golf course on the Tryst Ground and the famous Glenbervie course almost at the entrance to the village as one approaches from Stirling. Crownest Park has a Lido, tennis courts and putting green. The Dobbie Hall is one of the finest and most up-to-date public halls in Central Scotland.

LARGO, UPPER and LOWER, village and resort of E. Fife, on Largo Bay, distinguished as the birthplace of Alexander Selkirk (original of Robinson Crusoe) and the setting of the Scots fisherman's song, "The Boatie Rows". Selkirk was a native of Lower Largo, where he is commemorated by a statue. At Upper Largo is an ancient parish church, parts of which date from 1400. A pleasant walk leads through romantic Kiels Den. Largo Law (965 ft.) is a landmark and a viewpoint. Adjoining the village is Lundin Links.

Largs.　　　　　　　　(*W. S. Thomson*).

LARGOWARD, a village of Fife, 5 miles NE. of Largo.

LARGS, an important Clyde resort 15 miles S. of Greenock on the Ayrshire coast. Here was fought the decisive battle of Largs (1263), when Alexander III routed King Haco of Norway, and finally broke the Norwegian power in Scotland. Largs caters well for tourists with pavilion and illuminations, trim sea front with broad grass verges, two golf courses, bathing, sea-fishing, trout-fishing, tennis and bowls. Largs is a point of call for numerous Clyde steamers. The Royal Largs Yacht Club holds two regattas in the Clyde fortnight.

Points of interest are Kelburn and Knock Castles, Brisbane Glen and the Skelmorlie Mausoleum (with 17th century ceiling painting) in Largs Old Churchyard.

LARIG GHRU ("gloomy pass"), a wild and awesome mountain pass among the Cairngorms (2,733 ft. high), bleak but magnificent scenery, though rough going for the traveller.

LASSWADE, a village of Midlothian, charmingly situated on the North Esk, *c.* 2 miles SW. of Dalkeith. In the churchyard of the (ruined) Norman church is the tomb of Drummond of Hawthornden (*q.v.*). Scott lived in Lasswade for some years.

Overleaf: The Tay Valley at Dunkeld

LATHERON, LATHERON-WHEEL, neighbouring small coastal places in Caithness, 18 miles SW. of Wick.

LAUDER, a royal burgh and angling resort of Berwickshire, *c.* 9 miles NNW. of Melrose. There is fishing in the Leader Water and other streams. Formerly a walled town, Lauder was granted its charter by William the Lion and was the scene, in 1483, of a high-placed plot against some of James III's favourites, in which the Earl of Angus, undertaking to "bell the cat", seized the intended victims and hanged them over Lauder Brig—himself going down in history as Archibald "Bell-the-Cat". There is a 16th century church and a fascinating town hall. Thirlestane Castle (17th century) seat of the Earl of Lauderdale, is nearby.

LAUDERDALE, anciently the western district of Berwickshire.

LAURENCEKIRK, a pleasant old town of Kincardineshire, charmingly situated in the Howe o' the Mearns, on the slopes of Garvock Hill, 14 miles SW. of Stonehaven. It has a linen industry and was formerly famed for its snuff-boxes (Charles Triven), which are now collectors' pieces. There is an attractive park, tennis, bowls and fishing in the Luther Water. To the NW. is the site of the royal castle of Kincardine, of which only the foundations remain. Of the old royal burgh of Kincardine no trace is to be seen. Near here is the site of Haulkerton Castle, stronghold of the Falconer family, hereditary falconers to the ancient kings. The old name of Laurencekirk was Kirkton of Conveth (St. Laurence), but in 1779 it became a burgh of barony under its present name.

LAURISTON, a small place 7 miles N. of Montrose in Kincardineshire, with near by the romantic gorge of Den Fenella.

LAWERS, BEN (3,984 ft. with a cairn on its summit raising it to 4,000 ft.) stands on the north shore of Loch Tay (Perthshire), and is renowned for its Alpine plants. The (easy) ascent may be made from Lawers, about halfway along the loch on the north side, and is rewarded by glorious panoramic views. Winter sports (tow-rope) are popular here.

LAXFORD BRIDGE, a road junction of Sutherland at the head of Loch Laxford, a deep sea inlet on the west coast.

LEADBURN, a moorland village 14 miles S. of Edinburgh.

LEADHILLS, a mining village of Lanarkshire, one of the highest villages in Scotland, *c.* 20 miles S. of Lanark. Symington, the steamship pioneer, and Allan Ramsay, author of "the Gentle Shepherd", were born here.

LEDI, BEN, a mountain (2,873 ft.) to the W. of Callander, Perthshire.

Ben Ledi.

LEITH, the port of Edinburgh, lying to the north of the city on the south shore of the Firth of Forth, has been, since 1920, included in the city of Edinburgh with which it is connected by the broad thoroughfare of Leith Walk. It is mainly commercial and the harbours and docks form the second largest port on the east coast of Scotland.

Leith has the distinction of being the town where golf reputedly originated.

LENDALFOOT, a small coastal place in Ayrshire, *c.* 6 miles S. of Girvan on the Water of Lendal.

Nearby is Carleton Castle with its tale of a bluebeard baron who killed seven wives by pushing them over the cliff, but himself met the same fate at the hands of the eighth.

LENNOX, anciently a district incorporating Dunbartonshire with part of Stirlingshire, Perthshire and Renfrewshire, which gave name to the Earls of Lennox.

LENNOXLOVE. See Haddington.

LENY, PASS AND FALLS OF, a mountain pass 3 miles NW. of Callander, Perthshire, flanked on the west by Ben Ledi; Falls of Leny are near Callander.

LERWICK, the chief town and port on the east side of the mainland of Shetland. It occupies a sheltered position on Bressay Sound, opposite the Island of Bressay. Steamers from the mainland and Orkney call frequently and there are sailings from Lerwick to the northern islands of the group. Fishing is the most important occupation, and foreign boats are often to be seen in the harbour.

Though it is certain that Lerwick existed as a settlement from early times, it was totally destroyed and rebuilt during the 17th century, and there is little of antiquarian interest. The Town Hall was opened in 1883 and has stained glass windows depicting scenes from the history of Shetland.

Up-Helly-Aa, a festival held annually in January, is of ancient origin. Celebrations include a torchlight parade with a full-size replica of a Viking ship at the head.

Lerwick is a centre for the handknitted woollen goods and weaving for which Shetland is famed.

LESLIE, a small Fifeshire burgh, *c.* 9 miles N. of Kirkcaldy, with manufactures of paper and plastics, linen and rayon. The "Kirk" on its "Green" is claimed as the setting of the poem, *Christ's Kirk on the Green,* attributed to James V.

LESMAHAGOW, an attractive wooded village 5 miles SW. of Lanark, on the Glasgow–Dumfries road. The name commemorates a 6th century Christian missionary, St. Mahago. The alternative name of Abbey Green (not commonly used) recalls the Abbey founded here in 1160 and long since vanished. There is a golf course here.

LEUCHARS, a village and railway junction of Fife, 4 miles NW. of St. Andrews. It has a Norman church and quarries of red sandstone, also a 9-hole golf course with fine wide views. Leuchars Aerodrome is near here. To north and north-east is the extensive Tents Moor, part of which is a nature reserve, and part occupied by the Forestry Commission.

LEVEN, a seaport, golfing and holiday resort, on the Firth of Forth, at the west end of Largo Bay, and at the mouth of the River Leven. Industries include foundries and paper-mills, also golf - club making. Leven is visited for its magnificent sands and sand dunes, its golf (two 18-hole courses—open tournaments in summer) and its picturesque ceremony of crowning the Rose Queen and installing the Warden and his Lass—just as in the Border towns. Letham Glen is a delightful public park. There are facilities for boating, bathing, fishing, tennis and bowls.

LEVEN, a river of Fife, issuing from Loch Leven (Kinross-shire) and entering the Firth of Forth at Leven.

LEVEN, a river in Dunbartonshire, which runs from the foot of Loch Lomond, through the industrial Vale of Leven, and enters the Clyde at Dumbarton.

LEVEN, LOCH, a sea loch between Inverness-shire and Argyll, running inland from Loch Linnhe. At Ballachulish (Argyll) there is a ferry to North Ballachulish (Inverness-shire) which saves a wide detour round the loch on the Oban–Fort William road. The entrance to Glencoe is on its south shore. The little isle of St. Munda holds the burial place of the MacDonalds. Kinlochleven at the head of the loch has an aluminium factory.

LEVEN, LOCH, Kinross-shire, an inland loch ($3\frac{5}{8}$ miles by 2 miles) famous for trout fishing, and as a wildfowl resort and nature reserve. St. Serfs is the largest of the islands, with ruins of a priory. Castle Island is where Mary Queen of Scots was imprisoned in 1567 after her surrender at Carber, and abdicated from the throne in favour of her son, in 1568 making her dramatic escape to Niddrie Castle.

LEVERBURGH, a small town and fishing port on Harris, renamed after Lord Leverhulme, who unsuccessfully attempted to expand its trade.

LEWIS, the larger, northerly portion of the northernmost island of the Hebrides, included in the County of Ross. Called Eilean an Fhraoich, "isle of heather", it is roughly 100,000 acres in extent, a wild region of heathery moors, winding fiords and countless freshwater lochs teeming with fish. The coast is mainly rock and cliff, interspersed with sandy bays and green machair. There are no great mountains as in Skye: Ben Mhor (1,874 ft.) in the E. and Mealasbhal (1,800 ft.) in the W., are the highest summits. There are almost no trees, though moor and moss hold traces of the ancient forest which once clothed Lewis—burnt down, says tradition, by a Norse invader with "scorched earth" ideas. Stornoway is the only town, unexpectedly large, busy and modern in its wild environment.

Easy of access by air and sea, Lewis has many attractions for the tourist. Archaeologically its chief glory is the fine Stone Circle at Callanish on East Loch Roag. Anglers delight in its richly stocked fishing waters, while artists feel the spell of its rolling brown landscape, high headlands, and lonely lochs.

LEWIS, BUTT OF, the extreme north point of the "Long Island", has a lighthouse (120 ft.) built by Thomas Stevenson, father of Robert Louis Stevenson. In the rocky point is a natural opening called the Eye of the Butt. Legend says that once the Island lay far to the south, but a tow-rope through the "Eye" enabled a doughty jarl to bring it where it is now! Here, beyond the moors and the heather are many crofts and a number of villages— Eoropie, Knockaird, Lionel, Cross— all within a few miles. The islet of Sulisgeir, where young gannets (solan geese) are taken and salted for winter use, is some 40 miles north.

LIATHACH, a mountain (3,456 ft.) NE. of Upper Loch Torridon, Ross-shire.

LIDDESDALE, the romantic and beautiful valley of the Liddel Water which rises near Peel Fell, in the Cheviots, and which for several miles forms the boundary between England and Scotland. From Canonbie, Dumfriesshire, near which the Liddel enters the River Esk, an interesting excursion follows the "links of green Liddesdale" to Kershopefoot, Mangerton and Newcastleton.

LILLIARD'S EDGE. See Ancrum.

LILLIESLEAF, a pretty village of Roxburghshire, c. 6 miles SE. of Selkirk.

LINCLUDEN COLLEGE, 2 miles NW. of Dumfries, in Kirkcudbrightshire. These ruins stand on the banks of the Cluden near its confluence with the Nith. Founded in the 12th century, as a convent for Benedictine nuns, Lincluden was converted into a collegiate church at the end of the 14th century. It was for a considerable time under the patronage of the Earls of Douglas who spent lavishly on the buildings. Little is left of the 12th century nunnery, but choir and transepts remain of the church, which is of later date. Of interest is the tomb of Margaret, daughter of Robert III, and Countess of Douglas.

LINDORES ABBEY, a fragmentary ruin in Fife near the shore of the Firth of Tay, c. 10 miles E. of Perth.

Lindores was founded in the 12th century and was of great importance in the Catholic church of Scotland. At the Reformation there was a ceremonial burning of the mass books and vestments, recorded by John Knox, and after the last abbot died in 1596 ownership passed from the church.

LINLITHGOW, a royal burgh, palace and loch of West Lothian, 17 miles W. of Edinburgh, 3 to 4 miles distant from the Firth of Forth at Bo'ness.

The town of Linlithgow, indissociable from the palace, famed also for its fine old church and its wells, received its charter from David I, was thrice burnt by the English, but rose to be a place of consequence, preoccupied with the comings and goings of kings and queens, with royal courts and sittings of parliament. Here too, Edinburgh University functioned in 1645–46 while the city was ravaged by plague.

The romantic and singularly complete ruin of the palace stands on a small eminence, surrounded on three sides by the little loch (barely 1 mile long). Oddly enough, its site was chosen by Edward I of England, who planted a tower here to keep the "rebellious Scots" in check. Its capture in 1313, by a countryman's stratagem of armed men hidden in a wagonload of hay, is one of the more picturesque episodes in Scottish history. Though burned by

Linlithgow Loch.

Bruce it survived to be incorporated in the palace begun by James I in the 15th century—a large, formidable, rather plain structure built round a courtyard, with square towers at its outer angles. Here Mary, Queen of Scots was born, as was her father James V. Remains include not only the Great Hall (94 ft. long), Dining Room, King's Hall, Chapel, but also the domestic quarters, kitchens, bakeries and wine cellar. Other features to be looked for are Queen Mary's birthplace, Queen Margaret's Bower, in which James IV's queen waited, weeping, for news of Flodden;

the impressive stone gateway built by James V bearing the arms of Scotland and the insignia of James's four Orders of Knighthood [the Thistle (Scotland), Garter (England), Golden Fleece (Spain) and Fleur-de-Lys (France)] and the fine gothic fountain in the courtyard, which first ran with wine during the reign of James V and again during the '45 when Prince Charles Edward was entertained here. Also there is the secret staircase, the dungeon and the torture-chamber.

The lovely old church of St. Michael, 15th century gothic, lies close to the palace, its tall square tower adjoining the palace gateway.

To the tower, pinnacled and embattled, James IV added an open crown, which has since disappeared. The interior is rich and beautiful—note the vaulting of the aisles, the clustered pillars, the window tracery. It was here, in the south transept, that an apparition warned James IV of the impending disaster of Flodden. St. Michael's is still in use as a parish church, and is sometimes open to visitors.

Near by is the old Town House (1668), and other features of interest are the modern county buildings (Linlithgow being the county town) and the still numerous wells, including the Cross Well and St. Michael's Well with its warming inscription, "St. Michael is kinde to Strangers". The town has paper-making, tanning, pharmaceutical and distilling industries, two 9-hole golf courses, and a bowling green.

Seasonal highlights are the Riding of the Marches, the Annual Sports Meeting, and the Children's Gala in July in the Peel public park, near the Loch and the Palace.

Parts of the loch serve as a swimming pool and children's paddling pools.

LINLITHGOWSHIRE, the former name of West Lothian.

LINNHE, LOCH, a fine sea inlet of Argyllshire, extends 31 miles NE. from the Sound of Mull, forms part of the line of navigation of the Caledonian Canal. It has narrows at Corran and sends off Lochs Creran, Leven and Eil. At its head is Fort William, and at its foot the island of Lismore.

LINTON, a small village 6 miles S. of Kelso, which in olden times, according to tradition, had a "laidly worm" (dragon) slain by a local laird who thrust a burning peat down its throat.

LISMORE, an island (11 miles by 2 miles) in Loch Linnhe, an important ecclesiastical centre from the earliest times, and for centuries the seat of the Bishop of Argyll. Its name signifies "the big garden". There is a lighthouse on the south point of the island. The 17th century *Dean of Lismore's Book* is a famous manuscript collection of legendary and historical poems in Gaelic and English.

LOCHABER, a district in south Inverness-shire in which is Ben Nevis.

LOCHALINE (loch-ay'lin), a village on the Sound of Mull, near the mouth of Loch Aline. Nearby is picturesquely situated Ardtornish Castle, ancient stronghold of the Lords of the Isles. Fuinary, 3 miles W., is the locus of the well-known Gaelic song "Farewell to Fuinary", written by the Scottish divine Norman MacLeod (d. 1862) on leaving his beloved manse of Fuinary.

LOCHALSH. See Kyle of Lochalsh.

LOCH-AN-EILEAN, (eel'an), a small loch near Aviemore with an island on which are the ruins of a stronghold of the Wolf of Badenoch.

LOCHAWE. See Awe, Loch.

LOCHBOISDALE. See Uist, South.

LOCHCARRON, a small place on the north-west shore of Loch Carron, in Ross and Cromarty.

LOCHEARNHEAD, a pretty village at the head of Loch Earn, 13 miles NW. of Callander, popular for water-skiing. Ben Vorlich is to the SE.

Loch Linnhe.

Loch-an-Eilean.

LOCH FELL (2,256 ft.), a mountain of Dumfriesshire 6 miles E. of Moffat.

LOCHGAIR, a small village on Loch Gair, in mid-Argyll, some 10 miles from Lochgilphead. It has excellent fishing.

LOCHGELLY, a burgh 7 miles NE. of Dunfermline, on the now declining Fife coalfield.

LOCHGILPHEAD, a small burgh at the head of Loch Gilp, an arm of Loch Fyne, formerly interested in the herring fishing, now a holiday resort and shopping centre, sharing the administrative responsibilities of the county with Inveraray and Dunoon.

The region in which it stands is rich in historic as well as in prehistoric interest; this is the original home of the Scots who settled Caledonia in the early centuries of our era—their capital was at Dunadd, close to where Lochgilphead now stands. There is sea, loch and river fishing, rough shooting, boating and bathing.

LOCHGOILHEAD, a small holiday place at the head of Loch Goil, Argyllshire, with a steamer pier.

LOCHINDORB, a famous small fishing loch NW. of Grantown. The ruined castle on the island dates back to the 14th century and earlier; it was formerly a stronghold of the Wolf of Badenoch, the predacious Alexander, Earl of Buchan.

LOCHINVAR, a lake in north Kirkcudbrightshire with a ruined castle, famed in Scott's poem *Young Lochinvar*.

LOCHINVER, a small port, fishing village and tourist centre at the head of Loch Inver (west coast of Sutherland). There is excellent fishing and climbing. Behind the village rises the fantastic outline of Suilven. Just N. of the entrance to Loch Inver is Achmelvich, with fine sands. The Falls of Kirkaig are to the S.

LOCHMABEN, a royal burgh in Annandale, Dumfriesshire, 10 miles NE. of Dumfries, with five small lochs in the neighbourhood. The castle is claimed to be the birthplace of Robert the Bruce, though there is evidence that the honour may belong to Turnberry.

LOCHMADDY, a village on Loch Maddy (North Uist) with a hotel, coastguard station and large, modern pier.

LOCHNAGAR, a dark, wild, picturesque mountain (3,786 ft.) of Aberdeenshire, south of the Dee near Balmoral; popularised by Byron in his poem *Lochnagar*. It may be climbed from Braemar (via Clunie Water and Ballater), from Ballater (via Loch Muick and Allt-na-Guibhsaich) or from Crathie. At the foot of its precipitous north-east face is little Loch-na-gar, "Goat Loch" from which it takes its name.

LOCHRANZA, a pleasant resort on a deep sea inlet at the

Opposite: Loch Lomond from Balmaha. (*Tom Weir*).

north end of Arran with a castle of the name associated with Robert Bruce. There is a golf course, tennis courts, dance hall and cinema and interesting walks to the Cock of Arran and Catacol Bay.

LOCHWINNOCH, a small industrial town 9 miles SW. of Paisley, on the shore of Castle Semple Loch.

LOCHWOOD TOWER, a ruined Border stronghold of the Johnstones, 6 miles S. of Moffat, Dumfriesshire.

LOCHY, LOCH, a loch (10 miles long) in the Great Glen, first of a chain running from near Fort William almost to Inverness. The River Lochy flows from the south-west end to enter Loch Linnhe.

LOCKERBIE, a small town in Dumfriesshire, c. 15 miles NE. of Dumfries, important for its lamb fairs. The fierce battle of Dryfe Sands (1594) in which the Johnstones defeated the Maxwells, is referred to in the phrase "a Lockerbie lick".

LOGIERAIT, a village on the River Tay, 5 miles SE. of Pitlochry, in Perthshire. It was once the seat of a Regality Court, from which the powerful Lords of Atholl meted out the harsh justice of their times. The huge, hollow "Ash Tree of the Boat of Logierait" is said to have been the gallows tree.

LOMOND, BEN, a mountain (3,192 ft.) to the east of Loch Lomond, its massive green bulk visible from most parts of the loch, easily climbed by the track from Rowardennan (allow 4 to 5 hours for the double journey). Magnificent views from the summit include the Peaks of Arran, Paps of Jura, Ben Cruachan, the Cobbler, Ben Lui, Stobinian and wide stretches of the Lowlands.

LOMOND HILLS, the highest hills in Fife, in the W. near the Kinross border, comprising West Lomond (1,713 ft.) and East Lomond (1,471 ft.).

LOMOND, LOCH (24 miles by $\frac{3}{4}$ to 5 miles), the largest of Scotland's freshwater lochs, and the largest inland water in Britain. Lies between Dunbartonshire and Stirlingshire. The best approach is by Balloch, thence to Ardlui by car or bus (west shore only) or by loch steamer, if sailing.

Not the least of its charm lies in the "Thirty Islands" scattered over its surface between Luss and Balloch. They include Inchmurrin, with the ruins of Lennox Castle, Inch Cailleach (site of a nunnery), Inch Tavannach (site of a monastery), Clairinch, Inch Fad and Inch Lonaig.

Ascending the loch on the west shore one passes—beyond the large and imposing Loch Lomond Youth Hostel (Auchendennan House)—the hamlet of Arden, Glen Fruin, through which a road runs to Helensburgh, Glen Finlas, Rossdhu (seat of the Colquhoun chief), the charming village of Luss, Inverbeg, and, a little beyond, a path striking upward to Loch an Uaine. Tarbet stands at the east end of the narrow isthmus between Loch Long and Loch Lomond. The important Loch Sloy hydroelectric scheme is a few miles farther on, thence the road skirts Ben Vorlich to Ardlui at the head of the loch.

The north part of the east shore is wild and solitary. Between Ardlui and Rowardennan (c. 12 miles) there is no road, and no village but little Inversnaid, lying snug at the foot of a winding glen leading to the Trossachs. Inversnaid is reached either by ferry from Tarbet or by road via Aberfoyle. To the N. is Rob Roy's Cave, in which Bruce also was a fugitive. To the S. rises Ben Lomond with Ptarmigan between "the Ben" and the shore. On Ptarmigan's slopes is the cave called Rob Roy's Prison. From Rowardennan one may start the ascent of Ben Lomond; here, too, the road begins, running south through Balmaha, Pass of Balmaha and Drymen, back to Balloch.

Loch Lomond district, called "The Lennox", has a long history. In the 13th century Magnus, the Norse King of Man, portaged his galleys across the Arrochar–Tarbet isthmus to make war on the Highland glens. Then and in later years this was the country of MacGregors, Colquhouns, MacFarlanes—all fighting clans—and the scene of many gory battles (notably that in Glen Fruin in 1603 between the MacGregors and the Colquhouns) and of countless raids and forays by the light of "MacFarlane's Lantern"— the moon.

LONG, LOCH, an arm of the sea 24 miles long, running N. from the Clyde, dividing Argyllshire from Dunbartonshire. About halfway up, Loch Goil branches off to the NW.

LONG, LOCH, a small sea-loch in the south-west of Ross-shire, running NE. from Loch Alsh.

LONGFORGAN, a village in east Perthshire. 15th century Castle Huntly is now a corrective training centre for boys.

LONGFORMACUS, a Lammermuir village of Berwickshire, 7 miles NE. of Duns.

LONG ISLAND, THE, the alternative name for the Outer Hebrides, said to have been at one time a single long island, comprises Lewis and Harris, North Uist, Benbecula, South Uist, Eriskay and Barra.

LONGNIDDRY, a charming little town, garden city and golfing resort 14 miles E. of Edinburgh, in East Lothian. The golf course is its best feature, notable even in this golfing county. There are also bowling and putting greens.

LONGSIDE, a small east Aberdeenshire village, c. 6 miles W. of Peterhead.

LORA, FALLS OF, seawater falls or rapids at the narrow mouth of Loch Etive at Connel. Here, where the Connel Bridge crosses the loch, the water at low tide races fiercely and turbulently through its narrow channel.

LORN or LORNE, a district in Argyllshire lying roughly between Loch Etive on the N. and Loch Awe on the S., with Oban as the only place of any size.

LORN, LINN OF, a sea passage between the island of Lismore and the Benderloch Peninsula, Argyllshire.

LOSSIEMOUTH, a fishing port and holiday resort on the Moray Firth, c. 5 miles N. of Elgin on the River Lossie. It occupies a fine bold site with sea on three sides, has a good harbour and a considerable fishing industry. The naval air station is being modernised and developed further. The town is fairly recent growth, built up from several small old villages and a more modern one, Branderburgh. Today it is a delightful seaside resort bright and bracing, with 2 miles of magnificent sands backed by the 18- and 9-hole golf courses of the Moray Golf Club. There is boating, bathing, sea-fishing, angling (salmon, sea-trout, brown trout) in the River Lossie, tennis, bowls and putting. As yet it is comparatively unspoilt. Eastward over the bridge across the Lossie lies the fishing quarter, and here are more sands and extensive sandhills. Westward beyond the bathing beach is Covesea (cow'si) Lighthouse.

Ramsay MacDonald, first Labour prime minister of Britain, was born at Lossiemouth in 1866. He is buried in a tiny old churchyard to the south of the town.

LOTH, a small village 4 miles SW. of Helmsdale on the coast of Sutherland, is where the last wolf in Scotland was killed.

LOTHIANS, THE, a district of south-east Scotland, covered by the counties of West Lothian, Midlothian and East Lothian, named from the part of ancient Northumbria between Forth and Tweed, annexed to Scotland in 1018.

LOWES, LOCH OF THE, a small lake in Selkirkshire, divided from St. Mary's Loch, into which it flows, by a narrow strip of land.

LOWLANDS, THE, the counties of Scotland lying S. and SE. of a line drawn from Stonehaven to Dumbarton, although some people regard Aberdeen, north of Stonehaven, as being part of the Lowlands. As the division is diagonal many parts of the Lowlands are north of the Highlands, and on the Firth of Clyde the east side is Lowland while the west side is Highland. Despite the name, Lowlands, there are several ranges of hills of considerable height, especially in the southernmost counties.

LOWTHER HILLS, a range of hills in north Dumfriesshire and south Lanarkshire. Lowther Hill (2,377 ft.) and Green Lowther (2,403 ft.) are the highest points.

LOYAL, BEN, a mountain (2,504 ft.) near Tongue, in Sutherland, one of the best-known summits of the

NW. and a famous climb. Its four wild peaks of storm-worn granite make a distinctive outline. To the E. lies Loch Loyal.

LOYNE, a glen, loch (hydroelectric dam) and river, this last a tributary of the Moriston (*q.v.*).

LUBNAIG, LOCH, a beautiful loch in Perthshire, NW. of Callander. It is 5 miles long and ½ to ¾ miles broad. In the north it is fed by a river running from Loch Voil through Strathyre, and the River Leny discharges from the southern end. On the south-west of the loch is Ben Ledi.

LUCE ABBEY, on the Water of Luce, *c.* 3 miles N. of Luce Bay, Wigtownshire, is an ancient Cistercian Abbey founded in 1190. The Abbey was once of considerable size, and the former garden and orchard are now the glebe. The remains of the buildings are not very extensive —part of the Scottish Episcopal church, the cloister walls and the decorated chapter house, the latter in a better state of preservation.

LUCE BAY, a large bay on the Solway Firth, in Wigtownshire. The extensive Sands of Luce lie at the head of the bay.

LUI, BEN, a mountain (3,708 ft.) to the east of Dalmally (Argyll).

LUICHART, LOCH, a loch of central Ross and Cromarty, a reservoir link in extensive hydroelectric scheme workings.

LUING, an island of Argyll, S. of Seil Island. Like Seil, it was formerly noted for its slate quarries. West of the island is Luing Sound.

LUMPHANAN, a cattle-rearing village of south Aberdeenshire, *c.* 25 miles W. of Aberdeen. On the hill to the north-west of the village is Macbeth's Cairn, where he is reputed to have been slain after his defeat at Dunsinane.

LUMSDEN, a small Aberdeenshire village 12 miles S. of Huntly.

LUNAN, a seaside village on Lunan Bay, Angus, 6 miles S. of Montrose. At the north end of the bay, and at Red Head, just south of it, is fascinating rock scenery.

LUNCARTY, a small village, 4 miles N. of Perth, traditional scene of the defeat of the Danes by Kenneth III in 990. The story goes that a peasant named Hay, armed with a plough-yoke, rallied the breaking ranks of the Scots and turned the fortunes of the day. Several families of Hays still claim this heroic ancestor.

Loch Lubnaig.   *Overleaf: Loch Maree.*

LUNDIN LINKS, a small place adjoining Largo (Fife), 2 miles NE. of Leven, noted for its fine sands, golf links and its standing stones.

LUSS, a pretty village on the west side of Loch Lomond.

LYBSTER, a fishing village of Caithness, *c.* 14 miles SW. of Wick.

LYNE, a village, *c.* 5 miles W. of Peebles, with an old church and remains of a Roman camp.

LYON, a river and glen in Perthshire to the N. of Loch Tay, leading from Loch Lyon, a hydroelectric reservoir of the Breadalbane scheme.

MACDHUI, BEN, the highest point (4,296 ft.) of the Cairngorms (*q.v.*)

MACDUFF, a small town and prosperous fishing port on the Moray Firth, facing Banff across the estuary of the Deveron. It has an excellent and interesting harbour recently extended, with a fish market. Angling is available in the Deveron. At the east end of Macduff there is a good golf course, and below it, on the shore, the attractive Tarlair swimming pools, over which towers the "Needle's E'e" rock: the mineral spring here no longer flows.
Macduff was built in 1783 around the nucleus of a hamlet called Doune or Down, by an earl of Fife who named it from one of his titles Road traffic is carried W. by an imposing bridge over the Deveron.

MACHRIE, a seaside hamlet on the west coast of Arran, with a golf course and stream fishing.

MACHRIHANISH, a pleasant little resort on the west coast of Kinytre, on Machrihanish Bay. It has a famous golf course bordering the dunes and an aerodrome.

MACKINNON'S CAVE, a huge cavern on the west coast of the island of Mull, near Gribun.

MACLEOD'S MAIDENS, MACLEOD'S TABLES. See Dunvegan.

MAESHOWE, a tumulus on the mainland of Orkney, 9 miles W. of Kirkwall, near the shores of Loch Harray. It is a circular mound, 115 ft. in diameter and 24 ft. high, surrounded by a 45 ft. wide ditch. It is entered by a passage 36 ft. long which leads to a central chamber 15 ft. square with three small cells off it. Much of the structure is built of huge stone slabs, the rest of irregularly-coursed masonry, the whole being covered with earth. On some of the stones of the main chamber are runic inscriptions.

MAIDENS, a small coastal village, *c.* 7 miles N. of Girvan, in Ayrshire, in growing favour as a resort, with facilities for sea-fishing and boating. Here Bruce landed from Arran when he came to do battle for Scotland, summoned it is said by a mysterious beacon, popularly ascribed to supernatural agency, on Bogle's Brae.

MALLAIG, an important fishing station and route centre on the west coast of Inverness-shire, near the entrance to Loch Nevis, a rail terminus connecting with steamers for Skye and other islands of the Outer and Inner Hebrides.

MAMBEG, a small place on the west shore of the Gareloch, Dunbartonshire.

MAM SOUL, a mountain (3,862 ft.) NW. of Loch Affric, Inverness-shire.

MAR, an ancient district of Aberdeenshire giving name to the Earls of Mar.

MAR LODGE, a former royal residence and skiing centre on Deeside.

MAREE, LOCH, a freshwater loch (18 miles long) near the west coast of Ross-shire, joined to Loch Ewe (sea-loch) by the short River Ewe. Its picturesque wooded islets include Eilean Suthainn (1 mile long with three small lochans), Eilean Ruairidh and the small but interesting Eilean Maree, with the ruins of an early Christian chapel. The hotel is nearly opposite. Salmon, sea-trout and brown trout abound in loch and river.

MARKINCH, a small Fifeshire burgh, *c.* 7 miles N. of Kirkcaldy, with industries of papermaking, blanket weaving and whisky blending. For the visitor there is fishing, tennis and bowls. It has a fine old 12th century church with a Norman tower.

MARWICK HEAD, a headland on the NW. of the mainland of Orkney, on which is a memorial to Lord Kitchener who was drowned when the *Hampshire* sank off the coast in 1916.

MAUCHLINE, a village of Ayrshire, 12 miles NE. of Ayr, has many links with Burns, including Poosie Nansie's Inn—scene of *The Jolly Beggars*—and the churchyard setting of *The Holy Fair*. Gavin Hamilton's house, where Burns married Jean

Armour, and the nearby house in which they afterwards lived, may be seen, along with the ruins of Mauchline Castle.

MAXWELLTOWN, formerly a burgh in Kirkcudbrightshire is now part of the town of Dumfries (*q.v.*).

MAXWELTON HOUSE, a mansion *c.* 12 miles NW. of Dumfries is where Annie Laurie, celebrated in song, was born.

MAY, ISLE OF, a small island (1 mile long) in the Firth of Forth, off the coast of Fife between Anstruther and Crail. It has a lighthouse and remains of a 13th century chapel dedicated to St. Adrian, whose stone coffin is said to have floated from its burial place on the island, and drifted to the Fife shore (see Anstruther). It is noted also for its bird life, and has a bird watching station.

MAYBOLE, a small manufacturing town (boots and shoes and agricultural implements), standing high amid delightful surroundings, *c.* 8 miles S. of Ayr. It has a 9-hole golf course, tennis, bowls, good fishing in local waters, sea-bathing at (4 miles) the splendid sands of Culzean Bay. Culzean Castle (pron. kil-ane; part of it the Scottish home of Mr. Eisenhower) is situated on a cliff overlooking the sea. The castle is open to the public and its grounds are included in a National Park. The Tolbooth, Tower and remains of the old collegiate church in Maybole are noteable, also the Provost's house where John Knox engaged the Abbot of Crossraguel in a theological discussion lasting three days!

2 or 3 miles SW. are the very fine (and singularly complete) ruins of Crossraguel Abbey (13th century) including the massive gateway, nave and chancel of the church and a graceful chapter house with a beautiful groined roof. Casillis House is about 3 miles NE. of Maybole.

MEALL FUARVONIE, a mountain (2,284 ft.) on the western shore of Loch Ness (Inverness-shire).

MEARNS, THE, another name for Kincardineshire.

MEIGLE, a village of Perthshire, c. 16 miles NW. of Dundee. Here is a museum in which is a group of sculptured stones, said to have marked the grave of Queen Guinevere, wife of King Arthur. According to tradition she was imprisoned on Barry Hill, nearby.

MEIKLEOUR, a hamlet 4 miles S. of Blairgowrie in Perthshire, distinguished by the famous beech hedges on the main Perth – Blairgowrie road. The hedges are ¼-mile long and 80 ft. high, and are seldom without their interested and amazed admirers.

MELFORT, PASS OF, a picturesque rocky pass between Kilninver and Kilmelfort, some 12 miles S. of Oban. The River Oude flows through it into Loch Melfort. Motor coach tours run regularly from Oban to this notable beauty spot.

MELLON CHARLES, a small place on Loch Ewe, Wester Ross, with fine bathing sands.

MELNESS, a hamlet on the west shore of Tongue Bay, Sutherland, where the French sloop *Hasard* ran aground while bringing help to Bonnie Prince Charlie. Rabbit Island can be reached on foot at low tide.

MELROSE, a small town on the River Tweed, 7 miles NE. of Selkirk, visited for its beautiful abbey and its position in the heart of the Scott Country. There is golf, fishing, tennis, putting and bowls. A 3-day Festival in June includes the crowning of the Melrose Queen in the grounds of the abbey.

Founded in 1136 by David I, "Fair Melrose" is the loveliest of the southern Scottish abbeys. Like the others it suffered the full effects of Border warfare,

Beech Hedges,
Meikleour.

Melrose Abbey.   (*Scottish Tourist Board*).

and like them was finally destroyed by the Earl of Hertford (1544–45). The considerable remains comprise the eastern part of the abbey church—nave, transepts, chancel—a fragment of the tower and two of its piers (exquisitely carved), also the chapter house and reredorter. Features to note are the beautiful stone screen between nave and choir, the large, finely traceried 5-light window in the south transept, and the fine fretted stone roof in the chancel. Beneath the 5-light east window rests the heart of Robert the Bruce, which Douglas was carrying to the Holy Land when he was overcome by the Moors in Spain. Close by are the tombs of the Douglases, and of Michael Scott the Wizard. The abbey was presented to the nation by the Duke of Buccleuch in 1918. Existing ruins are mainly 14th and 15th century, with only slight fragments of the original church.

To the N. Melrose extends across the Tweed as Gattonside. Fruit is grown here. Gattonside Moss is of interest to botanists. To the S. are the three peaks of the Eildon Hills.

MELVICH, a crofting village on the north coast of Sutherland, 17 miles W. of Thurso, at the mouth of the River Halladale, with angling facilities.

MENNOCK, a village, pass, and stream in Dumfriesshire, south of Leadhills.

MENSTRIE, a small distilling town at the foot of the Ochils, birthplace (1734) of Sir Ralph Abercromby the famous general.

MENTEITH, LAKE OF, a small loch eastward of Aberfoyle. Here, on the island of Inchmahome, Mary Queen of Scots spent her early childhood with her companions before she sailed for France. A little garden is shown, said to be the one she tended with her own hands. R. B. Cunninghame Graham, Scottish writer and patriot, is buried on the island. On the north shore of the loch is Port of Menteith.

MERRICK HILLS, a range of hills in south Ayrshire. The best-known summits are Merrick (2,764 ft.), Kirriereoch (2,562 ft.) and Shalloch-on-Minnoch (2,520 ft.).

MERSE, THE, a plain N. of the Tweed, in Berwickshire and Roxburghshire, where the river forms the boundary between England and Scotland.

METHIL. See Buckhaven.

METHLICK, a village on the River Ythan (Aberdeenshire), 8 miles NW. of Ellon. It has fishing in the Ythan (salmon, sea-trout, finnock). Nearby is the ruined old castle of Gight, the home of Lady Catherine Gordon, mother of Lord Byron. Lower down the river, the fine Adam mansion of Haddo House (seat of the Marquis of Aberdeen) stands in beautiful and extensive grounds.

METHVEN (mef'en) a village 6 miles W. of Perth, noted for the remains of its 15th century church, and for Methven Castle with its fine old trees, including the famous Pepperwell Oak (400 years old). 4 miles up Glenalmond is the well-known public school of Trinity College, Glenalmond. A little to the east is Huntingtower, familiar from the ballad of the same name.

MEY, a hamlet in the north of Caithness, 13 miles E. of Thurso. Nearby are the Loch of Mey, Mey Bay, and the Men of Mey, jagged rocks off St. John's Point. Here is the Castle of Mey, a picturesque 17th century structure owned by Queen Elizabeth the Queen Mother.

MHOR, LOCH, a freshwater loch to the east of Loch Ness.

MIDCALDER, a small town on the River Almond, 12 miles SW. of Edinburgh. There is an ancient parish church and nearby is the mansion of Calder House, where John Knox first administered the sacraments according to the Protestant rite.

MIDLOTHIAN, formerly Edinburghshire, a Lowland county extending 12 miles along the southern shore of the Firth of Forth. There are hill pastures on the Pentland Hills (Scald Law 1,898 ft.) and Moorfoot Hills (Blackhope Scar, 2,137 ft.); lesser heights around Edinburgh include Arthur's Seat (823 ft.). A few small rivers—Esk, Water of Leith, and Almond—water the northern plain with its dairy-farming and market and nursery gardening. Papermaking, electronics and plastics manufacture, and precision engineering are important industries and there are coalmines in the E. Edinburgh is the administrative centre of the county, but is itself a county of a city. Other towns are Dalkeith, Musselburgh, Penicuik and the Calders.

MILLPORT, on Great Cumbrae, in the Firth of Clyde, is the only town on the Cumbraes, a pleasant little resort on Millport Bay. The most noteworthy building is the Scottish Episcopal Cathedral of the Isles. There are golfing, boating and bathing facilities, and a good steamer service.

MILNATHORT, a small town in Kinross-shire, near the north end of Loch Leven.

MILNGAVIE (mil-gī'), a pleasant little town of Stirlingshire, on the Allander Water, *c.* 5 miles N. of Glasgow, of which it is practically a suburb. Mugdock Castle, to the north, is a picturesque structure embodying an ancient tower. Craigallion Loch and the Whangie are other easy objectives.

MILTON OF CLOVA, a small place in Glen Clova, Angus, *c.* 18 miles NW. of Forfar.

MINARD, a village on Loch Fyne, once a centre of the herring fishing industry, now mainly concerned with afforestation.

MINCH, THE, and LITTLE MINCH, THE. The Minch or North Minch is a sea channel between the Outer Hebrides and the mainland, 25 to 45 miles wide, with great depth and a rapid current. The Little Minch, its southern extension, lies between Skye and the shores of Harris and North Uist.

MINGARY CASTLE, a ruined fortress in Argyllshire, on the south coast of the Ardnamurchan Peninsula, opposite the Sound of Mull. It was a seat of the MacIans, a branch of the Macdonalds, and it was here that the chieftains of the Isles submitted to James IV in 1495.

MINGULAY, a small island with precipitous cliffs at the southern end of the Outer Hebrides.

MINTLAW, a village of east Aberdeenshire, 8 miles W. of Peterhead, is the site of a 13th century Cistercian Abbey, recently re-dedicated.

MISTY LAW HILLS, a range of hills in west Renfrewshire, the Hill of Stake (1,711 ft.) being the highest point.

MOFFAT, a small town in Annandale, Dumfriesshire, 21 miles NE. of Dumfries. It is an angling and golfing centre, surrounded by lovely country, ideal for hill-walking. Mineral springs were discovered here in 1633, and during the 18th century Moffat was a popular spa. The wells are to the NE. of the town. It was in Moffat House that James Macpherson worked on the Ossianic poems published in 1760–63, which caused a great controversy in literary circles. Macadam, inventor of "macadamising" of roads, is buried in the churchyard. To the N. of the town is the Devil's Beef Tub.

MOIDART, a small lonely sea-loch and a peninsula on the west coast of Inverness-shire, just to the north of the wild Argyllshire district of Ardnamurchan. North-east of the loch is the Moidart Peninsula. Kinlochmoidart is near its head.

MONADHLIATH, a range of mountains north of the Spey valley in Inverness-shire with several summits around 3,000 ft., including

Moffat.

Chailleach (3,045 ft.) and Carn Mairg (3,093 ft.).

MONIAIVE, 16 miles NW. of Dumfries, was created a burgh of barony under charter of Charles I and has an old market cross. There is a monument to James Renwick, a native of Moniaive, who was the last Covenanter to be executed (17th February 1688).

MONIFIETH, a resort 5 miles E. of Dundee, on the north shore of the Firth of Tay. To the east are Barry Links and Buddon Camp, a renowned military training ground. Here also are Buddon Ness, and lighthouses.

MONKTON, an Ayrshire village, on the Northern boundary of Prestwick International Airport. Has an old ruined church, with Romanesque doorway.

MONREITH, See Port William.

MONTGARRIE, a small village in the Howe of Alford, Aberdeenshire.

MONTROSE, an ancient town and popular seaside and golfing resort of Angus. Its castle (long vanished) had associations with William the Lion and James VI. To the W. is the lakelike Montrose Basin, across which the road is carried by a bridge. Tourist attractions include 4 miles of magnificent sands, two 18-hole golf courses (one of championship standard) and a 9-hole pitch-and-putt course, tennis, bowls, bathing, boating, fishing in the North and South Esk and local waters (salmon, sea-trout, brown trout).

Loch Morar.

MONYMUSK, 19 miles WNW. of Aberdeen, a charming and secluded little village just off the main road. The Norman parish church is part of a priory founded in 1078 by Malcolm Canmore, has a fine round-headed doorway and a granite tower, most of which belongs to the original structure. The House of Monymusk, a delightful mansion said to have been built from the stones of the priory, stands in the Don valley, and the "Woods of Paradise" bring visitors from far and near to view the magnificent trees, planted in 1720 and still flourishing, except for a few destroyed by a phenomenal gale in 1953.

MOORFOOT HILLS, a range of moorland hills in the southern part of Midlothian and the north of Peeblesshire.

MORAR, a hamlet, loch and river on the south-west coast of Inverness-shire. The loch is small but reputedly the deepest in Britain. The short river connects it with the sea. Morar stands at the mouth of the river and it is noted for its fine sands and angling (river, loch and sea).

MORAY, an ancient province in the north-east, comprising roughly the modern shires of Moray and Nairn, and parts of Inverness and Banff. Of its powerful rulers (mormaers), predecessors of the later earls, Macbeth is best remembered. The Diocese of Moray had, from the 13th century, its splendid cathedral at Elgin; the modern Episcopalian united Diocese of Moray, Ross and Caithness has its cathedral at Inverness.

MORAYSHIRE, formerly Elgin-shire, a north-east county with a north seaboard about 35 miles long on the Moray Firth. Along the coast is a low plain, the Laigh of Moray, from which the surface rises to 2,328 ft. (Cromdale Hills) on the southern border. Rivers are the Spey, Lossie and Findhorn. The climate is notably mild and dry, and the district enjoys fame both for agriculture and holidaymaking. The Spey valley is renowned for its whisky distilleries. Manufactures include woollens at Elgin and fruit and vegetable preserving at Foch-abers. Moray combines with Nairn for most administrative purposes.

MORAY FIRTH, the triangular bight of the North Sea having at its apex Inverness, at the head of the Inner Moray Firth (Inverness Firth). Seawards it extends to a line from Tarbet Ness (Easter Ross) to Lossiemouth (Moray) or even to a line from Duncansby Head (Caith-ness) to Kinnaird Head (Aberdeen). It gives name to a smoked haddock.

MORE, BEN, the name of several mountains, most notably Ben More Assynt (3,273 ft.) at the head of Loch Assynt (Sutherland), a peak (3,843 ft.) in Perthshire to the east of Crianlarich, and the highest summit (3,185 ft.) of Mull.

MOREBATTLE, a village (angling centre) of Roxburghshire, 8 miles NE. of Jedburgh. Nearby is Corbet Tower.

MORHAM, a village 3 miles SE. of Haddington, which claims to be the birthplace of John Knox (but see Haddington).

MORISTON, GLEN, a large well-wooded glen in Inverness-shire, running W. from Loch Ness, traversed by the River Moriston, which flows from Loch Cluanie at the head of the glen. Invermoriston is at the foot of the glen. Lochs Cluanie, Loyne, and Dundreggan are reservoirs in the Moriston power scheme.

MORVEN or MORVERN, a dist-rict of northern Argyll, rather smaller than Mull, from which it is separated by the Sound of Mull and Loch Sunart. Like Mull it is wild and mountainous and sparsely popu-lated, and is itself almost an island. Lochaline is on its southern shore.

MORVEN, a mountain (2,862 ft.) in south Caithness, c. 9 miles N. of Helmsdale.

MOSSGIEL, a farm north of Mauchline, Ayrshire, the home of Robert Burns from 1784–88.

MOSSPAUL, a small place on the Ewes Water, c. 10 miles N. of Langholm, Dumfriesshire.

MOTHERWELL and WISHAW, industrial towns to the SE. of Glasgow, now united in a single burgh.

MOUSA, an island off the east coast of the mainland of Shetland, which has a celebrated broch in an excellent state of preservation. It is 43 ft. 6 ins. high, and 50 ft. in diameter at the base, 40 ft. at the top. It is entered by a passage at the foot, and contains cells, stairs and galleries. It is built of flat stones and no mortar was used.

MOY, a small village on the shores of Loch Moy, Inverness-shire, 10 miles SE. of Inverness. Moy Hall, at the north end of the loch, is the seat of the chief of the Clan Mackintosh. On an island in the loch are ruins of an ancient castle.

MUCHALLS, a picturesque holi-day place on the cliffs, 4 miles N. of Stonehaven, noted for its fine rock scenery. It has a 9-hole golf course.

MUCK (Muic, boar—probably from its shape), a small and isolated farming island S. of Eigg, off the coast of Inverness-shire. Some lobster fishing is carried on.

MUCKLE FLUGGA, the most northerly lighthouse in Britain, on a rock off Hermaness, Unst, Shetland.

MUICK, a loch, glen and river, with a linn, of Aberdeenshire. The latter runs into the Dee, near Ballater. Birkhall, a royal residence, is near the foot of the glen.

MUIRKIRK, a coal-mining town 26 miles E. of Ayr.

MUIR OF ORD, a growing village of Ross-shire, 15 miles north of Inverness. Here the main north road sends off branches to Garve (for Kyle of Lochalsh, Gairloch and Ullapool), and to the Black Isle (for Fortrose and Cromarty). There is a pleasant golf course on the moor where large stock markets formerly took place.

MULL, the largest of Argyll-shire's islands, roughly 30 miles by 29 miles, separated from the mainland by the Sound of Mull. It is very mountainous and wild, with numerous lochs and inlets and rivers. The wide bight on its west side includes Loch Tuath and Loch na Keal, separated by the island of Ulva (the "Ulva's Isle" of Campbell's poem, *Lord Ullin's Daughter*), and Loch Scridain to the S. Iona and Staffa (*qq.v.*) lie off the west coast.

The only burgh on Mull is Tobermory (*q.v.*). The steep eastern (landward) side has very few people, but many of the ancient clan strongholds were here (*e.g.*, Duart Castle). Mull has an old and stormy clan history, and is still held by two septs of the clan MacLean. The island is a paradise for the sportsman with rod or gun, or for the climber (highest summit, Ben More, 3,185 ft.). Mull is now served by a drive on/drive off car ferry from Oban to Craignure on the south of the island, with a connection to Lochaline on the mainland. The normal steamer service still operates from Oban to Tobermory. Several roads are being reconstructed or developed.

MULLARDOCH, LOCH. See Cannich.

MUSSELBURGH, a quaint old fishing town, also an old golfing town, of Midlothian, at the mouth of the River Esk, 5 miles E. of Edinburgh. Race meetings (Mussel-burgh Races), are held here in the season. The noted public school of Loretto takes its name from the chapel of Our Lady of Loretto, which stood on the site, and includes in its buildings Pinkie House.

NAIRN, an old royal burgh and county town of Nairnshire, a favourite golfing and holiday resort, at the mouth of the River Nairn, 16 miles E. of Inverness. There are good sands, three golf courses (two 18-hole), fishing in the Nairn, Findhorn, Lossie, Spey and in local lochs, bathing, boating, tennis, bowls. The old Town Cross is in the High Street, which at its east end leads down to the picturesque Fishertown. The most interesting historic feature is Cawdor Castle (5 miles SW.) traditionally the scene of the murder of King Duncan by Macbeth. The existing structure dates from the 15th to 17th centuries. Also in the vicinity are Kilravock (kil-rok') and Dalcross castles.

NAIRNSHIRE, a pleasant maritime county on the Moray Firth, E. of Inverness-shire; a breezy, broomy county of wide spaces, gentle hills and fir woods. Nairn is the only town. The north-west corner is watered by the River Nairn, centre by the River Findhorn, both of which afford excellent fishing.

NAN UAMH, LOCH ("loch of the caves"), a beautiful rocky sea-loch on the west coast of Inverness-shire. Prince Charlie's frigate *La Doutelle*, with the prince and his seven followers on board, anchored here on 25th July 1745. A cairn commemorates the departure of the defeated prince from here in 1746.

NAVER, a loch, river and strath in Sutherland. The lovely loch, 6 miles long, is skirted by the road on the north shore. The River Naver flows from the north-east end of the loch, through Strath Naver to the north coast, and enters the sea near Bettyhill.

NEIDPATH CASTLE, a keep situated on the Tweed, 1 mile W. of Peebles. The castle, till 1312 a

Dulsie Bridge, Nairn.

stronghold of the Frasers, in the early 15th century passed to the Hays of Yester. As a Royalist garrison it suffered attack and defeat by Cromwell. It is open to the public.

NELL, LOCH ("loch of the swans"), a small freshwater loch SE. of Oban, offering excellent fishing. The artificial island at the Kilmore end is the remains of a prehistoric lake-dwelling, and has a concealed underwater causeway. Nearby is the 300-foot-long serpentine grassy hill called the Serpent's Mound, probably an ancient burial mound.

NESS, LOCH, an inland loch, 24 miles long, extending from Fort Augustus to within a few miles of Inverness, and occupying about half the length of the Great Glen. The Loch Ness Monster has been seen in recent years by both tourists and natives, and is almost too well authenticated to be classed among the local legends. From the loch the River Ness flows 6 miles, through the town of Inverness, to the Inner Moray Firth.

NETHYBRIDGE, a village 10 miles NE. of Aviemore, spring headquarters of the Scottish Ski Club Rally, an attractive centre for walking. Abernethy church and the ruined Castle Roy are ¾ mile to the north-east.

NEVIS, BEN, the highest mountain (4,406 ft.) in Britain, SE. of Fort William (*q.v.*). There is an easy ascent by a track. Much more difficult, but rewarding in its magnificent views, is the so-called Allt a

Mhoullin route. Other still more dangerous routes are for practised rock-climbers only. Glen Nevis, through which flows the Water of Nevis, flanks the mountain on the S. and W.

NEVIS, LOCH, a wild sea-inlet of Inverness-shire, in the mainland opposite the south end of Skye.

NEW ABBEY, a picturesque village, 6 miles S. of Dumfries, with the ruins of Sweetheart Abbey. The Abbey, in Early English and Decorated styles, was founded for the Cistercian Order in 1273 by Devorguilla, who is buried, with her husband's heart, before the high altar—hence Dulce Cor or Sweetheart Abbey. Although practically roofless, all the main arches, a 90 ft. central tower, parts of the transepts, etc. remain.

NEWBATTLE ABBEY, a mansion 1 mile SE. of Dalkeith, on the site of a 12th century Cistercian foundation, the crypt and basement of which are incorporated in the present building. The Abbey is now used as a residential college for adult education.

NEWBURGH, a village and small seaport at the mouth of the River Ythan, 12 miles N. of Aberdeen. It is a good angling centre with trout and finnock in the Ythan—also pearl mussels. The largest pearl in the Scottish Regalia was taken from the Ythan, and presented to James VI by an Aberdeen provost. Aberdeen University has a zoological field station here.
NE. of Newburgh are the Forvie Sands, covering a buried village, and beyond this stretches a coastline of sand dunes interspersed with magnificent rocks and cliffs.

NEWBURGH, a royal burgh of north Fife, on the Firth of Tay, an attractive little place with a linoleum industry and a small harbour.

NEWCASTLETON, a village of Liddesdale, Roxburghshire, *c.* 20 miles S. of Hawick. To the S. of the village is Mangerton Tower, one of the many Border fortresses that once guarded Liddesdale.

NEW CUMNOCK, a mining village in Ayrshire, 5 miles SE. of Cumnock, situated near the confluence of the Nith and the Afton.

NEW DEER, a pleasant agricultural village and route centre 12 miles NNW. of Ellon in Aberdeenshire. The village of Old Deer lies 5 miles to the E.

NEW GALLOWAY, an attractive little royal burgh, situated on the Ken, 17 miles N. of Kirkcudbright. With Loch Ken and the Rhinns of Kells (2,668 ft., 2,446 ft. etc.) in the vicinity, the village is a good centre for angling and climbing, while the beauty and interest of the surrounding countryside reward the walker. Kenmure Castle and Kells churchyard (Covenanter's grave) lie respectively a little to the S. and N.

NEWHAVEN, a fishing port founded by James IV, on the Forth between Granton and Leith, famous for its "fishwives' choir" and for the "Peacock Inn".

NEWMILNS, a town of Ayrshire, 8 miles E. of Kilmarnock, with lace and muslin manufactures.

NEW PITSLIGO, a large village of Aberdeenshire, 20 miles WNW. of Peterhead, formerly the centre of an (illicit) distilling industry. Remains of a Roman settlement have recently come to light.

NEWPORT, a burgh and pleasantly situated resort of north Fife, on the Firth of Tay, at the south end of the Tay Road Bridge, between Fife and Dundee. It has tennis, bowls and golf at Scotscraig golf course (3 miles).

NEWTONMORE, a village 3 miles W. of Kingussie on the Spey. It has a golf course, good trout-fishing in the Spey and other waters and is a skiing and pony-trekking centre.

NEWTON STEWART, a picturesque little weaving town (mohair) of Wigtownshire, situated on the banks of the Cree, 4 miles from its mouth. There are golf and fishing facilities. It is an excellent centre for visiting such beauty spots as Loch Trool, and Bargaly Glen. To the E. is Cairnsmore of Fleet (2,331 ft.). Two bridges (one a suspension) cross the river, on the other side of which is Minnigaff, an old village with a ruined church; in the churchyard are many carved stones.

NEWTON ST. BOSWELLS, a village of Roxburghshire, 3 miles SE. of Melrose, once noted for its great gipsy fairs. St. Boswells (1 mile away) adjoins St. Boswells Green, with its considerable expanse of "green". Across the Tweed from here is Dryburgh Abbey (*q.v.*). Nearby is Lessudden House (16th–17th century).

NIGG, a scattered village on the east side of Nigg Bay, on the Cromarty Firth. There is a golf course, good sands and bathing, and a ferry (by arrangement) to Cromarty on the south side of the firth.

Newton Stewart and the Cree.

NINE MILE BURN, a hamlet 9 miles SW. of Edinburgh on the south slopes of the Pentland Hills, over which there is from here a path to Balerno.

NITH, a river flowing through Dumfries to the Solway Firth, known for its tidal bore and for its " haaf-net " fishers. At New Cumnock it is joined by the "sweet Afton" of the poet Burns.

NITHSDALE, the westernmost of the three principal districts of Dumfriesshire, constituted largely of the valley of the River Nith.

NORTH BERWICK, East
Lothian's renowned and popular seaside resort, an ancient royal burgh, on the Firth of Forth, 22 miles E. of Edinburgh. The chief occupation is golf : the burgh has two 18-hole courses and a golfing tradition running back for more than three hundred years. There is also a wide choice of golf links in the neighbourhood. Seaside amenities include two delightful sandy beaches and a small but well-appointed swimming pool, sheltered by the Platcock Rocks. One also has putting, tennis, bowls, and entertainments in the pavilion adjoining the swimming pool, and an endless succession of events—galas, golf and bowling competitions, fêtes, parades and regattas.

The town itself is interesting, with its narrow High Street and red-tiled Town Meeting House in Quality Street, its quaint old harbour, busy mainly with pleasure craft. There are slight remains of its ancient church—like Alloway Kirk, a haunt of witches and wizards. No fewer than 94 were involved in a

SCENES NEAR OBAN.

Top left: *Ruins of Coeffin Castle, Lismore.*
Lower left: *Dunstaffnage Castle (Print).*
Lower right: *Sanctuary Cross, Kilchomain, Islay.*

famous trial (1591), accused of dancing to the strains of a Jew's harp on the Anchor Green before the Kirk.

Outstanding feature of the landscape is Berwick Law (612 ft.), a conical volcanic hill rising abruptly from the flat, and offering splendid views. Seawards the Bass Rock catches the eye, and the smaller islands of Fidra (lighthouse), Craigleith and the Lamb. The imposing ruins of Tantallon Castle stand on a bold high headland to the SE., and date from the 14th century, figuring in history and Scott's *Marmion*.

NORTH QUEENSFERRY, a village at the north end of the Forth Rail and Road Bridges, formerly a ferry landing place. Quarrying is an industry and the village has some old-world features.

OA, MULL OF, a headland at the southernmost point of Islay. At Upper Killeyan, nearby, is a memorial to American soldiers drowned off the coast.

OAKWOOD, a hamlet in Ettrickdale, Selkirkshire, 5 miles SW. of Selkirk. According to Scott Oakwood Tower was the home of his namesake, Michael Scott the "Wondrous Wizard"; not however the present tower.

OBAN

A POPULAR resort on Oban Bay, on the west coast of Argyll. It is built on wooded hills overlooking the Bay, with a fine outlook over Kerrera to the mountains of Mull, glimpses of Loch Linnhe, the Sound of Mull and the Firth of Lorne.

Oban has considerable fisheries, an old distillery and a more recent woollen mill. It holds large sheep and cattle sales every year. There are two golf courses, tennis, bowls, good fishing waters within easy reach, yachting, boating, bathing and seafishing. This is the headquarters of the Royal Highland Yacht Club; yacht races and regattas are held, which with the Argyllshire Gathering (Oban Games) form the highlights of the Oban season.

Amenities include a fine stretch of bathing sands at Ganavan, 2 miles distant (frequent bus service), Dungallan Parks (also by the sea) and the pretty little Corran Park on the Esplanade. The Pulpit Hill above the Railway Pier is a vantage point, and the Cathedral of Trees at Glencruitten a feature of interest. Notable buildings are the fine Roman Catholic Cathedral (modern—Sir Giles G. Scott) and the roofless "Colosseum" called MacCaig's Tower. The

Oban from the Harbour.   *(Scottish Tourist Board).*

latter was built in the late 19th century by an Oban townsman, partly as a family memorial, but mainly to give work in a depressed period.

At the north point of the Bay is the ivy-clad ruin of Dunollie Castle, after many centuries still in the hands of the MacDougalls, one of whose treasured possessions is the Brooch of Lorne, taken from Robert the Bruce at Dalrigh.

Four miles N. of Oban is Dunstaffnage Castle, beautifully situated on a woody promontory of the Firth of Lorne. It is said to be an ancient capital of the Dalriadic Scots. The Stone of Destiny rested here before it was taken to Scone in 850. Hereditary Keepers are the Dukes of Argyll, Hereditary Captains the Campbells of Dunstaffnage. The present holder of the title is the 22nd Hereditary Captain. From Oban tours and cruises run to Staffa and Iona, to Tobermory, Fort William, Inverness, to Corrievreckan, Kyles of Bute, Inveraray, Dunoon; local tours of varying lengths to Easdale and Melfort, Loch Nell and Pass of Brander. One of the most popular day tours is the road-rail-and-water round trip to Glencoe, which includes a motor yacht cruise on Loch Etive.

OCHIL HILLS, a pastoral range in Perth, Fife, Kinross, Clackmannan and Stirling shires. Summits are Ben Cleuch (2,363 ft.), King's Seat (2,111 ft.) and Whitewisp (2,110 ft.).

OCHILTREE, a village 11 miles E. of Ayr. It was here that John Knox married his second wife, daughter of Lord Ochiltree.

OGLE, GLEN, a picturesque glen of Perthshire, traversed by the road between Lochearnhead and Killin.

OICH, LOCH, the central loch of the Great Glen chain, 4 miles long. About midway on its north-west shore, at the mouth of Glen Garry, is the ruined Invergarry Castle, where Prince Charles Edward lodged after Culloden. It stands on a picturesque rock called Craig an Fhithich, ("rock of the raven").

OLD DEER, a village 9 miles W. of Peterhead in Aberdeenshire, site of a Columban monastery founded in the 6th century. The famous Book of Deer (now in the Cambridge University Library) is a 9th century Latin MS transcript of parts of the New Testament, with Gaelic marginal references to current and monastic affairs—the first appearance in writing of Scots Gaelic. Deer Abbey is a ruined Cistercian monastery beside the South Ugie river, founded by William Comyn, Earl of Buchan, in the early part of the 13th century (open to visitors). Old Deer was also the scene of the Bruce-Comyn battle of Aikey Brae, fought in 1308. New Deer (*q.v.*) lies to the west.

OLDHAMSTOCKS, a pretty village in the Lammermuir Hills, 8 miles SE. of Dunbar.

OLD KILPATRICK, a village on the Clyde between Dumbarton and Clydebank, at the foot of the Kilpatrick Hills. It has a shipbuilding industry. St. Patrick's Well is a relic of the patron saint of Ireland, said to have been born here. Here Erskine Ferry crosses the Clyde on the southward route. On the south side of the river, among trees, is Erskine House, the Princess Louise Home for Limbless Soldiers and Sailors.

OLD MAN OF HOY. See Hoy.

OLDMELDRUM, a village 4 miles NE. of Inverurie (Aberdeenshire) with fishing in the Ythan, Urie and smaller streams (salmon, sea, brown and burn trout). Nearby is Barra Hill, where in 1308 was fought the Battle of Inverurie (see Inverurie).

ONICH, a little village at the mouth of Loch Leven, 1 mile W. of North Ballachulish, with fishing and boating facilities. At the Corran Narrows of Loch Linnhe (just to the northwest) a vehicular ferry plies to Ardgour.

OPINAN, a small place on the S. of Loch Gairloch, Ross-shire.

ORCHY, a river in Argyllshire which flows south-west from Loch Tulla through Glen Orchy, and Strath of Orchy, and runs into Loch Awe a little west of Dalmally. Bridge of Orchy, a hamlet, stands on the river about 3 miles S. of Loch Tulla.

ORD OF CAITHNESS, a hill on the coast of Caithness, 4 miles NE. of Helmsdale, over which the main road climbs steeply. It divides Caithness from Sutherland.

ORKNEY, or Orkney Islands, a group of some 70 islands forming a northern county of Scotland, separated by the Pentland Firth from Caithness. Besides the Mainland (or Pomona, 200 square miles), the main islands are Hoy, Sanday, Westray, North and South Ronaldsay, Rousay, Stronsay, Eday, Shapinsay, Burray, Papa Westray, Flotta, and Egilsay. The land is in general low (Hoy alone is hilly; 1,564 ft.), treeless, swampy in places, and windswept; great damage was done by a hurricane in 1953. On the W. the islands, notably Hoy, present lofty cliffs to the Atlantic. Prehistoric remains are found at Skara Brae, Maeshowe and the Ring of Brodgar. Until 1468 Orkney and Shetland were under Norse dominion. Lochs Stenness, Harray, Swannay, and Boardhouse offer good fishing. Kirkwall, the county town, and Stromness, both on the Main-

land, are the chief centres and ports.

ORMISTON, an attractive village 2 miles S. of Tranent, with an ancient church and mansionhouse (Ormiston Hall), a village cross and a monument to Robert Moffat, African missionary and father-in-law of David Livingstone.

ORONSAY, an island of Argyllshire, separated from the larger island of Colonsay by a narrow sea-passage, dry at low tide. It is named after Oran, confederate of St. Columba. There are ruins of a priory founded in the 14th century.

ORPHIR, on the mainland of Orkney, 9 miles W. of Kirkwall, has the ruins of an ancient circular church. It was partially pulled down and the stone used in the new church, but the apse and part of the walls still exist.

ORRIN, a river of southern Ross and Cromarty, which joins the Conon above Conon Bridge. Its glen contains a hydroelectric feeder dam.

OSSIAN, LOCH, a freshwater loch of Inverness-shire. Strath Ossian, at the north end of the loch is traversed by the stream Amhainn Ossian.

OUTER HEBRIDES. See Hebrides.

OVERSCAIG, a small angling place at the north-west end of Loch Shin, Sutherland.

OXNAM, a village in Roxburghshire, 4 miles SE. of Jedburgh, on the Oxnam Water, with the site of a Roman station near.

OYKELL, an excellent salmon and trout river of Sutherland and

Ross-shire, runs 35 miles eastwards past Oykell Bridge, and through Strath Oykell, to the Kyle of Sutherland and the Dornoch Firth.

OYNE, a village in Aberdeenshire, 24 miles NW. of Aberdeen, on the Gadie Burn, is a good base from which to climb Bennachie (*q.v.*).

PAISLEY

THE administrative centre of Renfrewshire, situated near the mouth of the River White Cart. Today it is a busy industrial town (thread, textiles, starch, flour products, chemicals, dyes, engineering and shipbuilding) but was a flourishing town in mediaeval times, and is known to have had a church, built by the Irish monk Mirin (Mirren) in the 6th century. In the Middle Ages the importance of Paisley centred on its Abbey founded in 1163 by Walter Fitz-Alan, High Steward of Scotland, magnificently rebuilt by the Stuart kings after its destruction by the English in 1307 and restored in 1859–1928. The Abbey today is one of the most famous churches in Scotland. The most notable features are the West Front, Nave and St. Mirren's Chapel.

Paisley was famed in the 18th century for its hand-loom weaving and in the 19th for its shawls, but the thread industry, begun in the 17th century and greatly developed since the 19th has been the main source of the town's prosperity.

Buildings of interest include the Observatory, the Public Library and Museum. John Wilson (Christopher North) was a native of Paisley.

PANNANICH WELLS, a small place on Deeside near Ballater, with mineral springs.

PAPA STOUR, an island off the west coast of the mainland of Shetland, divided from it by Papa Sound. On the south side of the island are impressive caves.

PAPA STRONSAY, a small island of the Orkney group, NE. of Stronsay.

PAPA WESTRAY, one of the northernmost islands of the Orkneys. On it is a chambered cairn considered one of the most interesting ancient burial places in Orkney.

PAPS OF JURA, three conical mountain peaks on the island of Jura, the highest, Beinn an Oir ("the mountain of gold") is 2,571 ft.

PATHHEAD, a small place 11 miles SE. of Edinburgh, with a fine Telford bridge over the Tyne. Crichton Castle, 2 miles SW., a large and impressive ruin, dates from the 15th and 16th centuries, and is open to visitors. It was built by Sir William Crichton, chancellor of Scotland during the minority of James II.

PEASE BAY, a fine sandy bay on the Berwickshire coast, 10 miles SE. of Dunbar, a popular picnicking place. Inland from it runs the beautiful, well-wooded ravine known as Pease Dean, spanned by an 18th century bridge, 127 ft. high.

PEEBLES

A HEALTH and holiday resort and county town of Peeblesshire, on the River Tweed, 22 miles S. of Edinburgh, picturesquely situated among green, steeply-wooded Border hills. There is salmon and trout fishing in the Tweed and other waters, golf, tennis, bowls, boating and pony-trekking. Peebles Hydro is the scene of the Scottish Lowlands Tennis Championships in July.

Peebles, a royal burgh since the 14th century, is not only an ancient town, it is also an ancient resort. James I, reputed author of the poem *Peblis to the Play*, must himself often have visited the place. Long before his time royal parties came to hunt in this part of the old Caledonian Forest.

Here history, romance and tradition are inextricably mixed. King Arthur's great victory at Peebles is as real as the successive burnings of the town by the English, or its bombardment by Cromwell, or its occupation by Bonnie Prince Charlie. Antiquities include the Mercat Cross, ivied ruins of the Cross Church, a 15th century bridge which still bears the mason's

marks, the tower of ancient St. Andrew's church, and a part of the old town wall. The Cross Church, built to enshrine relics of St. Nicholas found here (together with a 3rd century stone cross), was long a place of pilgrimage. The Cross Keys Hotel (formerly Yett Inn) is said to be the Cleikum Inn of Scott's *St. Ronan's Well*, and its hostess of Scott's days the original Meg Dods.

Neidpath Castle, superbly sited on a rock above a bend in the river, is another antiquity. Once it was famous for its yews—bows made from the wood of Neidpath yews are said to have been carried by the crusaders. A few of the ancient trees survive, but mostly they were cut down by the notorious "Old Q", 4th Duke of Queensberry, in 1795. The Chambers Institute (formerly the Queensberry Lodging—birth-place of Old Q) is the civic centre; it comprises town chambers, town hall, library, museum and picture gallery, and was gifted to the town by the publisher William Chambers, founder with his brother Robert of the Edinburgh firm; both were natives of Peebles. Mungo Park, the famous African traveller, prac-tised here as a surgeon, and there are literary associations with James I, Sir Walter Scott, and John Buchan. The "Play" of King James's poem, the Beltane Festival and crowning of the Beltane Queen, may still be seen in Peebles in June. The actual ceremony takes place on Saturday, and is followed by horse racing and other sports in the beautiful Hay Lodge Park.

Peebles is a good walking and excursion centre. Favourite walks lead up the Manor Water and into the hills to (*c.* 4 miles) the Black Dwarf's Cottage (see Scott's *Black Dwarf*), to Manor Church with the "oldest bell in Scotland", and King Arthur's battlefield of Cade-muir; also eastward up the Tweed to Lyne (*q.v.*). The old mansion of Barns (now a youth hostel), scene of John Buchan's novel *John Burnet of Barns*, and Drochil Castle (*q.v.*) also lie to the west.

PEEBLESSHIRE, or Tweed-dale, an inland county of the Southern Uplands, drained by the Tweed and its tributaries. Its grassy hills (Broad Law 2,754 ft., Minchmoor 1,856 ft., Dollar Law 2,680 ft., etc.) provide pasture land for sheep. Woollens are manufactured. Antiquities include hill forts, the castle of Neidpath, and the House of Traquair.

PENCAITLAND, a pretty village of East Lothian on the River Tyne, 6 miles SW. of Haddington, with a partly 13th century church.

PENICUIK, a town of Midlothian, on the North Esk, 10 miles S. of Edinburgh, famous for paper-making. An obelisk in the grounds of Penicuik House commemorates the poet Allan Ramsay (d. 1758).

PENNAN, a small picturesque fishing village of north Aberdeen-shire, on Pennan Bay, near Pennan Head, *c.* 10 miles E. of Macduff.

PENTLAND FIRTH, an arm of the sea dividing the mainland of Scotland and Orkney. It is notorious for rough seas, and there is a lighthouse on the Pentland Skerries at its eastern end.

PENTLAND HILLS, a range of hills running south-west from Edin-burgh for some 16 miles; a noted walking and rambling region. The highest summit is Scald Law (1,898 ft.); others are Allermuir, Caerketton and Carnethy Hill (1,890 ft.). On the lower slopes of Carnethy is Rullion Green, where the Coven-anters were defeated in 1666.

Pentland walks are famous. In every direction the hills are intersected by tracks and footpaths, sometimes following a stream, or skirting one of the many reservoirs in the region—Threipmuir, Glencorse, Loganlee and Harperrig. A favourite ex-cursion from Edinburgh takes one to Glencorse Reservoir, beneath whose waters, it is said, lies the chapel of St. Katherine in the Hopes, built by the St. Clair who founded Rosslyn Castle. The Pentlands are Robert Louis Stevenson's "Hills of Home", and a short walk from Edinburgh (Fairmilehead) takes one to the cottage at Swanston, where his childhood holidays were spent. Interesting little villages lie among the foothills.

PERTH

A HISTORIC royal burgh and county town of Perthshire, at the head of the Tay estuary, 46 miles N. of Edinburgh, a road and rail junction and also, in a small way, a port. It has cattle markets, brewing and distilling, as well as linen, glass and dyeing industries and salmon fisheries, and was formerly engaged in the most picturesque of all Scots industries—pearl fishing. (Scottish river pearls, milk-white and beautiful, and rather expensive, may still be bought in Perth).

The old name of the town was St. Johnstoun (St. John's Town), and its ancient and interesting church of St. John, founded, it is thought, in Pictish times, is the first aim of the sightseer. It has suffered many vicissitudes, was restored in the 19th century, and finally reconstructed as a War Memorial Church after the First World War. The town itself is rich in history. Traditionally the Scottish capital until 1437, it was held by Bruce, Edward I of England, Montrose, Claverhouse and the Jacobites. Prince Charles Edward and his following were here in 1745. The

County Buildings stand on the site of Gowrie House, scene of the "Gowrie Conspiracy" to capture James VI. Then in Curfew Row is the Fair Maid's House of Scott's novel *The Fair Maid of Perth*.

Perth today deserves its soubriquet of "The Fair City". Fine buildings and handsome streets, set in attractive scenery, are flanked by the North and South Inches, not really "inches" or islands at all, but spacious parks on the banks of the Tay. Sports include horse-racing (in Scone Palace grounds), fishing, golf, tennis, bowls and boating. There is a good repertory theatre.

Scone, ancient capital of Scotland, is now included in the environs of Perth. Here Scots kings were crowned on the Stone of Destiny, the Coronation Stone, brought hither from Dunstaffnage by Kenneth Macalpin. Edward I carried it off to Westminster Abbey (1297), where it still lies, forming part of the Coronation Chair. In 1950 it was removed from the Abbey, by Scottish patriots, but was afterwards returned. Traditionally it was Jacob's pillow at Luz, hence its sacred character.

Perth Aerodrome is at Scone, and Perth Races are held in the Palace grounds.

Other places of interest near Perth are Huntingtower, renowned in history and ballad, and the ruins of Elcho Castle. Dunsinane (1,012 ft.) in the Sidlaws, site of Macbeth's castle, is 7 or 8 miles NE. of Perth.

Kinnoull Hill.

PERTHSHIRE, a central county, partly Highland, partly Lowland. The Grampian Highlands (Ben Lawers 3,984 ft., Ben More 3,843 ft., Ben-y-Gloe 3,671 ft., Schiehallion 3,547 ft.) are diversified with Lochs Tay, Rannoch, Earn, and in the south the various lochs of the Trossachs. The north of the county is drained by the River Tay and its affluents, and is used for forestry, hill sheep-grazing and deer forests. There are in operation hydroelectric schemes at Tummel-Garry and Lawers. Alongside the Sidlaw and Ochil Hills are the fertile lowlands of Strathmore, the Carse of Gowrie, and the Carse of Forth. Agriculture, fruit-growing, sheep-farming, Tay fisheries, some textile manufactures, and catering for the tourists employ the inhabitants; there are many tourist resorts (Crieff, Pitlochry, Dunblane and Callander) as well as the county town of Perth. In winter the slopes above Glenshee, at Drumochter and on Ben Lawers are much frequented by skiers.

PETERCULTER, and CULTER (not dissociable) on the River Dee, 5 miles SW. of Aberdeen, form a pleasant village, with an unexplained brightly-coloured effigy of Rob Roy in a niche of the rock. Two miles W. is Drum Castle, 17th century, incorporating a formidable 13th century tower.

PETERHEAD, the most easterly Scottish town, a seaport and centre of the herring and white fishing industry, on the Buchan coast, 32 miles NNE. of Aberdeen. It owes its foundation in the late 16th century to George Keith, 5th Earl Marischal; another George Keith, 10th and last Earl, was exiled after the '15 when James, the Old Pretender, landed at Peterhead.

Of especial interest is the great National Harbour of Refuge to the S. of the town, enclosed by a fine breakwater built by convicts from the prison at Burnhaven, nearby. The quarries of pink Peterhead granite to the SE. should also be seen, and the castles of Ravenscraig and Inverugie.

To the tourist this bracing old sea town—more than once raised to the status of resort—has much to offer: sun and sea, tonic air, fishing in the River Ugie (sea-trout and finnock), golf (18-hole and 9-hole courses), and splendid rock scenery.

PHILIPHAUGH, a mansion 3 miles SW. of Selkirk. The plain nearby is where the celebrated battle of Philiphaugh was fought, in which Montrose was routed by the Covenanting army.

PINT STOUP (Rock Stack). See Arbroath.

PITCAITHLY, a small place 1 mile SW. of Bridge of Earn, Perthshire, with mineral springs.

Fish Ladder, Pitlochry.
(W. A. Sharp).

PITLOCHRY, the geographical "Heart of Scotland", a delightfully situated holiday resort 28 miles NNW. of Perth on the Great North Road, in hilly, well-wooded country, sheltered yet bracing. During the summer its Festival Theatre is an added attraction for visitors, with its slogan, "Stay six days and see six plays". Its stage is six inches longer than that of the Royal Opera House, London. To the N. is the Pass of Killiecrankie, to the W. the Falls of Tummel. At Pitlochry is Loch Faskally, the final reservoir of the Tummel - Garry hydroelectric scheme. The power station at the dam bears the Gaelic motto of the North of Scotland Hydro-electric Board, *Neart nan Gleann* ("Power of the Glens").

The fish-ladder, 900 feet long and comprising 35 pools, is of great interest to visitors. Less than a mile from Pitlochry is the ancient village of Moulin, believed to have been inhabited in the time of the Picts.

PITSLIGO, a small place 5 miles W. of Fraserburgh, Aberdeenshire, with a 17th century church and ruins of an old castle, parts of which date back to the 16th century. Pitullie Castle ruins are near by.

PITTENWEEM, a small fishing port, resort and old royal burgh of Fife, on the east coast between Anstruther and St. Monance. Near the parish kirk, which has an ancient tower, are the ruins of a once-famous priory. St. Fillan's Cave is on the shore.

PLADDA, a rocky island with a lighthouse off the south coast of Arran.

PLOCKTON, a farming village of Wester Ross on Loch Carron, 5 miles N. of Kyle of Lochalsh, set amid beautiful scenery.

PLUSCARDEN ABBEY, a fine ruin on the banks of the Black Burn 6 miles SW. of Elgin, in Morayshire. It was a Cistercian monastery founded by Alexander II in 1230, and its well-preserved ruins are now restored and in use as a Benedictine Abbey. Special features are the 16th century tabernacle and the chapter house with a central pier like that of Elgin cathedral.

Opposite: Pitlochry. (*The Scotsman*).

POLTON, a small village of Midlothian, 10 miles SE. of Edinburgh, for some years the home of De Quincey.

POLWARTH, a village 3 miles SW. of Duns (Berwickshire). Its church, standing in the Marchmont policies, is noted in history for an exploit of Lady Grizel Baillie, who, as a young girl, night after night carried food to her father, a fugitive after the Monmouth Rebellion, as he lay in the vaults of Polwarth church.

POMONA, the name of the mainland of Orkney.

POOLEWE, a village at the head of Loch Ewe in Wester Ross, near the north-west end of Loch Maree. There is excellent loch and sea-loch fishing and salmon fishing in the River Ewe. The climate is exceptionally mild. While the mountains of Ross are noted for their Alpine flora, at Inverewe Gardens on the shores of Loch Ewe subtropical trees and flowers are successfully grown. The Gardens are the property of the National Trust. Isle of Ewe is in Loch Ewe.

POOLS OF DEE. See Dee (Aberdeenshire).

PORT APPIN, a small place at the mouth of Loch Laich in the Appin district of Argyllshire. It has a pier and steamer communication with Oban.

PORT ASKAIG, a quaint village and port of Islay, on the Sound of Islay, with a ferry to Feolin in Jura.

PORT BANNATYNE. See Rothesay.

PORT CHARLOTTE, a village on Loch Indaal in Islay. Highland Games are held in July. Here are the graves of American soldiers lost when the troop-carrying *Tuscanai* was torpedoed in February 1918.

PORT ELLEN, a village of Islay, at the head of its south-east peninsula, the Oa. There is a golf course at Machrie (which also has a hotel). Good bathing is available. Distilling, fishing, lobster-fishing are carried on. A famous Norse warrior is believed to rest beneath the Carragh Ban (White Stone) between Port Ellen and Kintraw.

PORTENCROSS, a small coastal place of Ayrshire, 8 miles S. of Largs, where a ship of the Armada was sunk.

PORTESSIE, a fishing village on the Moray Firth, 2 miles NE. of Buckie.

PORT GLASGOW, this busy industrial Clydeside town came into being literally as the port for Glasgow before the river was deepened to allow navigation to the city itself.

PORT GORDON, a small fishing village and holiday resort of Banffshire, 2 miles SW. of Buckie. There is angling in the Spey.

PORTKNOCKIE, a fishing village on the Moray Firth. See Cullen.

PORT LOGAN, a small seaside place on Port Logan Bay, 12 miles S. of Stranraer. The Mull of Logan is to the NW. of the village. There is a famous tidal fish-pond (1788) on the opposite side of Logan Bay.

PORTMAHOMACK, a resort, 9 miles E. of Tain on the Dornoch Firth. Seabathing, sea fishing and touring make it a favourite holiday place. There are interesting antiquities nearby. Two miles away on Tarbat Ness is a lighthouse.

PORT MARY, a tiny place on the Solway Firth, 7 miles SE. of Kirkcudbright, from which Mary Queen of Scots sailed for England in 1568.

PORTNAHAVEN, a small Islay village at the south end of the Rhinns peninsula. There is a lighthouse on Orsay Island off the south coast.

PORTOBELLO. See Edinburgh.

PORTPATRICK, a resort on the west coast of the Rhinns of Galloway, 8 miles SW. of Stranraer, once a busy port for Ireland. Tradition says that St. Patrick once crossed from Ireland to Portpatrick in a single stride. Ruins of Dunskey Castle are near by.

PORTREE, the chief place in the Isle of Skye, a well-wooded and picturesque little town looking over its beautiful harbour, with views of the Cuillin to the S. Golf is available. Portree is a fine touring centre for coach, steamer and motorboat trips. N. of the harbour is Prince Charlie's Cave. Farther N. in the Trotternish peninsula is the landmark of the Old Man of Storr—an inland rock-stack on the top of a high cliff. Near the northern extremity of this peninsula is the Quiraing (*q.v.*).

PORT SETON, a fishing village and holiday place, *c.* 2 miles E. of Prestonpans (East Lothian). The chief attractions are the quaint old harbour, 2-mile stretch of sand and large modern swimming pool.
Port Seton takes its name from the great family of Seton, whose splendid home of Seton Palace was replaced by the present Seton

Castle (18th century). After Rizzio's murder in 1566, Mary Queen of Scots came to Seton Palace with Darnley; next year, after Darnley's murder, she brought Bothwell.

PORT SKERRA, a small fishing village on the north coast of Sutherland, 18 miles W. of Thurso, with fine rock and cliff scenery.

PORT SONACHAN, a small village on the south-east shore of Loch Awe, Argyllshire.

PORTSOY, a small fishing port 7 miles W. of Banff on the Moray Firth, with angling, boating, bathing and remarkably fine rock scenery. A salmon-pink granite and so-called Portsoy marble (a variety of serpentine) are quarried here.

PORT WILLIAM, a small seaside village on Luce Bay, 11 miles SW. of Wigtown. At Monreith nearby are Monreith House, famed for its gardens, and the old church of Kirkmaiden.

POTARCH BRIDGE, a small place with an inn on the River Dee.

PRESTONPANS, an ancient town of East Lothian, 10 miles E. of Edinburgh on the Firth of Forth, long famous for its salt pans, oysters, and pottery. These and other industries have, however, largely given place to coalmining. From Prestongrange coal seams are followed under the Firth. There is a modern civic centre and housing estate (1962).
Preston village on the landward deserves to be visited for its interesting Cross and a number of fine old houses of the 17th

Errochty Power Station.

HYDROELECTRIC DEVELOPMENT

Scotland, with its abundant water resources in its upland regions, provides ample scope for hydroelectric development, and many schemes are now in being. Apart from those in Galloway (see page 122) and Lochaber (see Fort William), these are operated by the North of Scotland Hydroelectric Board. This public body was established by Act of Parliament in 1943 to undertake all future development of water-power in the Highlands and Islands, and its activity has been such that no visitor to the Highlands will long remain unaware of it. Numerous reservoirs have been made, which with their dams and power-houses, aqueducts, tunnels, fish-passes, etc., have become a new and by no means unpleasing feature of the Highland scene. Some of the "new" lochs, indeed—for example, Faskally, Benevean and Glascarnoch—are in themselves scenic attractions, while in many places the roads constructed as part of the schemes have opened new and beautiful country to the tourist. Care has been taken to preserve natural beauty as far as possible, and in many cases power-stations are concealed, either partly (as in the illustration above) or completely (see Cruachan).

century and earlier; also the massive 15th century keep of Preston Tower. The Battle of Prestonpans (1745), a notable Jacobite victory, was fought near here.

PRESTWICK, 2½ miles N. of Ayr, one of the most popular resorts on this fine coast, famous for its airport and its golf. The airport is internationally known, large and modern, admirably situated and equipped, with its own hotel, frequent Transatlantic flights and communications with practically every part of the world. Golf, too, reaches international status; many championship contests have been fought out on the fine Prestwick course, including the Open Championship. Of the four golf courses one, St. Ninian's, is municipally owned.

Besides golf, Prestwick has excellent sands, a sea-bathing "Lake", tennis courts, bowling and putting greens, and children's amusements, galas, carnivals and firework displays are held.

Prestwick as a town is quite old; it has a good Mercat Cross, set among colourful flower-beds. Old St. Nicholas' Church is of interest, also the Wallace Monument and Kingcase Well, site of a lazar house built by Robert the Bruce, who was here cured of leprosy.

Prestwick Airport.
(*Scottish Tourist Board*).

PROSEN, GLEN, a glen of Angus, traversed by the River Prosen.

QUEENSBERRY, a mountain (2,285 ft.), 7 miles SW. of Moffat. Nearby is Wee Queensberry (1,675 ft.).

QUEENSFERRY. See South Queensferry and North Queensferry.

QUINAG, a mountain (2,653 ft.) of Sutherland, to the north of Loch Assynt.

QUIRAING, THE, an extraordinary mountain mass near the north tip of the Isle of Skye; a vast tumbled fantasy of rocks of every conceivable shape, with a central turf-topped table surrounded by high rock walls. This is one of the

most intriguing of Skye scenes. To the E. is Staffin Bay; to the W. in Kilmuir churchyard, is a memorial to Flora Macdonald, and just to the N. is Flodigarry Hotel, part of which was her home after her marriage.

QUOICH, LOCH, a freshwater loch and hydro-electric reservoir of Inverness-shire, drained by the River Garry (*q.v.*).

RAASAY, an island of Inverness-shire, separated from the mainland by the Inner Sound and from Skye by the Sound of Raasay. The island is 16 miles long and about 2 miles broad, with high cliffs along the east coast. Brochel Castle ruins are on the east coast and there is a wonderful panorama from the summit of Dun Caan Hill (1,456 ft.), the highest point of the island.

RAHANE, a small village on the west side of Gare Loch, Argyllshire.

RANNOCH, LOCH, a loch in north-west Perthshire, 9½ miles long. On its south shore is the famous Black Wood of Rannoch, survival of the ancient Caledonian Forest. Kinloch Rannoch is a pleasant little village at the loch's east end. Loch Rannoch forms part of a hydroelectric scheme involving the river Tummel and Loch Ericht.

RANNOCH MOOR, a high, wild, expanse of heather and peat moss in north-west Perthshire, about 20 miles square, sprinkled with numerous lochs and peaty pools. It may be crossed either from Rannoch Station or from Kinghouse Inn at the head of Glencoe and Glen Etive. This is a lovely (if desolate) hike, only to be attempted when the weather is right, as the track is boggy and ill-defined and the ground treacherous. The largest of the lochs are Lochs Lydoch (or Laidon) and Ba, famous for trout. The wanderings of Alan Breck and David Balfour (in R. L. Stevenson's *Kidnapped*) brought them to Rannoch Moor.

RATTRAY, lies on the east bank of the River Ericht, opposite Blairgowrie (*q.v.*) of which it is practically a suburb.

REAY, a pretty village on the north coast of Caithness, 10 miles W. of Thurso. Nearby are the Achvarasdal Ferneries of the botanist Robert Dick, and Dounreay nuclear power station.

REAY FOREST, an extensive deer forest stretching from Ben Arkle to Ben Hee in north-west Sutherland—the ancient hunting ground of the Mackays. It is now in process of afforestation.

RED HEAD, a bold headland on the coast of Angus, 6 miles N. of Arbroath.

REDSCAURHEAD, a village 3 miles N. of Peebles where, in a wayside cottage, the designer of Edinburgh's Scott Monument, George Kemp, served his apprenticeship to a joiner and millwright.

REEKIE LINN (FALLS), these are falls on the River Isla, 3 miles N. of Alyth, Perthshire.

RENFREW, the county town of Renfrewshire, and a royal burgh.

Opposite: *Loch Rannoch.* (*W. S. Thomson*).

It is of ancient foundation and received its charter in 1396. The title Baron Renfrew was once borne by the heir apparent to the throne of Scotland, and is still used by the Prince of Wales. Today there is little of antiquarian interest remaining, and the town is rapidly becoming a suburb of Glasgow. There are shipyards, boiler, soap, rubber and furniture industries. Renfrew airport formerly the civil airport for Glasgow, has now been demolished the new Abbotsinch airport nearby taking its place.

RENFREWSHIRE, a western county on the left bank of the Clyde estuary between Glasgow and the Firth of Clyde. There is hilly moorland in the south-east and west; the coastal plains are fertile. There are mining, engineering, shipbuilding, sugar-refining, motor and cotton textile industries, as well as agriculture. Hillington is a modern industrial estate; Paisley is the largest town and Renfrew the county town; other populous centres are Greenock, Port Glasgow, Barrhead, Johnstone and Gourock.

RENTON, a village in the pleasant and peaceful Vale of Leven, *c.* 2 miles N. of Dumbarton, famous as the birthplace of Tobias Smollett. It shares in the long-established Vale industries of dyeing, bleaching and calico-printing. Smollett, one of the earliest of British novelists, was born at old Dalquhurn House (to the E.), in 1721. There is a monument to his memory in Renton School playground. Dalquhurn (dal-hurn´) is now a centre of local industry. Salmon and trout are caught in the river.

REST-AND-BE-THANKFUL, a long hill in Glen Croe, Argyllshire, on the main road from Loch Lomond to Inveraray. On the N. is Ben Arthur (The Cobbler, 2,891 ft.) and on the S., Ben Donich (2,774 ft.). The old road, originally built by General Wade's soldiers, may be seen on the south side of the fine new one. A stone seat at the summit is inscribed "Rest and be Thankful".

RHINNS OF GALLOWAY. See Galloway.

RHU, a picturesque village on the east side of the Gare Loch, 2 miles N. of Helensburgh. Here is the clubhouse of the Royal Northern Yacht Club.

RHYNIE, an Aberdeenshire village 9 miles S. of Huntly, birthplace of "Mackay of Uganda" (1849–90), missionary. The Tap o' Noth lies prominently to the NW.

RIDDON, LOCH, a beautiful loch of Argyllshire running N. from the Kyles of Bute.

RODEL. See Harris.

ROGART, a village 7½ miles W. of Golspie, Sutherland.

ROMANNO BRIDGE, a small village *c.* 10 miles NW. of Peebles. Cowie's Linn is a pretty waterfall.

RONA, SOUTH, an island to the N. of Raasay, separated from the mainland by the Inner Sound and from Skye by the Sound of Raasay.

RONALDSAY, NORTH, the most northerly island of the Orkneys, divided from Sanday by the North Ronaldsay Firth. There is a small broch and other rather scanty remains of antiquarian interest.

RONALDSAY, SOUTH, the southernmost of the larger islands of the Orkneys, to the SE. of Scapa Flow. Agriculture and fishing are the main occupations. There are some standing stones, ruined brochs and other antiquities.

ROSEHEARTY, a village on the north coast of Aberdeenshire, 4 miles W. of Fraserburgh. There is fishing in the River Rathen and elsewhere. The ruins of Pitsligo Castle are near here, also the cave where the last Lord Pitsligo hid after the '45.

ROSEMARKIE. See Fortrose.

ROSNEATH, on the Gare Loch opposite Helensburgh, is a tiny secluded village, most easily reached by ferry from Rhu Point. Rosneath Castle was formerly the residence of Princess Louise, Duchess of Argyll, who also remodelled the Ferry Inn.

ROSLIN, a village 8 miles S. of Edinburgh, famous for its beautiful chapel, and, in a lesser degree, for its castle.

Rosslyn Chapel was founded in 1446 by Sir William Sinclair, 3rd Earl and Prince of Orkney, who intended it to be the choir of a large and important Collegiate Church of St. Matthew. Actually no more than this was ever built. As it stands Rosslyn is a gem of gothic architecture, enriched with flying buttresses and double rows of pinnacles, but chiefly remarkable for the great wealth and variety of the stone carving with which it is adorned. Lintels, transoms, capitals of the graceful clustered pillars—all are covered with lively imaginative sculptures; the Seven Virtues, Seven Deadly Sins, Dance of Death, etc. Even the stone vaulting of the roof is covered with flowers and foliage, a different flower in each bay. Richest of all is the so-called Prentice Pillar, to which clings the legend of the gifted apprentice and the jealous master who kills him. But the older and probably more accurate reading is "Prince's Pillar", the prince being the Prince of Orkney.

The chapel (skilfully restored and now in use as an Episcopal Church) stands on the brink of a pretty wooded glen on the North Esk and is open to the public on weekdays only. A little way below it is Rosslyn Castle, built in 1330 by another St. Clair, restored 16th, 17th, 18th centuries.

The castle which is open to the public, has a restaurant in the Great Hall. Across the river are the ruins of Woodhouselee Castle.

ROSS AND CROMARTY, a Highland county stretching from the Moray Firth to the Minch, and including Lewis (but not Harris) in the Outer Hebrides. The shores are indented by the

Beauly, Cromarty, and Dornoch Firths in the east, and by Lochs Alsh, Carron, Torridon and Broom on the west. The country is mountainous, with many peaks of over 3,000 ft. (Cairn Eige, 3,877 ft.). Loch Maree is noted for its scenery; Loch Luichart is the centre of an extensive hydroelectric undertaking. The east side of the county, including the Black Isle, is fertile; the remainder is deer forest or rough grazing for sheep and cattle. Dingwall is the county town; Stornoway is larger. Tain, Invergordon, Fortrose, Cromarty, Kyle of Lochalsh are other centres. The scenery is magnificent and there are abundant facilities for river and loch angling, climbing and shooting.

ROSYTH, a naval base on the north shore of the Firth of Forth, near Inverkeithing and the Forth Bridges; reaching great size and importance in recent wars. To the S., close to St. Margaret's Hope anchorage, is the ruined Rosyth Castle, which figures in Scott's *Abbot*; to the E. the Donibristle Naval Air Repair Yard, near the old castle of Donibristle. Part of Rosyth has been developed as a garden city. It was the scene of the Battle of Pitreavie, a Royalist defeat, in the Civil War.

ROTHES, a village at the head of Rothes Glen, *c.* 10 miles SSE. of Elgin. It has an ancient castle (occupied in 1296 by Edward I of England) and a distilling industry. There is fishing in the River Spey.

Rum.

234

ROTHESAY

ON a lovely bay at the entrance to the Kyles of Bute, Dunoon's chief rival among the Clyde resorts and noted for a climate which has given it the name of the "Madeira of the Clyde". This resort offers a wealth of first-class hotels, including the magnificent Glenburn Hydro, and comfortable boarding houses as well as a number of more homely establishments which extend a real Scottish welcome to visitors and provide the best of holiday fare.

There is safe bathing from every part of the front, and for cooler days there is an indoor salt-water swimming pool where medicinal treatment of ozone, sunray and seaweed may also be obtained. The former bathing Lido is now operated as a fun-fair during the summer season.

Sea angling and boating are indulged in with great enthusiasm by old and young. Motor launches and "drive-yourself" craft are hired at reasonable rates from the various stations along the promenade.

Behind the famous esplanade, which runs the whole length of the front, are the putting greens

Rothesay Castle.

and lawns of the esplanade gardens. These never lose their charm for visitors, while the steeply ascending Serpentine takes one quickly to vantage points on the high ground above the town or along the winding paths through Skipper's Wood. In the Pavilion, a large modern dance and conference hall, celebrity concerts are a feature, and there are numerous other places of entertainment, including the Winter Garden Theatre on the esplanade which presents up-to-date musical revues, often in Highland costume, from May to September.

Rothesay Castle dates from the 11th century and has important associations with Wallace, Bruce and the Stuart kings. Its ruins are an impressive feature of the central part of the town. The museum and library cater for those visitors interested in the history of the island, and here too is a good selection of local sea birds and wild life as well as exhibits from the interesting archaeological sites on Bute.

There is a breezy 18-hole municipal golf course on Canada Hill with a well-appointed clubhouse. Rothesay is within easy reach of the fine sands of Ettrick Bay with bathing facilities and a large pavilion, Scalpsie Bay and

Opposite: Rothesay. (Aerofilms).

Rothesay Bay. (L. S. Paterson).

Kilchattan Bay and the Kyles of Bute.

Regular steamer services and smaller craft run to the Kyles, Loch Striven, Arran, Ayr, Loch Goil and Loch Long. Fares are moderate and meals are served on board.

Inland waters include the fine Loch Fad with Edmund Kean's cottage on the shore, and freshwater fishing is available here in Loch Ascog and Greenan Loch.

Other points of interest near Rothesay are Mount Stewart, modern home of the Bute family, Kerrycroy village (4 miles), Port Bannatyne and Kames Castle, Ascog Bay (3 miles), St. Ninian's Bay and Cockle Shore (4 miles), Rhudabodach with its ferry to Colintraive and Kames Hill, highest point in the island.

Highlights of the season are the yachting regattas in July and the illuminations in August and September.

ROTHIEMURCHUS, a fairly extensive deer forest and a small hamlet, on the south-east bank of the Spey opposite Aviemore.

ROUSAY, an island of the Orkneys separated from the mainland by Eynhallow Sound. Rousay is rich in antiquities, which include the very fine Mid Howe Broch, on the south-western shore of the island, and a large number of chambered cairns.

ROWARDENNAN. See Lomond, Loch.

ROXBURGH, a pleasant little village near the River Teviot, in the county of Roxburghshire, once an important royal burgh. Its history is the history of Roxburgh Castle. This famous old place, former royal residence and birthplace of

Alexander III, suffered the usual vicissitudes of a Border keep, and after a lengthy spell of English governance, was taken and destroyed by the Scots (1460). The (slight) remains stand on an eminence called the Marchmound, 2 miles NNE. of the village. Higher up the river are the Covenanters' Caves.

ROXBURGHSHIRE, a southern county stretching from the English border in the south to the Tweed and beyond in the north. The surface is upland (Auchopecairn, 2,382 ft.; Eildon Hills, 1,385 ft.), drained to the Tweed by the Teviot, and to the south-west, through pastoral Liddesdale, by the Liddel. Sheep-farming and tweed and woollen industries are the chief occupations. Visitors are attracted to the abbey ruins at Jedburgh, Kelso, and Melrose, and by associations with Scott. Jedburgh is the county town; Hawick is the chief centre of population and industry; Kelso and Melrose are other towns. Roxburgh itself, once an important burgh with a castle (of which scant remains survive) that was one of the chief Border strongholds, is now represented by only a village of the name, near Kelso.

ROY, a stream of Inverness-shire traversing Glen Roy, famous for the "parallel roads of Roy" (raised beaches). Roy Bridge stands at the foot of the glen.

RUBERSLAW (HILL), a hill (1,392 ft.), 5 miles E. of Hawick, a haunt of the Covenanters.

RUM, a bare and hilly island off the west coast of Inverness-shire, c. 8 miles by 7 miles. Askival (2,659 ft.) is the highest of four peaks all over 2,000 feet. The island is now a nature reserve and visitors are not encouraged.

RUMBLING BRIDGE (FALLS). See Dunkeld.

RUMBLING BRIDGE. See Devon, River.

RUTHERGLEN, a busy industrial town and old historic royal burgh of Lanarkshire, some 3 miles S. of Glasgow and now practically continuous with the city. It dates at least as far back as the 12th century, and has associations with Wallace, Queen Mary and the Covenanters and was frequently a storm centre in the wars in which they were involved. However its monuments have mostly perished; only the steeple remains of the old church, and the castle has entirely disappeared. A little to the E. is Cambuslang.

RUTHWELL, a village of Dumfriesshire, 7 miles W. of Annan. In the church is a Runic Cross, carved with animals, birds, biblical scenes and runic verses, and a poem believed to be the oldest existing written English.

RYAN, LOCH, a sea-loch in Wigtownshire, separating the northern peninsula of the Rhinns of Galloway from the mainland. Stranraer is at the head of the loch.

SADDELL, a village on the east coast of Kintyre, with a 12th century abbey and an ancient castle.

ST. ABBS, a cliff village with smugglers' caves about 2 miles south of St. Abb's Head (lighthouse).

Royal and Ancient Clubhouse.

ST. ANDREWS

A HISTORIC old sea-town of north-east Fife, a royal burgh since 1140, also the "home" of golf and a first-rate holiday resort, on St. Andrews Bay. It has the oldest university in Scotland (1412), and the world's leading golf club (The Royal and Ancient).

St. Andrews first appears in history as a Culdee settlement of the 8th century, but traditionally it owes its foundation to St. Regulus or Rule, who landed here in the 4th century with some relics of St. Andrew, *viz.*, "an arm-bone, three fingers, a tooth and knee-pan". Later links are with the Stuart kings and queens, the martyrs of the Reformation, the Covenanters, and the '45. Here Patrick Hamilton and George Wishart were burned at the stake, and were afterwards avenged by the slaying of Cardinal Beaton. Three miles away at Magus Moor, more than a century later, took place the historic murder of Archbishop Sharpe.

University life is very much a part of the town; when vacation is past, the familiar red gowns are everywhere. The fine University Chapel (restored) was built in 1512; in 1645 a parliament was held in what is now the university library—the old Parliament Hall. Near the beautiful and secluded buildings of St. Mary's College (1538) is an ancient thorn tree said to have been planted by Mary, Queen of Scots.

Ruins of the 12th century cathedral and priory, though not extensive, convey something of their former beauty and importance, especially the west front of the cathedral and The Pends, part of the magnificent old main gateway of the priory. On a rock above the shore stands the castle (formerly the Bishop's Palace), now a ruin featuring a "bottle" dungeon and an underground passage. Nearby is St. Rule's Cave. Of interest, too, are Queen Mary's House, the old Town Kirk (contemporary with the university), the curious high tower of St. Rule (in the cathedral precincts), 1130, and the fine mediaeval West Port.

As early as the mid-16th century St. Andrews was renowned for its golf, and so it is still. Of its four golf courses (the Old, the New, the Eden, and the Jubilee, all open to visitors), the classic Old Course retains first place in the affections of golfers throughout the world. Appropriately, golf-club making is an important industry. There are also facilities for putting, bowls, tennis, boating and bathing, angling and sea-fishing. The Step Rock Swimming Pool, a 100-foot-long tidal pool with natural rock barriers is exceedingly popular, though it was formerly the Witches' Lake, where witches suffered their sink-or-swim trial

The Castle, St. Andrews.

before being burned. To the right and left respectively are the East and West Sands, the latter one of the most perfect stretches of sand in Britain.

St. Andrews has a theatre and cinemas, a promenade, a large caravan site and a number of public parks. The theatre, which is very small, was built out of a byre and is appropriately called the Byre Theatre.

Among countless seasonal events are the Kate Kennedy celebrations in April, Royal and Ancient meetings in May and September, swimming galas and Masque of St. Andrews in July and August, Lammas Fair and Scottish Hard Courts Tennis Championships also in August, and golf competitions and tournaments all the time.

Beyond the East Sands are Kinkell Braes, popular with geologists and picnickers.

ST. BOSWELLS. See Newton St. Boswells.

ST. CYRUS, a coastal village of Kincardineshire, 6 miles N. of Montrose, with a fine sandy bay. It has rich and varied flora.

ST. FILLANS, a pretty village and holiday resort at the east end of Loch Earn, 12 miles W. of Crieff, with facilities for golf, fishing, boating and touring. It has a large underground power station, part of the Breadalbane hydroelectric scheme.

Antiquities in the neighbourhood include the ruined Culdee chapel of St. Fillan. Ardvorlich House, 4 miles distant on the south shore of the loch, figures in Scott's *Legend of Montrose*, and stands in a glen running up into the hills, a good place from which to climb Ben Vorlich.

ST. KILDA, a group of islands 52 miles W. of Harris, the last outpost of the Western Isles, and even in the Hebrides a synonym for remoteness. Behind the wave-washed cliffs, in some places 1,300 ft. high, the interior is rocky and bare. Yet until 1930, when they were evacuated to the mainland, some 45 people lived a hardy self-supporting existence there, with sea-birds as the main item of their diet. Today St. Kilda is a strictly protected wild-life sanctuary, with the largest gannet population in the world, a breeding place of rare birds, including the St. Kilda wren, and the domain of a wild and unique breed of sheep. The unique St. Kilda mouse did not survive the departure of human beings. A rocket-tracking station has been built on the main island.

ST. MARY'S LOCH, a charmingly situated little loch, 3 miles long, at the head of the Yarrow Water in Selkirkshire. It is a favourite excursion place, and there is fishing available (salmon, sea-trout, brown trout, pike and perch). At the head of the loch is Tibbie Shiels Inn, made famous in the early 19th century by Scott, Hogg, De Quincey, and the many other poets and writers who frequented it. The Inn stands on the narrow isthmus between St. Mary's Loch and the tiny (but fishable) Loch of the Lowes, and near it

St. Mary's Loch.

is a monument to James Hogg, the Ettrick Shepherd.

ST. MONANCE, a small old fishing place on the east coast of Fife, 3 miles NE. of Elie. It has a boat-building industry, caravan site, bathing, putting, bowls, and golf at Elie (18-hole course) and Anstruther (9-hole).

There is a remarkable little church on the shore which was built by David II in the 14th century. It is small and solid with a short square tower surmounted by an octagonal spire.

ST. VIGEANS, a village 1 mile N. of Arbroath. The much-restored 11th century church has many celtic stones, the inscription on one of which, the Drosten Stone, is said to be the only extant legible example of the Pictish language.

SALEN, a small place on the north shore of Loch Sunart, Argyllshire.

SALEN, a small port on Salen Bay in the Isle of Mull, with a good pier. Ben More can be climbed from here. On the north point of the Bay stands ruined Aros Castle, a once formidable stronghold of the Lords of the Isles.

SALINE, a village of west Fife, 5 miles NW. of Dunfermline. It has a 9-hole golf course with fine views.

SALTCOATS, an old burgh (1528) and popular seaside resort 1½ miles SE. of Ardrossan on the Ayrshire coast, formerly a salt-working town. As a resort it is admirably placed and planned. The outstanding attractions are the very fine bathing beach and promenade, and the large swimming pool (Saltpans Bathing Station), modernly equipped, flood-lit and illuminated. There is another pool on the East Beach.

Aquatic sports take precedence, boating, bathing, sea-fishing, but Saltcoats also has a testing 18-hole golf course, tennis courts, bowling

Overleaf: Skye: Loch Scavaig and the Cuillins.

greens, bands and entertainments in Melbourne Park, walks in the Holm Plantation, and cinemas. The tower at the end of the Old Harbour is a favourite viewpoint.

SALTOUN, EAST AND WEST, villages some 6 miles SW. of Haddington, in East Lothian, associated with the famous Scottish patriot Fletcher of Saltoun (d. 1716), whose tutor, the historian Gilbert Burnett (afterwards Bishop of Salisbury) was parish minister. Saltoun Hall is the imposing seat of the Fletchers who have held the estate since 1643. An interesting industry is silver fox farming (since 1924).

SANDAY, a northern island of the Orkneys with numerous ancient monuments.

SANDBANK, a small resort on the south shore of the Holy Loch, Argyllshire, famous for yacht and boat building.

SANQUHAR (sang′ker), a small town and royal burgh (1484) of Dumfriesshire near the junction of the Nith and the Crawick. It has a golf course. There is a commemorative granite monument (1860) on the site of the former Town Cross to which the Covenanters (many of whom in the 17th century found frequent retreat in the nearby Lowther Hills) affixed two Declarations—that of 1680 renouncing allegiance to Charles II, and that of 1685 witnessing against James VII's usurpation of the government. Two miles W. are remains of part of the Devil's Dyke (*q.v.*).

SCALLOWAY, a village with a golf course, formerly the capital of

Shetland, attractively situated on a bay 6 miles W. of Lerwick. The ruined castle (1600) built by the wicked Earl of Orkney, Patrick Stewart, stands above the village.

SCALPAY, the largest (3½ miles long) of a group of islands in East Loch Tarbert, Harris.

SCALPAY, an island off the east coast of Skye, south of Raasay, with a chapel on the site of a Culdee cell.

SCAPA FLOW, a sea basin in the Orkneys, S. of the mainland, with an area of about 50 square miles. It was an important base in both World Wars and the scene of the scuttling of most of the German fleet in 1919.

SCARBA, a small island to the N. of Jura (Argyllshire).

SCAVAIG, a large sea-loch on the south-west coast of Skye, vastly impressive with the wild Cuillin rising on its western shore. At its head the River Scavaig flows (less than ¼ mile) from Loch Coruisk.

SCHIEHALLION, a mountain (3,547 ft.) in Perthshire, S. of Kinloch Rannoch.

SCONE. See Perth.

SCOURIE, a crofting village on Scourie Bay, west coast of Sutherland, with angling facilities. The island of Handa, to the N., is a famous bird sanctuary; 2 miles S. is Badcall, overlooking a scatter of islets in Edrachillis Bay. Inland is Ben Arkle (2,580 ft.) and Ben Stack (2,364 ft.).

SCRABSTER, a quaint fishing village with its own fish market, 2 miles NW. of Thurso. The mail steamer for the Orkneys leaves from Scrabster pier.

SEAFORTH, LOCH, a majestic and beautiful winding loch between Lewis and Harris on the east coast of the island. It gave its name to the Seaforth Highlanders.

SEAMILL, a small Ayrshire coastal resort adjoining West Kilbride, with a golf course.

SEIL ISLAND, an island in the Firth of Lorne. It is said to be connected to the mainland by what is the "only bridge over the Atlantic", but two others are known on the west coast.

SELKIRK, a historic royal burgh, county town of Selkirkshire, on the banks of the Ettrick Water at the foot of the beautiful vales of Ettrick and Yarrow, 11 miles N. of Hawick. The town is chiefly preoccupied with agriculture and the manufacture of tweeds and woollens. There is excellent fishing and golf, and it is a centre for touring some of the most romantic country in the Borders.

Selkirk's market "square" is a triangle, dominated by the handsomely-spired Town Hall, before which is a statue of Sir Walter Scott, in his robes of office as sheriff of the county. In the High Street is the statue of Mungo Park, the African explorer, born at Foulshiels to the N., and nearby is the Flodden Monument (1913), with the simple inscription "O Flodden Field".

The visitor may wonder why, in a tweed-making town, all the men should bear the title of "souters" (shoemakers). The reason is that an early trade of the town was the making of "single-soled shoon", and the name of the makers—so long nearly synonymous with a burgher of the town—has survived longer than the trade itself! The Souters of Selkirk appear in history with the '45, when they were called upon to make 2,000 pairs of "shoon" for Prince Charlie's army. The Common Riding in June commemorates Flodden, and is accompanied by races, at which large crowds attend.

SELKIRKSHIRE, a county of the Southern Uplands, drained by the Tweed, Ettrick and Yarrow, and covering the chief part of the old "Ettrick Forest". Broad Law (2,754 ft.), on the boundary with Peeblesshire, is the highest point; St. Mary's is the largest loch. Stockrearing and woollen manufacturing are the chief occupations. Selkirk and Galashiels are the main towns. The county is rich in historical and literary associations, especially in Border Ballad lore. Sir Walter Scott was sheriff-principal; James Hogg, (1770–1835), the Ettrick Shepherd, was born and is buried in the Vale of Ettrick.

SETON, a castle 1½ miles W. of Longniddry, on the site of former Seton Palace. The Palace had associations with Mary, Queen of Scots, who was there in 1566 with Darnley after Rizzio's murder, and in 1567 with Bothwell after Darnley's. In the grounds is the unfinished collegiate church of Seton (15th century).

SHANDON, a hamlet on the Gare Loch (Argyllshire), 3 miles SE. of Garelochhead, with a golf course.

SHERIFFMUIR, the site, 2¼ miles E. of Dunblane, of an indecisive battle (1715) between Jacobites and Hanoverians.

SHETLAND, or ZETLAND,

a group of more than 100 islands and skerries forming the northernmost Scottish county, the capital of which is Lerwick. The largest of the islands are Mainland, Yell, Unst, Fetlar, Bressay, Whalsay and Foula. The cliff scenery is very fine and the sounds and voes or firths are so numerous that no spot is more than three miles from the sea. The surface is more rugged than that of Orkney, the highest points being Ronas Hill (1,486 ft.) on Mainland, and Sneug (1,372 ft.) on Foula. Shetland ponies are reared, chiefly on Unst. Herring fishing and knitting are the leading industries, and fish processing is being developed.

Full information regarding the excellent angling for brown and sea trout may be obtained from the Zetland Anglers' Associa-

tion, Lerwick. The best lochs and voes are probably those of Spiggie, Tingwall, Laxdale and Weisdale on the Mainland and Snarravoe, Cliff, and Burrafirth in Unst.

The islands are remarkable for their prehistoric remains which include the Jarlshof and Mousa brochs.

Many birdwatchers and ornithologists go to Shetland. Most of the commoner sea birds—gulls, fulmar and gannets—are here in abundance as well as the rarer skuas, puffins, Iceland gulls, terns and great black-backed gulls. Noss (off Bressay) and Hermaness (Unst) are bird sanctuaries.

In upwards of a dozen districts there are annual yacht regattas, the Shetland boats evolved from Scandinavian designs being un-decked, clinker built and up to 20 ft. in length, remarkable for beauty, speed and safety in open water.

The islands are served by steam-ship from Aberdeen and Leith to Lerwick and also by aircraft from Edinburgh, Glasgow and Aberdeen to Sumburgh. Steam-er services also connect Lerwick with the Orkneys and with the northern islands of Yell, Whalsay and Unst.

SHIEL, LOCH, a freshwater loch between Inverness and Argyll near the west coast. It has associations with Prince

Charles Edward. Glenfinnan (*q.v.*) is at its head.

SHIELDAIG, the name of a mountain (Ben Shieldaig), a glen, a village and a small sea inlet and island of Loch Torridon, Wester Ross.

SHIN, a loch and river of Sutherland. The loch (20 miles long) is the largest in the county. The river is famed for its salmon. Tourist centres are Lairg and Invershin. There is angling at Overscaig. Loch Shin is a hydroelectric reservoir, and Cassley power station is situated near the NW. end of the loch. See Lairg.

SHOTTS, a town of Lanarkshire, 6 miles NE. of Wishaw, formerly a large mining centre, now developing new industries, such as diesel-engine manufacture.

SIDLAW HILLS, a hill range of Angus, to the NW. of Dundee.

SKARA BRAE, a prehistoric village on the west coast of the mainland of Orkney. Excavations (1855–67, 1927–30) have revealed stone-built huts in clusters, connected by paved paths, belonging to a people of early pastoral economy. The village was eventually overwhelmed by sand dunes.

SKELMORLIE, the most northerly of the Ayr coast resorts—small but attractive. Like West Kilbride and Seamill it serves a dual purpose, "seaside" at shore level and "country" behind its high red cliffs. There is a golf course. Places of interest include Skelmorlie Castle,

Jarlshof, Shetland. (*Aerofilms*).

parts of which date from 1502. Skelmorlie adjoins the Clyde steamer centre of Wemyss Bay.

SKERRYVORE, a lighthouse on a lone rock 10 miles SW. of Tiree.

SKIPNESS, a village on the east coast of Kintyre. It is a peaceful little place, with fine views of Arran, and the remains of a 13th century castle and an ancient chapel.

SKIRLING, a delightful little place to the NE. of Biggar, in Peeblesshire. It has a village green, some prehistoric forts, and an atmosphere of serenity and charm.

Sgurr nan Gillean.   (*W. S. Thomson*).

SKYE

EILEAN a Cheo ("Isle of Mist"), the second largest (50 miles by about 45 miles) of the Western Isles, included in Inverness-shire. It consists of a nucleus and a number of large peninsulas each with its district name—Trotternish (N.), Vaternish (NW.), Duirinish (W.), Minginish (SW.) and Sleat (S.). Between these are fine sea-lochs, Snizort, Dunvegan, Bracadale, Scavaig and Eishort, as well as many smaller lochs and beautiful bays. It is, however, its mountains that draw the visitor to Skye. The stark ridge of the Cuillin is perhaps the most savagely beautiful mountain scene in Scotland. Among the chief summits are Sgurr nan Gillean (3,167 ft.), Bruach na Frithe (3,143 ft.) and Sgurr Alasdair (3,251 ft.). Many lives have been lost on those baffling peaks, and much of the Cuillin should be left to the practised rock-climber. In the north is the Quiraing (*q.v.*).

Apart from the mountains, Skye is an island of crofters and fishermen, with an ever-growing sense of its tourist value. On the east are the islands of Raasay, Scalpay, South Rona, and in the south-west is the little island of Soay which gives its name to a breed of sheep. The scenery is delightful, mainly hilly, with lonely but beautiful glens, and woods of pine and birch. The little townships of Portree, Broadford, Dunvegan and Kyleakin, are very picturesque. There is a good network of main and secondary roads, covering all the important places in the island.

Skye has an ancient history. It was held by Norsemen until the 12th century when it came under the rule of Somerled, first Lord of the Isles. For centuries it was almost an independent kingdom. Then James V paid a ceremonial visit with his fleet, anchored off Portree, set up a royal pavilion on the shore, and won the islanders over. Later the Jacobite influence waned. From Skye, in 1746, Prince Charles Edward embarked, after safe conduct to Portree as Flora Macdonald's servant.

The approach from the mainland is by ferry from Kyle of Lochalsh to Kyleakin, Glenelg to Kylerhea or Mallaig to Armadale. Also there are extensive steamer communications between Skye, the mainland and the other islands of the Outer and Inner Hebrides. To welcome visitors to the island, Skye Week is held annually in the last week of May.

SLEAT, SOUND OF, a sound between south-west Skye (Sleat) and the mainland.

SLIGACHAN, a village at the head of Loch Sligachan, 18 miles WNW. of Broadford in Skye. There are angling facilities. Various hill tracks, none of them easy walking, lead to Loch Coruisk. Sligachan is generally regarded as the "gateway to the Cuillin".

SLIOCH, a mountain (3,217 ft.) overlooking Loch Maree in Wester Ross.

SLOY, LOCH, a loch in the mountains, 2 miles W. of north Loch Lomond, whose waters are utilised to supply power, through Inveruglas power station, for Glasgow.

SMA' GLEN. See Crieff.

SMAILHOLM, a small village 7 miles E. of Melrose, with a 16th century tower, which is the scene of Scott's ballad *Eve of St. John* and also figures in *Marmion*.

SMOO CAVE, a three-chambered cave near Durness, Sutherland.

SOLWAY FIRTH, an inlet (40 miles long) of the Irish Sea, separating south-west Scotland from north-west England. It has exceptionally strong tides and valuable salmon fisheries.

SORN, an attractive Ayrshire village with a 17th century church (jougs still on the walls), and a castle dating in part from the 15th century.

SOUTHEND, a village on the south coast of Kintyre peninsula, traditionally the spot where St. Columba first set foot in Scotland. There is a golf course.

SOUTH QUEENSFERRY, a small but ancient royal burgh at the south end of the Forth Bridges (*q.v.*), 9 miles W. of

Edinburgh. Here was a ferry much used by Malcolm Canmore's queen, Margaret—hence its name. The more recent ferry has been replaced by the Forth Road Bridge (1964). The Episcopal Church is part of an old priory founded in the 14th century. The Hawes Inn appears in Scott's *Antiquary* and Robert Louis Stevenson's *Kidnapped*. The mansions of Dundas Castle and Hopetoun House are in the neighbourhood. To the west is Blackness, with some historic associations and an ancient castle. The old church at Abercorn has interesting features, including the tomb of General Thomas Dalyell, royalist victor of Rullion Green (1666), who 15 years later raised the Scots Greys.

SOUTRA, a hill and high pass where the Edinburgh–Lauder road crosses the Lammermuir Hills, on the borders of Berwickshire, East Lothian and Midlothian. The highest point offers magnificent views.

SPEAN BRIDGE, a village and railway junction where the bridge crosses the River Spean not far from its mouth at Loch Lochy, on the Inverness–Fort William road. There is good fishing. To the left of the Inverness road, 1 mile from Spean Bridge, is an impressive and moving Commando Memorial (1950).

SPEY BAY, a small village and resort at the mouth of the River Spey. It has salmon fishing, and there is a golf course. It is becoming increasingly popular as a holiday resort.

SPEY, RIVER, one of Scotland's longest, swiftest and loveliest rivers. It flows from the tiny Loch Spey among the foothills of the Monadhliath Mountains, traverses a good part of Inverness-shire, forms the boundary between Banff and Moray, and enters the sea from the latter county 5 miles W. of Buckie. On its banks are Newtonmore, Kingussie, Aviemore, Boat of Garten, Grantown-on-Spey, Craigellachie and Fochabers. The scenery of mountains, rocks and pinewoods is richly romantic, and the river has good salmon fishing.

SPOTT, an East Lothian village near Dunbar, with an old Watch House. Scene of the last Scottish witch-burning, the place being marked by a wayside stone.

SPYNIE, the ruins of Spynie Palace, 3 miles N. of Elgin, were once the seat of the Bishops of Moray. The oldest part is the formidable keep.

STACK, a loch and mountain (Ben Stack, 2,364 ft.) of north-west Sutherland.

STAC POLLY, a mountain (2,009 ft.) of Sutherland, S. of Lochinver.

STAFFA, a pillared island of black basalt off the west coast of Mull nearly N. of Iona, which is much visited for its peculiar formation and its caves, especially the famous Fingal's Cave, 66 ft. high and 220 ft. deep. This is a sea-cave, round which one can walk on a railed-off ledge of rock above the level of the sea. Of the many distinguished visitors to Fingal's Cave, including Scott, Keats, Wordsworth and Verne, perhaps the best known is Mendelssohn, whose Hebrides (or Fingal's Cave) Overture is a memorial of his visit.

STANLEY, a village and railway junction, 7 miles N. of Perth on a richly wooded stretch of the Tay.

STENNESS, LOCH, an excellent angling loch on the mainland of Orkney, with, near it, two groups of standing stones, the Ring of Brodgar and the Ring of Stenness.

STENTON, a pretty East Lothian village in the Lammermuirs, 5 miles SW. of Dunbar. There are remains of an old church near the modern one, and on the roadside near the entrance to the village is the curious old stone Rood Well.

STEVENSTON, a town 1¼ miles E. of Saltcoats, Ayrshire, with a golf course. Nearby are an explosives

Staffa: Fingal's Cave.   (*Aerofilms*).

factory and the Ardeer Chemical Works.

STEWARTON, a busy Ayrshire town 6 miles N. of Kilmarnock, engaged in the manufacture of knitted goods, and in the allied industries of spinning and dyeing. It was formerly noted for its bonnets. It caters for visitors with a golf course, tennis courts and a bowling green. Sightseers should not miss the ancient castle of the Cunninghames, after whom the district of north Ayrshire was named.

STIRLING

A HISTORIC royal burgh and county town of Stirlingshire, with a famous castle. It stands on a bold inland promontory overlooking the "Links of Forth", 36 miles WNW. of Edinburgh, and is the centre of a prosperous agricultural and ironworking region. It has good shops and recreational facilities, and there is an annual festival of music and the arts. It is the site of Scotland's newest university (opening 1967).

Stirling is dominated by its castle on a 360 ft. high rock. It was a key town from early times, guarding the gate of an important route running from the Firth of Forth to the Firth of Clyde at Dumbarton. During the Scottish Wars of Independence it rose to supreme heights, and here were struck the two great blows which won freedom for Scotland: Wallace's victory at Stirling Bridge (1297) and Bruce's at Bannockburn (1314), both battles fought, in the first instance, for the possession of Stirling Castle.

Mary, Queen of Scots, spent part of her childhood in Stirling, and was crowned there, in the High Kirk, in 1543, as was her son James VI in 1567. General Monk held the castle for Cromwell in 1651, and in 1746 it was unsuccessfully besieged by the last of Bruce's line, Prince Charles Edward.

The Castle, entered by a drawbridge from the Esplanade, embodies an old Royal Palace, Parliament Hall, Chapel Royal, the building which once housed the Royal Mint, and the Douglas Room, with a history and some interesting relics. From here an underground passage runs to Ballengeich, between the castle and Gowan Hill, recalling that it was from Stirling Castle that James V, in his guise of the "Gudeman of Ballengeich", sallied out to adventure among his subjects. Visitors should see also Queen Mary's Look-Out, with the Queen's initials and the date (1561), the Ladies' Rock (another vantage point), the 11th century arch at the old entrance to the castle, and the King's Garden, including the "King's

Stirling Castle: Palace and Inner Gate.

Knott" (remains of a formal garden). From the Castle Esplanade (with a magnificent view and a statue of the Bruce), steps lead down to the Castle Wynd, where is Argyll's Lodging (1640), a classic example of a Scots town house of the period. Nearly opposite is the curious old ruin called Mar's Work (16th century) and the old and interesting church of the Holy Rude, of which the long 5-bay nave (early 15th century) and the choir (early 16th century) are probably the oldest parts. The tower still bears the marks of General Monk's guns. Adjoining is the cemetery, with a monument to the Wigtown Martyrs.

Points of interest in the town are Darnley's House in Broad Street, the old Mercat Cross, Town House and the Old Burgh Buildings, the Guildhall (Cowane's Hospital) where are preserved the old Standard Scots Weights and Measures, and Smith's Institute including a fine Art Gallery and a Museum with many fascinating relics.

While Stirling is an excellent base for touring central Scotland, a certain amount of sightseeing can be done in the immediate neighbourhood. Less than a mile away are the ruins of Cambuskenneth Abbey, founded by David I in 1147, with a 15th century tower and west doorway. It is said that this once rich and beautiful abbey, where the Scottish Parliament sometimes sat, was demolished after the Reformation by the Earl of Mar for the building of the so-called Mar's Work in Stirling (see above). James III and his queen are buried in the abbey.

Towering above the village of Causewayhead (1½ miles, across the river) is the Wallace Monument, a high tower standing on the 340 ft. Abbey Craig, where Wallace took up his position before Stirling Bridge. The tower, about one hundred years old, commands wide and lovely views. Within is a museum containing among other relics Wallace's "two-yard sword" (in prose, 5½ ft.).

STIRLINGSHIRE, a county of Central Scotland, bounded on the north mainly by the River Forth and on the west by Loch Lomond. In the highland north-west is Ben Lomond (3,192 ft.); in the south are the Campsie Fells (Earl's Seat, 1,896 ft.), Kilsyth and Fintry Fells, drained by the Endrick to Loch Lomond; and in the east are the rich Carses of Stirling and Falkirk. Coal and iron were formerly mined. Industries include ironworks (Falkirk and Carron), oil-refining and chemicals (Grangemouth) and textile and plastic manufacture. Notable battles were fought at Stirling (1297), Falkirk (1298 and 1746), and Bannockburn (1314).

STOBINIAN, a mountain (3,827 ft.) twin peak of Ben More, Perthshire.

STOBO, a village on the Tweed, 6½ miles SW. of Peebles. Stobo Castle is a handsome modern structure standing in beautiful grounds. The church, founded in the 13th century, still has relics of the Norman original, with the jougs still hanging in the church porch.

STOER, a small crofting village on Stoer Bay, 7 miles NW. of Lochinver, on the west coast of Sutherland. There is a fine rocky coast, and magnificent seascapes. Of interest are the Old Man of Stoer, off Stoer Point, and the lighthouse on the Point, also the ancient burial ground on Oldany Island in Clashnessie Bay to the north-west.

STONEHAVEN (old name "Stanehyve"), a holiday resort and county town of Kincardineshire, on a rock-protected bay, 14 miles S. of Aberdeen. For the holidaymaker there is an 18-hole golf course, a large open-air swimming pool, fishing, tennis, hill-riding, bowls, pavilion and dance hall. There is fine rock and cliff scenery around the coast.

The old town clusters in the lee of Downie Head, with the new town high above it to the north-west. The main points of interest are in the old town: the Town House in the High Street, with its tall and decorative steeple, the recently restored 17th century Tolbooth beside the quay and the harbour itself. The 18th century origins of the new town are credited to Barclay of Ury.

A curious old custom which goes back to pagan times is the swinging of "fireballs" on Hogmanay (New Year's Eve), now part of the general festivities.

Dunnottar Castle is 2 miles to the south.

Dunnottar Castle, near Stonehaven.

STORNOWAY, a prosperous, pleasantly situated burgh on the east coast of Lewis, and the largest town in Ross-shire. It has a fine harbour, large woollen mills, and an important fishing industry, and is also a favourite base for tourists. Stornoway Castle (Technical College) was presented to the town by Lord Leverhulme, a former owner of the island. The beautiful grounds, which include an 18-hole golf course, are open to the public. Stornoway has excellent fishing. The airport is 2 miles distant at Melbost, and steamers from Mallaig and Kyle of Lochalsh connect with trains from the south.

15 miles W. of Stornoway is the "Scottish Stonehenge", the famous Standing Stones of Callanish with the Broch of Carloway to the north-west. Near Callanish is a specimen "black house" with its primitive features carefully preserved. To the east is the Eye peninsula. Knock has remains of an ancient church. At Tiumpan Head (north end of the peninsula) is a notable lighthouse, offering fine panoramic views of the mainland.

STORR, a craggy height (2,360 ft.) on the east coast of Skye, 6 miles N. of Portree. At its east foot is the Old Man of Storr, a black pinnacle, 160 ft. high.

STOW, an attractive Midlothian village, 27 miles SE. of Edinburgh. It has an old church and a 17th century bridge.

STRACATHRO, a village 2 miles SE. of Edzell, Angus, where John Baliol in 1296 did homage to Edward I, gave name to a fine Scottish psalm tune.

STRACHUR, a village on Loch Fyne amid beautiful scenery. Its pier is 1 mile NW.

STRAITON, a village 7 miles SE. of Maybole, Ayrshire. Its church has a pre-Reformation aisle.

STRANRAER, a port and royal burgh at the head of Loch Ryan, Wigtownshire, with a mail-steamer service to Larne, North Ireland. There is a golf course. Stranraer Castle (16th and 17th centuries) in the centre of the town, was in 1682 the residence of Graham of Claverhouse. North West Castle, was the home of Sir John Ross, the Arctic explorer, and is now a hotel.

STRATHAVEN (stray'ven), a market town and holiday place of Lanarkshire, on the River Avon (a Clyde tributary) c. 16 miles SE. of Glasgow. It has woollen and rayon industries. There is a good golf course, and excellent fishing.
Strathaven has a quiet charm of its own, contributed to by the bow-backed bridge and narrow streets, 15th century ruined castle, and old mill. The farms and fruit-farms and pleasant Avondale uplands make an attractive setting.

STRATHBLANE, an attractive resort situated at the foot of the Campsie Fells, Stirlingshire. There is a golf course. At nearby Blanefield are calico-printing works.

STRATHDON, an angling village of west Aberdeenshire, at the junction of the Nochty with the Don. The lofty church spire is a local landmark.

STRATHEARN. See Earn.

STRATHFARRAR, GLEN, a fine glen (Ross and Inverness-shire) to the SW. of Beauly, traversed by the Farrar, which joins the Glass to form the Beauly (q.v.). Loch Monar at its head and Loch Beanna-charan midway in its course have been dammed (and enlarged) to form hydroelectric reservoirs.

STRATHGLASS. See Glass.

STRATHKINNESS, a Fifeshire village, 2 miles W. of St. Andrews.

STRATHMIGLO, a large linen-weaving village 2 miles W. of Auchtermuchty in Fife.

STRATHMORE, a fertile valley lying between the Sidlaw Hills on the S. and the Grampians on the N. Through it run the rivers Tay and Isla. It extends E. into Angus, where it is known as the Howe of the Mearns.

STRATHPEFFER, a small delightful resort 4½ miles W. of Dingwall in Ross-shire, formerly a well-known spa with renowned medicinal waters. It stands above the lovely valley of the Peffery, amid the foothills of Ben Wyvis. There is a pavilion and pleasure gardens (tennis, putting and bowls) and an 18-hole golf course at Ulladale, on the heights to the north.

Strathpeffer is a centre for sightseeing. The Falls of Rogie, Falls of Conon, Loch Achilty, Loch Luichart, Loch Garve, and Loch Ussie are places of much scenic beauty. Ben Wyvis (3,429 ft.) is an easy climb, and there are a number of still easier vantage points such as Raven's Rock, with wide and pleasing views. A fine vitrified fort on Knockfarrel is among the local antiquities.

The Tower of Fairburn, 5 miles S., beyond Marybank, commands a fine view. It also has the added interest of a connection with Coinneach Odhar, the Brahan Seer. When the Mackenzies were at the height of their power, Coinneach prophesied that their pride would be brought low, and their castle so reduced that a cow would calve on top of the tower, which prophecy was duly fulfilled.

STRATHY, a small place on the north coast of Sutherland, 17 miles W. of Thurso. Flagstone quarries, Strathy Bay and Strathy Point, with a lighthouse are nearby.

STRATHYRE ("Bonnie Strathyre" of the song), is a village and holiday place 9½ miles NNW. of Callander. There is fishing in Loch Lubnaig. Strathyre is a forestry centre.

STRICHEN, a large village of north Aberdeenshire, some 9 miles SSW. of Fraserburgh, on the River Ugie, where there is fishing. Mormond Hill (769 ft.) is a notable landmark in this flat and generally treeless region, and offers extensive views. On its slopes are the white cut-out figures of (S.) a horse (1700) and (E.) a stag (1870).

STRIVEN, LOCH, a sea inlet of Argyllshire in the south of the Cowal Peninsula. It is known as "Rothesay's weather glass" because rainstorms cross from the loch to the town.

STROMA, a small island in the Pentland Firth, NW. of John o' Groats.

STROME FERRY, on the southwest shore of Loch Carron, Rossshire, was the former railhead and port for Hebridean steamers, until it was superseded by Kyle of Lochalsh. On the north shore are the remains of Strome Castle.

STROMNESS, a fishing port of Orkney on the south-west coast of the mainland. There is a golf course. It has a good sheltered harbour and a small museum. John Gow, hero of Scott's *The Pirate*, was born here. Across Hoy Sound is the island of Hoy (*q.v.*).

STRONE, a holiday resort of Argyllshire, on the north of the entrance to the Holy Loch (Strone Point). It has a golf course. Geographers aver that, if a straight line is drawn south from Strone Point, it will not touch land until it reaches the coast of Spain.

STRONSAY, an island in the NE. of the Orkney group. At one time it was famous for medicinal springs, claimed to cure leprosy.

STRONTIAN, a village at the head of Loch Sunart in Morven, with facilities for fishing. The mineral strontium takes its name from this region, where its ore, strontianite, was discovered in the lead mines.

STRUAN, a village of Glengarry, Perthshire, 4 miles W. of Blair Atholl. To the north is Glen Bruar with the famous Falls of Bruar.

STRUY, a pretty little village 10½ miles SW. of Beauly, on the River Glass, 6½ miles NE. of Cannich, from which the glens of Affric, Cannich and Urquhart may be ascended.

SUILVEN, a mountain (2,399 ft.) in the west of Sutherland, near Lochinver, a famous climb, though on its Caisteal Liath side almost perpendicular. Its distinctive "sugarloaf" shape is due to its geological formation (Torridonian sandstone on a base of Lewisian gneiss).

SUMBURGH HEAD, the most southerly point of Shetland with a lighthouse, and nearby the civil airport for Shetland. On the east of Sumburgh Voe is Jarlshof (*q.v.*) settlement.

SUMMER ISLES, THE, a group of small islands in the estuary of Loch Broom, Wester Ross. They, may be reached from Ullapool, or Achiltibuie. The largest, Tanera More, is popular with picnickers.

SUNART, a sea-loch and district of Argyllshire. The loch runs from the north of the Sound of Mull 20 miles W. to E. between the districts of Ardnamurchan and Sunart on the N. and between Mull and Morvern on the S. The villages of Salen and Strontian both lie on the loch. The district is mountainous (Ben Resipol), and is situated between Lochs Sunart and Shiel, SW. of Ardgour district.

SUTHERLAND, a wild northern county, with, on the NW. indented rocky shores terminating in Cape Wrath (523 ft.), the north-west point of the British mainland. The surface is mountainous moorland, with heights which provide some exacting climbing (Suilven, Ben More Assynt, Ben Loyal, Canisp and many others). There are numerous lochs (Assynt, Shin, etc.), and straths in which flow the Oykell, Brora, Helmsdale and other rivers. Agriculture, sheep farms, deer forests, grouse moors and fisheries provide employment. There are rich mineral deposits as yet mainly undeveloped. The main towns are Dornoch, Golspie, Brora and Helmsdale, but many even of the smallest places have excellent sporting facilities, trout, sea-trout, and salmon fishing, deer-stalking, grouse shooting, golf and climbing.

SUTORS OF CROMARTY, THE. See Cromarty Firth.

SWANSTON, a picturesque hamlet at the foot of the Pentland Hills, with associations with R. L. Stevenson. Swanston Cottage was for several years the summer home of the Stevensons, and figures in *St. Ives*. Behind Swanston, on the lower slopes of the Pentlands, is the T Wood, planted in the shape of that letter.

SWEEN, LOCH, a sea inlet on the Argyllshire coast opposite Jura.

SWEETHEART ABBEY. See New Abbey.

SWINTON, a village of Berwickshire, 12 miles SW. of Berwick-upon-Tweed, on the Kelso road. It has an interesting old church. Nearby, on the banks of the Tweed is Ladykirk, whose church is said to have been built by James IV, who had narrowly escaped drowning while crossing the river at this point.

SYMINGTON (AYR), a village 5 miles SW. of Kilmarnock. Its restored church contains some Norman work.

SYMINGTON (LANARK), a village *c.* 2 miles SW. of Biggar. This is the best place from which to climb Tinto Hill (2,335 ft., its twin peaks joined by a ridge). There is a view indicator and a fine panorama over a wide expanse of country.

TAIN, an old historic town on the Dornoch Firth, a royal burgh and the former capital of Ross, said to owe its charter to Malcolm Canmore. There are wonderful sands, bathing and boating facilities, fishing on Loch Eye, a golf course, tennis, bowls and a cinema.

Sweetheart Abbey.

Tain preserves the ivy-covered walls of the Chapel of St. Duthac, brief refuge of Bruce's queen and daughter before their capture by the English, and place of pilgrimage for James IV and James V. Pilgrims often came barefoot and the "King's Causeway", specially constructed for the royal feet, is still to be seen. St. Duthac Memorial Church dates from 1569. The picturesque Old Tower of the Courthouse is of note, as is the historic Abbey of Fearn, 4 miles SE.

TALLA RESERVOIR, a reservoir supplying the city of Edinburgh, lying SW. of Peebles near the village of Tweedsmuir.

TANTALLON CASTLE. See North Berwick.

TARBERT (ARGYLL), an ancient village (formerly a burgh) on the narrow neck of land between the districts of Knapdale and Kintyre in Argyll. It stands between East and West Loch Tarbert, and has an important fishing industry, and also a tourist industry which it shares with West Tarbert, 1½ miles to the W. The ruined castle on East Loch Tarbert was once the home of Robert the Bruce.

TARBERT (HARRIS), the chief village of Harris in the Outer Hebrides, stands on the narrow neck of land between North and South Harris (here as elsewhere Tarbert signifies a portage). There is a pier on East Loch Tarbert, and there are facilities for angling.

TARBERT, EAST LOCH (ARGYLL), a small loch in Loch Fyne, with Tarbert at the head.

TARBERT, EAST LOCH (HARRIS). See Harris.

TARBERT, WEST LOCH (ARGYLL), a sea loch on the west of the Kintyre peninsula of southwest Argyll, which it nearly cuts off from the mainland. There is a steamer communication with Jura and Islay and the Outer Islands.

TARBERT, WEST LOCH (HARRIS). See Harris.

TARBET, a small place with a steamer pier on the west shore of Loch Lomond.

TARBOLTON, a village 7 miles NE. of Ayr, where Burns became a Freemason, founded his Bachelor's Club and wooed his Highland Mary (Mary Campbell, dairymaid at Montgomerie Castle). The thorn-tree where they parted still flourishes on the banks of the Ayr.

TAY, loch, river and firth of east central Scotland. The loch (in Perthshire) is 16 miles long, and is famed for its salmon and trout fishing. The river rises in Loch Tay, follows a winding course through Strath Tay, Perthshire (with Perth on its banks) to the Firth of Tay, which separates Angus from Fife. The Tay Rail Bridge, which carries the railway from Fife across the Firth of Tay to Dundee, is 2 miles, 50 yards long, and was built in 1882–87, to replace an earlier structure, blown down with a crossing train in a gale of 28th December 1879 (Tay Bridge Disaster). The Tay Road Bridge 1·6 miles long is the longest road bridge in Britain.

TAYCHREGGAN. See Awe, Loch.

TAYNUILT, a village on Loch Etive, 12 miles WNW. of Oban (*q.v.*). There is fishing and Ben Cruachan may be climbed from here. There are walks through Glen Lonan and Glen Nant (for the Tailor's Leap). Remains may still be seen of an 18th century iron-smelting furnace, for which forests of oak were grown, some of which still remain between Taynuilt and Achnacloich. Pieces of slag, like brightly coloured pebbles, may be found on the beach. Beside the parish church is a Nelson Monument erected by the English iron-workers after Trafalgar.

TAYPORT, a burgh of Fife, formerly known as Ferry Port on Craig, on the Firth of Tay, 3 miles E. of Newport and nearly opposite Broughty Ferry. The parish church is of interest, and there is an old Mercat Cross. Nature reserves of Tents Moor and Morton Lochs are near here.

TAYVALLICH, a small village near Keills and Carsaig Bay on Loch Sween, west Argyll. This is one of Argyll's most charming beauty spots.

TEITH, a river of Perthshire, running out of Loch Vennachar, through Callander to join the Forth 2 miles NW. of Stirling.

TEMPLE, a Midlothian village 6 miles SW. of Dalkeith, with a roofless 14th century church, chief Scottish seat of the Knights Templar.

TENTS MOOR, or TENTS-MUIR. See Leuchars.

TERREGLES, a mansion (1789) 1½ miles NW. of Dumfries, on the site of that in which Mary Queen of Scots "rested some few dayes" before going south to commit herself to Queen Elizabeth.

TEVIOT, a river of Roxburghshire, which flows north-east through Hawick, etc., to join the Tweed at Kelso. The district through which it runs is known as Teviotdale.

TEVIOTHEAD, a small place on the River Teviot, 9 miles SW. of Hawick, where there is a church-yard tablet to Johnny Armstrong (see Gilnockie) and a cairn in honour of songwriter H. S. Riddell (*Scotland Yet*).

THORNHILL, a neat little town just E. of the River Nith, with a golf course. There is a monument at the town centre surmounted by the winged horse of the Queensberry family.

THORNTON, a village, railway junction, cattle-marketing and important mining centre, 2 miles inland from West Wemyss (Fife), on the River Ore.

THREAVE CASTLE, built by the third Earl of Douglas in the 14th century, stands on an island in the River Dee (Kirkcudbrightshire). Tradition has it that James II used "Mons Meg" against it in 1455—when it certainly surrendered to him; Covenanters in 1640 devastated the interior.

THURSO, the most northerly town in Scotland, ancient burgh and port of Caithness, on Thurso Bay in the Pentland Firth. There is a fishing industry, and a good harbour. Formerly flagstones were exported in large quantities. Today the town's evident prosperity rests on its proximity to the nuclear reactor at Dounreay (*q.v.*). There is a new technical college.

Thurso draws the tourist with its fresh winds and sunshine, fine firm sands for bathers, facilities for golf, tennis, cricket, bowls, yacht-racing, with a two-day regatta in the season, and, of course, its fishing. The Thurso is a notable salmon river, and one also has sea-fishing and a choice of numerous small lochs. Probably unique in Britain are the "Midnight Sports" held usually in June, in the long summer twilight of the North.

Thurso is the birthplace of Sir William A. Smith, founder of the Boys' Brigade. Sir John Sinclair, compiler of the *First Statistical Account of Scotland* is commemorated in Sir John Square; Dick's Herbarium recalls the baker botanist (who came to Thurso at the age of 19) whose *Life* was written by Samuel Smiles, and reminds us that the rare Scottish primrose (pink or mauve in colour) here grows wild. Note the ruins in the Fisherbiggins of Old St. Peter's Church, with some fine window tracery: the Tower Bar and the Turnpike, relics of the 16th to 17th centuries; and "Ye Auld Fish Stane" let into the paving of what was once the Market Square.

Thurso Castle (now roofless) is modern, built on the site of an older Sinclair Castle. Owing to the prevailing winds, this handsome turreted structure turns its back on the sea—just as many of the small houses turn away from the street.

Westwards round the Bay is Scrabster (*q.v.*).

TIGHNABRUAICH, a picturesque little holiday place on the Kyles of Bute, well wooded and charming.

TILLICOULTRY, a small town of Clackmannanshire, standing at the foot of the Ochils, on the River Devon, $2\frac{1}{2}$ miles W. of Dollar. There are tartan and woollen manufactures. Behind the town is Ben Cleuch (2,363 ft.), the ascent of which is easily made.

TILT, a river of northern Perthshire, tributary to the Garry (at Blair Atholl) traversing the magnificent Glen Tilt.

TINGWALL, a hamlet *c.* 6 miles NW. of Lerwick, Shetland. On an island in Tingwall Loch, reached by stepping-stones, the "Althing" (Shetland open-air Parliament) used to meet.

TINTO HILL. See Symington (Lanark).

TIREE, a flat productive island of Argyllshire, 11 miles by 6 miles, mainly Gaelic-speaking. Tiree is noted for its good sands and fine sandy grasslands. It has considerable archaeological and historic interest, and is noted for its bird life. There are steamer connections with Oban, and an air service operates from the mainland.

TOBERMORY, the only burgh in Mull, a small place, delightfully situated on Tobermory Bay, well wooded and especially pleasing when seen from the sea. It has a pier and steamer connection with Oban; good anchorage for yachts. Though only in modern times a burgh, Tobermory is quite old and justly proud of its complex clan history.

Beneath the waters of Tobermory Bay is the wreck of the *Florida*, a galleon of the Spanish Armada, which was sunk in 1588. The treasure which the galleon is reputed to have carried has inspired many attempts at reclamation, but so far only several cannon, some skulls, and a few coins, etc., have been brought to the surface.

TOMATIN, a small place on the River Findhorn, some 16 miles SE. of Inverness, with excellent salmon and trout fishing in the river.

TOMDOUN, an angling centre on the River Garry, 10 miles W. of Invergarry (Inverness-shire).

TOMINTOUL, a high moorland village and resort of southwest Banffshire—the highest in the Highlands, being some 1,160 ft. above sea-level. There is fishing in the Rivers Avon and Livet (salmon, sea-trout, brown trout) and a number of smaller streams, hill walks and fine bracing air.

TONGUE, a wooded village on the Kyle of Tongue (inlet of the Pentland Firth) 37 miles N. of Lairg. Castle Varrich, whose history is unknown, stands on a promontory W. of the village. There is good fishing, sea-bathing and boating. Tongue House, for long a seat of the Mackays, is 1¼ miles N.

TORPHICHEN, a village of West Lothian, 2½ miles N. of Bathgate, is famous for its 15th century church of the Knights of St. John of Jerusalem, whose Scottish headquarters this was. Henry Bell,

Tobermory.

pioneer of steam navigation was born here in 1767 Nearby is Cairnpapple with its famous Bronze Age remains.

TORPHINS, a resort in Aberdeenshire, 7½ miles NW. of Banchory with a golf course.

TORRIDON, LOCH, a sea-loch of Wester Ross, with Upper Loch Torridon running eastwards from it. It is fed by the River Torridon. Liathach (3,456 ft.) lies to the NE. of the Upper Loch.

TORRIN, a village on Loch Slapin, Skye. Five miles distant is the stalagmitic Spar Cave, entered from the sea at low tide.

TORWOODLEE, 2 miles NW. of Galashiels, has a ruined broch.

TOWARD POINT, Argyllshire, the most southerly point of the Cowal Peninsula, with a lighthouse.

TRANENT, a mining town of East Lothian, 10 miles E. of Edinburgh.

TRAPRAIN LAW, a small conical hill (724 ft.) on Whittinghame estate in East Lothian. Here in 1919 excavations revealed evidence of an extensive Celtic community occupying the hill for several centuries. They also brought to light a rich hoard of Roman silver (now in the Antiquarian Museum in Edinburgh), thought to be the loot of 4th century pirates. King Arthur's capital of Loth (from which doubtless the Lothians are named) is said to have been here.

TRAQUAIR, a village of Peeblesshire, on the Quair Water, 1½ miles S. of Innerleithen. Traquair House claims to be the oldest inhabited house in Scotland, part of it said to be more than one thousand years old. The bed in which Mary, Queen of Scots, slept and the wooden cradle of James VI are still preserved. A curious and romantic interest clings to its great gates—closed and locked after the departure of Prince Charles Edward, never to be opened again until a Stuart should sit on the throne. Stone bears flanking those idle gates are said to have suggested to Scott the Bears of Bradwardine in *Waverley*. Traquair's old church has an outside stair to the gallery. Beyond the village are the witch-haunted Satyr Sykes and the beautiful Plora Wood (scene of Hogg's poem *Kilmeny*), with remnants of the old Ettrick Forest.

TREIG, LOCH, a freshwater loch of Inverness-shire. With Loch Laggan it supplies water for the Lochaber Power Scheme (see Fort William).

TRESHNISH ISLES, a group lying W. of Mull, *c.* 10 miles N. of Iona. The shape of the farthest west island, the Dutchman's Cap, explains its name.

TROMIE, a stream of SE. Inverness-shire, tributary to the Spey.

TROOL, LOCH, a small loch of western Kirkcudbrightshire in the Glen Trool National Forest Park (see page 281).

TROON, a well-known golfing and holiday resort—also a port with a fine harbour—on the Ayrshire coast, *c.* 10 miles NNW. of Ayr. It has no fewer than five 18-hole golf courses, mostly of championship standard, a large and beautifully appointed swimming pool (carnival illuminations, band, etc.) also two fine bathing beaches, N. and S. of its promontory, and delightful bowling and putting greens and tennis courts. The town itself is well laid out and pleasantly residential, with wide streets, good shops and handsome buildings. The bird sanctuary of Lady Isle lies off the coast.

TROSSACHS

A PASS in west Perthshire, made famous by Scott's *Lady of the Lake,* lies between Loch Achray and Loch Katrine, with Ben A'an on the north, Ben Venue on the south. The region is richly wooded in the west Highland sense, with stunted birch, hazel, and rowan interspersed with heather and honeysuckle. Grandeur is tempered by the purely picturesque, and they combine to make this one of the most visited of Scottish scenes.

The best route runs from Callander, and following the westward road at the little village of Kilmahog, passes the huge boulder on Bochastle Hill—legend says, a piece of Ben Venue thrown down by a Celtic hero appropriately named Samson!—and a little later Coilantogle Farm from which one may ascend Ben Ledi (2,873 ft.). So to Loch Vennachar, its east end the scene of the duel between Roderick Dhu and FitzJames. On the south are the Menteith Hills, on the north Stuc Odhar. Leaving Vennachar behind, the road crosses the ridge to Loch Achray, even more richly picturesque and tumbled, and continues to Brig o' Turk. Now down the shores of Loch Achray to the Trossachs Hotel at its west end—and here are the Trossachs proper. Ben A'an (1,750 ft.) rises to the north, not a great climb except on its rocky west face, but a vantage point for glorious views of the whole lovely glen.

Traffic must not pass beyond the Trossachs Pier, and those who wish to round the head of Loch Katrine must go on foot. The loch-level has been raised and the Silver Strand is no longer visible, but the loch itself is still enchanting, pleasant

Loch Lulnaig, Trossachs.   (*W. S. Thomson*).

to walk round, and even more delightful to sail on. A small steamer daily makes the return journey to Stronachlachar at the far end, passing wooded Ellen's Isle and sailing under the vast bulk of Ben Venue. On the slopes of the Ben are the Goblin's Cave and the Beallach nam Bo (Cattle Pass) through which Rob Roy drove his spoil after a foray. Glasgow's water is supplied by Loch Katrine, and near the Royal Cottage is the Aqueduct of the Glasgow Waterworks (1859). The journey ends at Stronachlachar Pier, except for the return trip, which is even more satisfying in its romantic beauty. From its numerous associations with the outlaw, the Trossachs is often known as "Rob Roy country".

TRUIM, GLEN, a glen of Inverness-shire traversed by the River Truim, a tributary of the Spey, also by the main road and the railway.

TULLA, a loch to the SW. of Rannoch Moor.

TULLIBODY, a Clackmannanshire village, 2½ miles NW. of Alloa, birthplace of Robert Dick, the botanist and geologist. The roof of the 15th century church was used by French troops, sent to help Mary of Guise against the Protestants, to replace a destroyed bridge across the Devon.

TUMMEL, a river, waterfall (Falls of Tummel) and loch of Perthshire. The river runs from the foot of the loch to the Tay near Ballinluig, and the Falls are on its upper course.

The extensive Tummel-Garry hydroelectric scheme utilises the water resources of the two river basins and a number of lochs as reservoirs (Ericht, Garry, Laidon, Rannoch, Tummel, Errochty, Faskally), and converges on Pitlochry. A high point on the loch's north side is known as the "Queen's View".

TURK, BRIG O'. See Trossachs, The.

Loch Tummel: Queen's View.

TURNBERRY, a famous golfing resort on the Ayrshire coast, 17 miles SW. of Ayr. It has a first-rate golf course. There are slight remains of Turnberry Castle (on Turnberry Sneuk) in which, it is said, Robert the Bruce was born. (Lochmaben also claims this honour.) According to one version of a famous tradition, it was here that the mysterious (and by implication unearthly) beacon was lit that brought him post-haste from Arran to begin the fight for Scotland and freedom.

TURNHOUSE, Edinburgh airport, situated *c.* 6 miles W. of the city centre.

TURRET, a loch and stream to the NW. of Crieff.

TURRIFF, a busy little market town of Buchan, Aberdeenshire, 11½ miles SSE. of Banff. Salmon, sea-trout and brown trout fishing is available in the River Deveron. Turriff has the remains of an ancient church and is remembered in history for the "Trot of Turriff" (1639), rout of a band of Covenanters, under the Master of Forbes, by a royalist force—the first real clash of the Civil War.

A visit to Eden Castle (4 miles) might be rewarding on a hot summer's day! It is said that, in fulfilment of an ancient curse (called down on an Earl of Buchan by a widow whose son he had drowned as a means of "reforming" him) there is always a wind blowing round the walls of Eden, even on the warmest and stillest day.

TUSHIELAW, a small place in Ettrickdale, 7 miles E. from St. Mary's Loch with a ruined tower, fortress of Adam Scott, notorious Border robber.

TWEED, a river (97 miles) of south-east Scotland flowing east from Tweedswell in south Peeblesshire, through or between the counties of Selkirk, Roxburgh, and Berwick, and then between Berwick and Northumberland, where it forms the Scottish border, till finally it enters England and reaches the sea at Berwick. It has a drainage area of 1,870 square miles, is fed by the Gala, Leader, Yarrow (and Ettrick), Teviot and Till, and for its last 10 miles is tidal. Its valley forms good pastureland for sheep, and its prosperous little towns (Peebles, Innerleithen, Galashiels, Melrose, and Kelso) are famous for the woollen cloth called "tweed" (said to be a mis-reading, by association, of "tweel"). Its banks, on both sides, are dominated by many castles, keeps or peels, such as Neidpath, Smailholm, and Norham, and the ancient feuds and border raids have steeped the river in romance and enriched the ballads and legends of both Scotland and England. Thomas the Rhymer, James Thomson, Hogg, and Scott have close associations with the Tweed.

TWEEDDALE, the upper basin of the Tweed: synonymous with Peeblesshire.

TWEEDSMUIR, a Peeblesshire village 12 miles SE. of Biggar. There are standing stones, and to the east the Tweedsmuir Hills (Broad Law, 2,754 ft.; Dollar Law, 2,680 ft.). John Buchan (later Baron Tweedsmuir) spent some of his early years in the district.

TYNDRUM, a Perthshire village 35 miles NW. of Callander on the Argyllshire border at the junction of Strath Fillan and Glen Lochy. It is a centre for touring, climbing and fishing.

TYNE, a small stream of East Lothian. It flows through Haddington and enters the sea near Tynninghame.

TYNNINGHAME, a pretty village of East Lothian, on the River Tyne near East Linton. In the grounds of Tynninghame House (seat of the Earl of Haddington) are the remains of a 12th century church, now used as a burial chapel.

UDDINGSTON, a Lanarkshire town 7 miles SE. of the centre of Glasgow, with ironworks.

UDNY, a small Aberdeenshire village 14 miles NW. of Aberdeen.

UIG, a village with pier for steamers and car ferry to Outer Hebrides at the head of Uig Bay, on the west coast of Trotternish (Isle of Skye).

UIG BAY, a beautiful bay on the west coast of Lewis, famed for its sands and its sunsets.

UIST, NORTH, a deeply indented island of the Outer Hebrides (18 miles by an average of just over 6 miles), separated from Harris by the Sound of Harris, in the west given up to sheep and dairy farming, with a number of crofting townships along the coast. The eastern half is a labyrinth of land and water, an intricate pattern of islands, peninsulas, sea and freshwater lochs of every conceivable shape. The largest sea-loch is Loch Maddy; the longest, Loch Eport. On the former is the main township, Lochmaddy. A much-broken north–south range of hills reaches 1,138 ft. in Ben Eaval. North Uist specialises in the production of beautiful tweeds and knitwear, has a dyeing, carding and spinning mill, and a seaweed processing factory. Sports include brown and sea-trout fishing and deer stalking. A good road runs round the island, with regular bus services, and connects by the North Ford causeway with Benbecula to the S.

Tourists may note the many monuments of prehistoric times, also the exceptionally interesting bird and plant life.

UIST, SOUTH, an island S. of Benbecula (Outer Hebrides), 21 miles long. It has a much indented east coast (Lochs Skiport, Eynort and Boisdale) and a chain of freshwater lochs stocked with salmon and trout. A good road runs down the west coast (viaduct link with Benbecula to the N.). Lochboisdale is a good fishing centre, and has steamer connections via Castlebay with Oban and Glasgow. N. of Loch Eynort, Ben Mhor (2,034 ft.) and Hecla (1,988 ft.) beckon the climber. On the shore below Hecla is a cave where, in 1746, Prince Charles Edward hid during his wanderings in the Western Isles. Farther south, nearer Pollacher, is another link with the '45—the birthplace of Flora Macdonald. In the north-west near Loch Bee there is a rocket range site.

ULBSTER, a small place on the east coast of Caithness, 7 miles SW. of Wick.

ULLAPOOL, a remote but delightfully situated little place on the north shore of Loch Broom (Wester Ross). It stands on a point running far out into the loch, has enchanting views over the loch to the Summer Isles. Ullapool is reached (*via* Garve) by a road from Dingwall. It is a splendid centre for motor-boat cruising and car and motor

Ullapool.

coach touring. Golf (18-hole course), sea, loch and river fishing, stalking, boating, pony-trekking and sea-bathing are available.

The ferry across the loch and an easy walk take one to Dundonnell, at the head of Little Loch Broom. In the north-east is the deer forest of Rhidorroch. Ben Dearg (3,547 ft.) and Sgur Mhor (3,637 ft.) are also in the parish.

ULVA, a small crofting island off the west coast of Mull between Loch Tuath and Loch na Keal. Formerly this was a thriving community and the site of a "College of Piping" under a famous instructor.

UNST, the northernmost island of Shetland, visited by anglers and ornithologists. Off the point of Hermaness (bird sanctuary) is Muckle Flugga, northernmost lighthouse in Britain.

UPHALL, a mining village of West Lothian, *c.* 13 miles W. of Edinburgh, with a pre-Reformation church (partly rebuilt) with some notable tombs. The 16th century mansion of Houston lies to the S.

URQUHART, GLEN, a glen of Inverness-shire, debouching on Loch Ness, with the ruined Castle Urquhart at its foot.

URR, river of Kirkcudbrightshire flowing south out of Loch Urr, 5 miles S. of Moniaive, to enter the Solway Firth S. of Dalbeattie. Beside the Urr Water, 2½ miles N. of Dalbeattie, is the Mote of Urr, an artificial mound, rising in concentric terraces and surrounded by a fosse: the fortification is said to date from early Saxon times.

VALLEYFIELD, a garden village of Fife, 5 miles W. of Dunfermline.

VANE, BEN, a Dunbartonshire mountain (3,004 ft.) to the N. of Ben Arthur (the Cobbler).

VATERSAY, a small island of the Hebrides, to the S. of Barra.

VENNACHAR, LOCH, a loch to the W. of Callander, with Invertrossachs House on its southern bank overlooked to the N. by Ben Ledi.

VENUE, BEN, a Perthshire mountain (2,393 ft.) to the S. of Loch Katrine.

VOIL, LOCH, a fine loch SW. of Lochearnhead (Perthshire).

VORLICH, BEN, a mountain (3,224 ft.) to the S. of Loch Earn (Perthshire).

VRACKIE, BEN, a mountain (2,757 ft.) to the N. of Pitlochry (Perthshire).

WALKERBURN, a small woollen-spinning village 8 miles E. of Peebles.

WANLOCKHEAD, a Dumfries-shire village on the Wanlock Water, 47 miles SW. of Edinburgh. It is the highest village in Scotland and lead and gold were once mined here.

WATTEN, a hamlet and loch (noted for trout fishing), 10 miles SE. of Thurso.

WEEM, a Perthshire village 1 mile W. of Aberfeldy, with above it the Loch of Weem (800 ft.; good view-point). In the church are monuments to the Menzies, whose seat (partly 16th century) lies to the west.

WEMYSS, EAST AND WEST (weems), are coastal villages to the NE. of Kirkcaldy, interesting because of the caves ("weems") from which their name comes. Mary Queen of Scots stayed in old Wemyss Castle, and first met Darnley there. Ruins of the so-called Macduff's Castle (beyond East Wemyss) emphasise the traditional local association with the Thane of Macduff.

WEMYSS BAY, a pleasant coast resort of Renfrewshire, just north of the Ayrshire border, makes an excellent centre for Clyde steamer sailings. Buses run to Gourock, Greenock and Largs. The 19th century Wemyss Castle to the north was the mansion of Lord Inverclyde.

Loch Voil.

Wemyss Bay shares the amenities of Skelmorlie which adjoins it on the south, and has a golf course and a fine hotel-hydro.

WESTBARNS, a coastal village of East Lothian, 2 miles W. of Dunbar.

WESTERGLEN, site, 2 miles SW. of Falkirk (Stirlingshire), of a regional broadcasting transmitter.

WESTERKIRK, a village in Eskdale, 6 miles NW. of Langholm, birthplace of Thomas Telford.

WESTERWOOD, a small place 6 miles W. of Falkirk with a Roman fort.

WEST KILBRIDE and SEA-MILL, on the Ayrshire coast between Largs and Ardrossan, together make a favourite Clyde resort. Transformed industrially by the Hunterston nuclear station nearby. Seamill has a sandy beach, boating and bathing, golf course and the coast road. West Kilbride, high above it has a concert hall and library and inland walks. Some interesting old castles and the notable antiquities called the Cup and Ring stones are objectives. There are good views of Arran and the Clyde.

WEST LINTON, a Peeblesshire village and holiday resort 8 miles SW. of Penicuik pleasantly situated in the Lyne Valley on the south-east fringe of the Pentlands. There is fishing in the Tweed, Lyne and Westwater. Part of its charm lies in its antiquity—800 years ago David I granted its church to the monks at Kelso. Its relics are rather less ancient—Lady Gifford's Well (17th century) and the 16th century Halmyre House (3 miles SE.).

WESTRAY, an island in the north-west of the Orkney group. Hotels (at Pierowall Bay), and a golf course.

The ruins of 16th century Noltland Castle, 1 mile W. of Pierowall, give evidence of its once fine hall, kitchen and staircase; in the 17th century the castle sheltered the last surviving officers of Montrose's army, and in 1745 it was burnt by Government troops. On Noup Head, the impressive NW. point of the island, is a lighthouse. Across Papa Sound to the NE., is the island of Papa Westray, with on the east of the Loch of St. Tredwall the ruins of a chapel belonging to that saint; there is also a neolithic cairn.

WHALSAY, an island of the Shetland group, off the north-east of Mainland, is a fishing station.

WHINNYFOLD, a small village near Cruden Bay (Aberdeenshire).

WHITEADDER, a small river rising in the Lammermuir Hills and flowing south to the Tweed 2 miles W. of Berwick.

WHITBURN, a town in West Lothian (coal mines, iron works), 9 miles W. of Midcalder.

WHITEHILLS, a small but thriving fishing village near Banff on the Moray Firth.

WHITEKIRK, an East Lothian village near North Berwick, with a fine old church and tithe barn. It was a place of pilgrimage.

WHITHORN, an ancient royal burgh of Wigtownshire, 9 miles S. of Wigtown, where in 397 St. Ninian set up his Candida Casa ("white house"), the first recorded Christian church in Scotland. The shrine of St. Ninian (who died here in 432) was visited, by king and commoner alike, through many centuries, until in 1581 an act of parliament rendered the pilgrimage illegal. The Pend (17th century) leads to the 12th century priory, which some archaeologists believe to incorporate the foundations of St. Ninian's building. This honour is, however, also claimed by the coastal village of the Isle of Whithorn (on a peninsula 3 miles SE.), where there is a 13th century chapel of St. Ninian.

WHITING BAY, a small seaside place on the south-east coast of Arran with a golf course, tennis, putting and bowling facilities and a dance hall. Glenashdale nearby is interesting ("Giants" graves).

WHISTLEFIELD. See Garelochhead.

WHITTINGHAME, a hamlet 6 miles E. of Haddington in East Lothian, chiefly notable for Whittinghame House, one of the loveliest of Scottish mansions—seat of Viscount Traprain and formerly of Earl Balfour, statesman and premier in the present century. It has been an approved school, and is now a boarding-school. The mansion lies at the foot of a ravine running into the Lammermuir Hills, and has an ancient castle in its grounds, and the famous old yew-tree within whose "shadowing shroud", it is said, Darnley's enemies plotted to kill him. The curious and interesting Stoneypath Tower is near here, a little south of the road to Garvald.

WICK (Norse *vik*, a bay), the county town of Caithness, a royal burgh since 1589 and a fishing station. There is an airport N. of the town, fishing in the Wick and in several lochs, and a golf course 3 miles N. at Reiss. At the height of the herring season (July–September) the harbour is a centre of attraction. A small but important industry recently started is the making of Caithness glass. The town itself, built on both sides of the River Wick, is set amid rocks and cliffs dotted with ruined castles. There is the 12th century tower called the Old Man of Wick just S. of the town. To the north, on Sinclair Bay, are Castle Sinclair and Castle Girnigoe, where a tyrant of former days kept his son in a dungeon, fed him on salt beef and denied him water! Then N. of Keiss (where there are prehistoric brochs) is Bucholly Castle, once held by Swayne the Pirate; and there is yet another castle at Freswick.
Southwards there are several small places with Norse-sounding names.

WIGTOWN, a royal burgh, small port, and the county town of Wigtownshire, situated on Wigtown Bay just N. of the mouth of the River Bladnoch: Wigtown Sands, which appear at low water, lie to the NE. In the parish churchyard are the

Overleaf: Eildon Hall near Melrose.

graves of the Wigtown Martyrs, Margaret McLauchlan and Margaret Wilson, who, because of their staunch adherence to the Covenanting cause, were tied to a stake at the mouth of the Bladnoch, and were eventually drowned by the rising tide. They, and other martyrs for their cause, are commemorated by the Martyrs' Monument above the town. 3 miles NW. of the town are the Standing Stones of Torhousekie, 19 monoliths in the form of a complete circle, inside which 3 blocks are enclosed.

WIGTOWNSHIRE, the extreme south-west county of Scotland, separated from Ireland by the North Channel. It is divided into three districts: the Rhinns of Galloway, the fertile "hammer-head" peninsula defined by Loch Ryan and Luce Bay; the Machars, the broad-based triangle of land between Luce Bay and Wigtown Bay; and the Moors, the remainder of the county, lying E. of Loch Ryan and N. of the Machars. The rivers, flowing south-east, are the Cree, Bladnoch and Luce; there are many small lakes. Much of the surface is generally level and of no great elevation, though the Moors are mainly bleak fells and high mosses. Nearly half the surface is arable, and there are sheep and dairy farms. The largest town in the county is Stranraer; others are Newton Stewart, Wigtown (the county town), Whithorn, and Portpatrick.

WINCHBURGH, a small town in the oil-shale district of West Lothian, 12 miles W. of Edinburgh.

WINDYGATES, a village near Markinch in Fife.

WISHAW, an industrial town of Lanarkshire, amalgamated with Motherwell (q.v.).

WORMIT, a village of Fife, at the south end of the Tay Bridge.

WRATH, CAPE, a stormy headland at the extreme north-west of Scotland with a lighthouse, and a rock-stack. Its name (so apt in English) is from the Norse word *hvarf*, a turning point.

WYVIS, BEN, a mountain (3,429 ft.) to the N. of Strathpeffer, Ross-shire. On its SW. lies Little Ben Wyvis (2,497 ft.). The elephantine Wyvis massif, 30 miles distant, dominates the northern horizon as the northbound traveller approaches Inverness.

YARROW, a stream of Selkirkshire flowing through the lovely Yarrow Vale. It joins the Ettrick to form a tributary of the Tweed. Yarrow Vale provides the setting for innumerable ballads, songs and poems, among them those of Scott, Hogg and Wordsworth. Yarrow is easily reached from Selkirk.

Interest is not only scenic. Some 3 miles from Selkirk one passes the mansion and battlefield of Philiphaugh, where in 1645 the Covenanting General Leslie defeated Montrose. Just beyond this is the Buccleuch mansion of Bowhill (to the south), and beyond Bowhill Newark Castle, a royal hunting tower in the days of James I, later a Scott stronghold—not a picturesque ruin. Across the river from Newark is the farm cottage at Foulshiels where Mungo Park was born. At Broadmeadows House a drove road crosses Minchmuir (1,856 ft.) to Innerleithen. The remains of Hangingshaw Tower of ballad fame and the 17th century Yarrow church are other points of interest, and at the crossroads (where stands an anglers' inn) one is within a mile of St. Mary's Loch. This is the country of James Hogg, the Ettrick Shepherd, and there are many reminders here both of his life and of his poetry.

YELL, an island of the Shetland group, lying to the NE. of Mainland, from which it is separated by Yell Sound. But for ½ mile of marshy ground which lies between them, Whale Firth on the west and Mid Yell Voe on the east would dissect the island. At Gloup, in the north there is fine cliff scenery, while good trout-fishing may be had on most of the island's numerous small lochs. Steamers call at Mid Yell and Burravoe, on the E., and there are ferry connections with Unst and Mainland. To the east of Yell is Fetlar, an island noted for pony-breeding.

YESTER. See Gifford.

YETHOLM, a village *c.* 8 miles SE. of Kelso (Roxburghshire), near the English Border, comprises Town Yetholm and Kirk Yetholm, really two villages, with the Bowmont Water (angling) flowing between them. Kirk Yetholm was formerly the home of the large and picturesque tribe of the Scottish Border gipsies, descendents of Johnny Faa and his band, celebrated in the old ballads. Cheviot (2,676 ft.) over the Border to the south-east, is the highest summit of the Cheviots.

YETTS OF MUCKHART, a Perthshire village and road junction at the south entrance to Glen Devon, 4 miles NE. of Dollar.

YTHAN, a river of Aberdeenshire, rising at Ythan Wells in the west of the county and flowing 35 miles east to enter the North Sea at Newburgh. The town of Ellon is near its mouth.

YTHAN WELLS, an Aberdeenshire village, *c.* 9 miles E. of Huntly. At Glenmellan, 1½ miles W., are remains of an encampment, the most northerly traces of Roman occupation in Britain.

ZETLAND, the alternative name for the Shetland Islands.

WINTER SPORTS IN SCOTLAND

THE winter sports enthusiast, be he skier or snow-climber, will find in Scotland every facility to suit his tastes—and all of them reasonably accessible from centres of civilisation.

FOR ski-ing, the best months are March and April, though the season runs from mid-December to the beginning of May, and often extends from November to early June. Popular areas are Glencoe (Kingshouse), the Cairngorms (Aviemore), Glenshee and the Devil's Elbow. There is also ski-ing in the Ben Lawers area and on Ben Wyvis. Ski-lifts are in operation at several places, and on the Cairngorm the "Ski Road" enables access to a height of 2,000 ft.: there are ski-ing centres at Glenmore Lodge, Newtonmore, and Carrbridge, at all of which instruction is given. Many other slopes—the Grampians, Pentlands, Campsie Fells, etc.—provide good runs for the skier. Several ski-tows are in operation.

THE Scottish Youth Hostels Association organises courses in ski-ing at Glenisla Hostel (Perthshire) and at Loch Morlich (Inverness-shire), at which hostels as at Garth, Killin, and Glendoll (Angus), skis may be hired.

THE snow-climber, to whom we recommend the first three months of the year, has at that time the choice of all the Highland mountains, except perhaps those in the Western Isles. Ben Nevis and Glencoe, in addition to providing snow-climbs of a difficult standard, offer rewarding ice-climbs. The climber is advised to refer to the guide books of the Scottish Mountaineering Club.

FURTHER details about ski-ing and ski-courses in Scotland may be had from:

> THE SCOTTISH SKI CLUB, 15 Hope Street, Edinburgh, 2.
> (Full membership: 10s. entrance fee; £1 annual subscription. Temporary membership (31st Aug. to 31st Aug.): 25s.)
>
> THE SCOTTISH COUNCIL OF PHYSICAL RECREATION, 4 Queensferry Street, Edinburgh, 2.
>
> THE SCOTTISH YOUTH HOSTELS ASSOCIATION, 7 Bruntsfield Crescent, Edinburgh, 10.

NATIONAL FOREST PARKS

IN order that the public may enjoy access to the fine mountain scenery and open countryside on land belonging to the Forestry Commission, National Forest Parks have been established in certain areas. These are open during daylight hours throughout the year, and camping and caravan sites are available. The lower slopes of the mountains are generally occupied by plantations, in which visitors are asked to keep to the paths, but the high ground is completely free for climbing and rambling. In Scotland are:

GLEN TROOL NATIONAL FOREST PARK (130,127 acres), centred on Loch Trool in Galloway among some of the wildest and most beautiful scenery in SW. Scotland, culminating in the Merrick (2,764 ft.), highest peak south of the Highlands. It also includes Clatteringshaws Loch, created by the Galloway hydro-electric scheme. Robert the Bruce defeated the English twice in the neighbourhood in 1307, at Glen Trool and Rapploch Moss; both places have memorial stones. The park is rich in wild life, including red deer, wild goats, many sea and loch birds, and a variety of flowers, some of them rare bog plants. There is a camp site at Caldons beside Loch Trool.

THE QUEEN ELIZABETH FOREST PARK (42,000 acres), named in honour of the Coronation in 1953, stretches from the E. shore of Loch Lomond eastwards to the outskirts of the Trossachs, the best centre being Aberfoyle. There is a camping ground at Rowardennan on Loch Lomondside and another near Aberfoyle. The park includes some of the finest scenery in the southern Highlands, covering Ben Lomond (3,192 ft.), Ben Venue (2,393 ft.), Loch Achray, and Loch Ard. This area was the terrain of the outlawed MacGregors, and is the background of Sir Walter Scott's *Rob Roy* and *The Lady of the Lake.*

NATIONAL FOREST PARKS (*Continued.*)

ARGYLL FOREST PARK (60,000 acres), situated on the Cowal penin-
sula, comprises the forests of Ardgartan, Glenbranter, Loch Eck,
Glenfinart, and Benmore; also the estate of Ardgoil, belonging to
Glasgow Corporation. The main camping site is at Ardgartan near
Arrochar, on Loch Long, a favourite centre for climbing Ben Arthur
("The Cobbler"). The park also includes Ben Ime (3,318 ft.) and
many other peaks, Loch Eck, Loch Goil, and the E. shore of Loch
Long. At Benmore there are interesting botanic gardens. The wild-
cat, polecat, peregrine falcon and golden eagle are found in the
remoter parts, and the flora is rich and varied.

GLEN MORE FOREST PARK (12,500 acres) lies on the NW. side of
the Cairngorms around Loch Morlich and is almost entirely mountainous, rising to 4,084 ft. in the Cairngorm. The nearest centre of
population is Aviemore, and there is a youth hostel and camping site
at Loch Morlich. Glenmore Lodge nearby is a residential centre of
the Scottish Council for Physical Recreation; beyond it are the slopes
of the Cairngorm, now becoming increasingly popular as a winter
sports centre, with a ski-lift. Adjoining on the west is Rothiemurchus
Forest, part of the Cairngorms Nature Reserve. Deer, mountain
hares, ptarmigan, grouse and capercailzie figure among the wild life,
and reindeer have been introduced experimentally.

THE BORDER FOREST PARK (126,000 acres), lies mostly over the
English border, but parts extend into Roxburgh and Dumfriesshire.
There are extensive remains of Hadrian's Wall, and many ruined
castles, peel towers and fortified farmhouses, relics of centuries of
border warfare. The main camping and caravan site is at Lewisburn,
4 m. S. of the border on the Bellingham-Kielder road.

SOME GAELIC TERMS IN PLACE NAMES

Aber, *confluence.*
Ald, Alt, Auld, *burn, stream.*
Ard, Aird, *height, promontory.*
Bagh, Bhaig, *bay.*
Baile, Bhaile, *town, hamlet* (Ballachulish).
Ban, Bhan, Bhain, *white, fair.*
Bard, Bhaird, *poet; meadow.*
Beag, Bheag, *small.*
Bealach, *pass between hills* (Balloch).
Beinn, Bheinn, *mountain.*
Beith, *birch.*
Ben, conventional for Beinn.
Beul, *mouth.*
Binnean, *small peaked mountain.*
Blar, Bhlair, *plain* (Blairgowrie).
Bo, *cow.*
Bodach, Bhodaich, *old man.*
Brae, Bread, *height* (Braemar).
Bruach, Bruaich, *bank, brae* (Tighnabruaich).
Buchaille, Bhuachaille, *herdsman* (Buchaille Etive).
Buidhe, *yellow.*
Cairn, Carn, *heap of stones* (Cairntoul).
Caol, *strait* (Colintraive).
Cas, *steep.*
Clach, Cloiche, *stone.*
Clachan, *place of stone, hamlet.*
Cladach, *shore.*
Cleuch, *ravine.*
Coill, Coille, *wood.*
Coir, Coire, *hollow in mountain-side, corrie.*
Creag, Craig, *rock.*
Cruach, *stack, heap.*
Dearg, *red.*
Drochaid, *bridge* (Drumnadrochit).
Druim, *ridge, back* (Drumnadrochit).
Dubh, Dhubh, *black.*
Dun, Duin, *fort, castle.*
Eilean, *island.*
Fad, Fhad, *long.*

SOME GAELIC TERMS IN PLACE NAMES
(*Continued.*)

Fas, *vegetation.*
Gair, Gearr, *short* (Gareloch).
Glas, *grey or green.*
Gorm, Ghorm, *green and blue* (Cairngorm).
Inch, Innis, *island, meadow by a river.*
Inver, Inbhir, *mouth of, confluence.*
Ken, kin, *head.*
Knock, *hillock.*
Kyle, *strait.*
Lag, *hollow.*
Lairig, *pass.*
Liath, *grey.*
Linn, *port.*
Lios, *garden* (Lismore).
Lomond, *beacon.*
Machar, Machair, *sandy plain* (Machrihanish).
Marn, Meall, *round hill.*
Monadh, *hill, mountain.*
Mor, Mhor, *great, big.*
Na, nam, nan, *of the*
Ob, Oban, *bay.*
Ramh, Raimh, *oar.*
Riabhach, Riach, *greyish, grizzled.*
Rudha, *promontory.*
Scuir, Sgor, Sgurr, *rocky peak.*
Sean, *old.*
Sron, Stron, *nose, point* (Strone, Strontian).
Stac, *conical hill.*
Stob, *point.*
Strath, *valley.*
Tairbeart, Ta(r)bert, *narrow isthmus.*
Tigh, Tay, Ty, *house* (Tighnabruaich),
Tobar, Tober, *well* (Tobermory).
Tom, *hill* (Tomintoul).
Uamh, *cave.*
Uig, *bay.*
Uisg, *water.*